# A Common Law

# A Common Law

## The Law of Nations and Western Civilization

### SECOND EDITION

## Ruben Alvarado

WordBridge
PUBLISHING
εν αρχη ην ο λογος
AALTEN, THE NETHERLANDS

WORDBRIDGE PUBLISHING
Aalten, the Netherlands
www.wordbridge.net
info@wordbridge.net

First edition published 1999 by Pietas Press, an imprint of WordBridge Publishing

ISBN 978-90-76660-54-7

The cover artwork is in the public domain

# Table of Contents

# Foreword

THE PAINTING on the front cover is "The Conspiracy of Claudius Civilis" by Rembrandt van Rijn. There we see Claudius Civilis, leader of the Batavians, a tribe living in the Betuwe region of the modern Netherlands. Claudius is pictured in the act of forming the oath-bound conspiracy which led to the revolt of the Batavians against the Romans back in the $1^{st}$ century AD, as recorded by Tacitus.

The Dutch ruling class gladly looked upon these freedom-loving Batavians as their forefathers, and used this myth to justify not only their revolt against Spanish tyranny, but also against the supposed tyranny of the church – even though it was the Reformed church which had given the nation the backbone to fight for independence in the first place. The Batavian myth was a secularized, anti-ecclesiastical version of reality.

Rembrandt, however, did not play along. The painting did not depict the Batavian forebears as noble aspirants to legitimate power, but as upstarts and usurpers, brigands and partners in crime. In effect, Rembrandt thus branded the new order represented by the burgher regime as a usurpation. Not surprisingly, this painting, done on commission to commemorate the new Amsterdam city hall, was displayed for only a short time before it was returned. It is thought that Rembrandt never received remuneration for the work.

"The Rise of the Dutch Republic" (the title of John Lothrop Motley's iconic and hagiographic book on the subject) is indeed the stuff of romantic legend, but the reality is a bit more complicated, and a bit more sinister. In actuality, the Dutch ruling class coopted the church's tradition of liberty and wedded it to a secular purpose, "True Freedom," thus turning freedom into an end in itself. Instead of viewing liberty as a means to a higher end, the Dutch Republicans, along with their spiritual progeny throughout subsequent history, viewed liberty as a disconnection from this higher end – at least, in terms of Jesus Christ as the Way, the Truth, and the Life. The Christian distinctive became secondary and private; the newfound understanding of liberty gave birth to a new form of civil religion, while it banished Christianity from the public square.

This gave us the Enlightenment. It also had momentous consequences for the development of the social order. The constitutional tradition of the West was necessarily transformed; stripped of its Christian foundation, it became an unstable compound, a cultural bipolarity bound together in dialectical back-and-forth relation.

Thus was obliterated the unity of Western Civilization. What then arose were two sub-civilizations, embodied in the two major entities comprising the West, Continental Europe and Anglo-America. How is it that the common inheritance of liberty was first acquired? How was it then transformed? And what does it matter? These are the questions this book addresses.

NOTE ON THE TEXT: The original text is included in its entirety. Commentary is interspersed throughout, set off by a different font and horizontal lines fore and aft. Interpolations are similarly formatted, between square brackets. The original page numbers are likewise included, in bold face, placed between angled brackets, like this: <1>. The "Original Index" is a facsimile thereof.

# A Common Law

# Introduction

THIS BOOK got its start from a line in Edmund Burke's *Reflections on the Revolution in France.* Burke there chides the revolutionaries in France for their overthrow of the country's ancient constitution, arguing that they would have been much better off seeking to restore it from its dilapidated condition. To do this they could have "looked to your neighbors in this land who had kept alive the ancient principles and models of the old common law of Europe meliorated and adapted to its present state – by following wise examples you would have given new examples of wisdom to the world."[1]

It was this phrase that caught my attention: "the old common law of Europe." I saw it echoed in Alexis de Tocqueville's *The Old Regime and the French Revolution,*[2] where de Tocqueville speaks of his surprise at discovering a "remarkable similarity" between the laws and institutions of medieval France, Germany, and England; that "the administration of all three countries derived from the same general principles; the political assemblies were composed of the same elements and invested with the same powers." De Tocqueville went on to point out the common class structure, comprising a nobility with the same positions, privileges, and appearance; cities with the same administrations; rural districts with the same modes of government; peasants in the same conditions. He concluded by saying "it is not, I think, going too far to say that in the fourteenth century the political, social, administrative, judicial, and financial institutions – and even the literary productions – of the various European countries had more resemblance to each other than they have even in our time, when the march of progress seems to have broken down all barriers and communications between nations have so vastly im- <2> proved."

De Tocqueville characterized this common social structure as the "ancient constitution of Europe" and he, like Burke, remarked that it had fallen into a state of dilapidation. But what was it about these statements that made

---

[1] Edmund Burke, *Reflections on the Revolution in France* (Indianapolis & New York: Liberal Arts Press, Inc., 1955 [1790]), p. 41.

[2] Alexis de Tocqueville, *The Old Regime and the French Revolution,* trans. Stuart Gilbert (Gloucester, MA: Peter Smith, 1978 [1856]), part I, chap. 4.

them such a revelation to me? Just this: I had never known of an ancient constitution of Europe, of a common law of Europe, something to which we could look back to for guidance. I only knew of a Europe of light and of darkness, of a Europe in which Liberty had struggled against absolutism, in which Enlightenment had finally triumphed over superstition, leading to the free societies of the modern world.

---

Continental Europe and the Anglo-American orbit once shared a common culture, rooted in the medieval past; they were not yet two separate entities with two separate traditions. The Enlightenment redefined that past, turning it into a period of darkness against which it contrasted a new regime of liberty. In reality, it had taken the tradition of "the old common law of Europe" and refashioned it according to its predilections. It made this version of history the only version.

---

In a classic work of historiography, Herbert Butterfield described this view of history – a view which I had been given and had received without question, without knowing there even was another view – as "the Whig interpretation of history."[3] Now the Whigs were the party in England which had championed parliamentary government as opposed to divine-right monarchy. Their patron saint was John Locke, the quintessential exponent of the social contract theory of the origin of the state – a theory which essentially made the individual will the source of all authority. Locke's philosophy became part and parcel of the Whig ideology, that elevated the individual will to a position of primacy and castigated all forms of authority not rooted in consent as tyrannical. It was this ideology which gave birth to the Enlightenment, which underlay all that period's attacks on church and state in their received forms as expressions of oppression and violation of conscience. Priest and King became the very embodiment of all that was messed up with the world. <3>

---

This "Whig" orientation, formed by de-emphasizing monarchy and the church – and public Christianity generally – transformed the common-law

---

[3] Herbert Butterfield, *The Whig Interpretation of History* (New York and London: W.W. Norton & Co., 1965 [1931]).

tradition, providing a new departure for the Western tradition of liberty, a truncated version of the original common law.

I think I can state with confidence that this view of history, as far as it goes, is still the one taught in schools in America (and probably everywhere else) to this day, proffered and accepted without question, as it has since the beginning of the U.S. "experiment," it being a major component of America's self-image. But it is wrong. And not only is it wrong, it provides the necessary room for its polar opposite to take root, grow, and prosper: to wit, the Marxist interpretation of history.

Whig one-sidedness opened the door to a dialectical opposite, emphasizing collectivism as opposed to individualism. The resulting alternative orientation, which, as we shall see, is the heart of the civil-law tradition, finds its most extreme expression in Marxism. Twenty years along and lo and behold! in the classroom, it is the Marxist interpretation of history which has triumphed, and superseded the Whig interpretation.

The Marxist gladly accepts the Whig's critique, but takes it a step further, in fact turning it against the Whig himself, criticizing his reliance on property and economic liberty, and substituting for that reliance a call for solidarity and community realized through the state.

In our day it is assumed that these two positions are polar opposites, Right and Left, and as such mutually exclusive; but the very prosperity of the latest fad in politics, the so-called Third Way represented by the reformed labor and socialist parties of the West, should tip one off to the underlying reality that these two, far from being mortal enemies, in fact need each other and could not subsist without each other. Their symbiosis lies in their common origin: a rejection of the Christian, theocratic, monarchical, ecclesiastical past.

Despite appearances to the contrary, this is not a healthy condition. Marxist and Whig may rule the roost but they do not rule the truth. The culture wars taking place within and without the political arena are insoluble in terms of the Marxist/Whig dialectic because they reach beyond this shallow Enlightenment dismissal of pre-modern Western civilization. The culture wars are a war over first principles. The time in which first principles were mutually agreed upon is over. We are searching for solid ground upon which to re-found our social and political institutions. In such a time there is nothing more salutary than historical investigation into such first principles. That is what this study is about. There really was a common law of Europe, which, I will argue, was not what it later was made out to be; but it got hijacked, and it was the Whigs <4> that did the hijacking, in doing so burning all the road signs from the getaway scene, destroying all evidence of their theft. The resultant stunted, truncated social order they created no longer serves its purpose. We now have to go back and pick up the thread, rediscover our roots, and then choose whether to continue on this path or not. That is the crisis of the West. Crisis in Greek – *krisis* – means decision. An informed decision at this juncture is our calling. Which shall we make?

# Chapter 1

# Liberalism and Its Discontents

AS WE PASS from one millennium to another, we cannot help but take stock of the one we are leaving behind. The second millennium Anno Domini ended with a century of the greatest wars the world has ever seen. Oddly enough, this century, the 20th, itself followed a century of peace, in its turn perhaps the greatest the world has ever seen. This, the 19th century, is often labeled the Age of Liberalism: it witnessed the establishment of the rule of law, with the nations submitting to a common and universal order. The 20th century, the century of World War, witnessed the nations rise up in rebellion against this universal order. Russia, Japan, Italy, Spain, Germany all chose for explicitly anti-liberal social and political orders. From Right and Left came the common diagnosis – liberalism is dead, has had its day, must be super-seded. But the common enemies of the liberal order were defeated in two world wars, which ended up delivering triumph to the USA and the estab-lishment of a Pax Americana incorporating many of liberalism's basic prin-ciples.

The conflict thus seemed to have come to an end. What became increas-ingly clear, however, was that in the world of theory liberalism remained un-der siege, just as in world of practice the Soviet Union and Maoist China threatened the very existence of the once-secure Pax Americana. For many it seemed just a matter of time before the postwar order succumbed to the com-bined theoretical, military, and economic might of the anti-liberal phalanx. But as the 20th century came to a close, a most astonishing development man-ifested itself. Not the liberal order but the antiliberal order collapsed. Capi-talism had triumphed over communism as it had over fascism. The Cold War was over. Conflict had ended. "Liberal Democracy" as it had come to be known had cleared the field. It was the End of History.[4]<6>

---

[4] See the appendix for a review of the book from which this phrase was taken: Francis Fukuyama's *The End of History and the Last Man.*

Or so it seemed. For even in its hour of triumph liberal democracy was being relentlessly subjected to critique from within, questioning its very legitimacy. And indeed, political success followed those who best managed to maintain the institutions of liberal democracy while preaching its corruption. In terms of practical policy, the liberal agenda of free markets, privatization, individualism predominated, but in terms of justification and legitimacy these measures were carried through only by putting the best anti-liberal face on them. It was almost as if politicians were having to apologize for effecting the measures voters put them into office to implement. But it was ultimately the voters apologizing to themselves, for this peculiar form of schizophrenia was first and foremost their own; the politicians only reflected the signals they themselves were receiving in the first place. There was one sure way of losing any political argument, and that was to couch measures explicitly in terms of the liberal philosophy out of which they sprang. Double-talk was the order of the day, and was accepted gladly, almost thankfully. It was almost as if people needed to believe they were doing anti-liberal things even as they assented to the most liberal of measures. This was a game only the most adept political chameleons could play, this appeasement of voter double-mindedness, this assuagement of voter guilt.

My targets here were Bill Clinton and Tony Blair. The terms of political debate have since changed dramatically: leftist politicians no longer feel the need, as they once did, to camouflage the positions they are advancing. Whether their newfound candor will prove palatable is another question.

Indeed, this was the greatest mystery of the age. Even at its triumph, capitalism remained deeply unpopular, even shameful. The people's hearts were elsewhere. They longed for a return to lost community, a caring society, a giving society, for commitment, for compassion. Though the Marxist reality was rejected, its ideal remained living and vibrant. Something deep inside compelled people to seek a social order fundamentally different from the one in which they lived. The moral high ground was held by those proclaiming agendas fundamentally at odds with the liberal order.

Is it any wonder that socialism and communism have again sprung up, seemingly from out of nowhere? It is part of a continuous cycle: the dialectic of modernism is ineluctably one of capitalism **and** socialism, in mutual dependency.

The popular schizophrenia of triumphant liberal democracy did not go unnoticed. One of the major proponents of the liberal agenda, Nobel <7> Prize winner Friedrich Hayek, was entirely conscious of the deep-rooted discontent and proposed an elegant explanation. Its roots, he averred, lay in man's evolutionary past. In terms of the evolutionary struggle for survival, man's strategy was group-oriented. Hobbes's concept of the isolated individual in the state of nature is a myth. "The savage is not solitary, and his instinct is collectivist."[5] An isolated individual could never have survived in the primeval environment. Survival mandated that groups stick together and that individuals sacrifice for the welfare of the group. The group nurtured values of solidarity and altruism. These are "instincts" which apply to "one's own group and not to others," a further element of the evolved survival strategy. Groups were small, able to be steered, able to be coordinated. Everyone knew everyone else. Goals were joint, explicit and understood.

Somehow, however, another form of social order came to supersede the closed group. It is the "extended order," the order of civilization. It favors not the group but the individual. It allows for the integration of large numbers of human beings precisely because it does away with group introversion. The groups which were the basis for human society in earlier evolutionary stages become subsumed in a larger order which counteracts the instincts of solidarity with "rules from above" establishing spheres of freedom – "several property, honesty, contract, exchange, trade, competition, gain, and privacy."[6] The extended order became established not because anyone thought it up but by virtue of an invisible, insensible process of selection acting across groups, whereby the groups in which individuals began behaving according to these rules began prospering to a greater degree than groups which didn't, eventually displacing them. The values of civilization thus work better than the values of primitive society – they sustain greater populations and enable

---

[5] Friedrich A. Hayek, *The Fatal Conceit: The Errors of Socialism* (Chicago: University of Chicago Press, 1988), p. 12.

[6] Hayek, *The Fatal Conceit*, p. 12.

population masses <8> to cohabit in peace. These rules are taught not by instinct, but are handed down by "tradition, teaching and imitation."[7]

It is precisely because the extended order runs against the grain of our
"evolved" collectivist instincts that human beings have such an underlying
bias against that order. The extended order is impersonal and does not necessarily extend its rewards to the most morally upright of its members. Some
gain, others lose, and it is not always entirely clear why. This is inherent to
the structure of the extended order. It functions not in terms of agreed goals
but in terms of agreed rules of conduct. Outcomes are anything but guaranteed. What is guaranteed is a sphere of freedom within which one may work
out his own destiny for better or worse.

The welfare function cannot be applied as it was in the old "micro-order"
because to do so would overthrow the basic structure of the extended order,
decentralized decision-making. Welfare redistribution entails the establishment of a supervisory intelligence able to grasp the totality of the market process and direct it to agreed concrete ends. But that would be to destroy the
market process itself. For one thing, such knowledge would have to be gained
by forcing market participants to submit total and accurate information to
the supervisory authority in a time scale which would not cause the system
to grind to a halt. And it would entail the imposition of a predefined scale of
merit whereby criteria other than exchange value would determine who got
what. "In such a world we would be deprived of those signals that alone can
tell each what, as a result of thousands of changes in the conditions in which
we live, we must now do in order to keep the stream of production flowing
and, if possible, increasing."[8]

All of this leads to the development of a residual antagonism to the extended order, even though people understand as never before that it is this
very order which has enabled mankind to survive and flourish. "The <9> per-
sistence of instinctual feelings of altruism and solidarity subject those who
follow the impersonal rules of the extended order to what is now fashionably
called 'bad conscience'; similarly, the acquisition of material success is supposed to be attended with feelings of guilt (or 'social conscience'). In the

[7] Hayek, *The Fatal Conceit*, p. 12.

[8] Hayek, *The Fatal Conceit*, pp. 74–75.

midst of plenty, then, there is unhappiness, not only born of peripheral poverty, but also of the incompatibility, on the part of instinct and of a hubristic reason, with an order that is of a decidedly non-instinctive and extra-rational character."[9]

The question arises – how, if Hayek's assumption of evolutionary origins is to be believed, is it that the original group-oriented survival strategy could ever have been supplanted by the extended order? What would have first spurred individuals to begin acting according to the rules of the extended order and what group would have allowed its members the freedom for that to happen? As Hayek himself recognizes, "Indeed, if our present order did not already exist we too might hardly believe any such thing could ever be possible, and dismiss any report about it as a tale of the miraculous, about what could never come into being."[10]

If evolutionary theory is to be believed, mankind developed out of lower forms of life and is therefore in direct continuity with them. Thus mankind's social order should have the same basic makeup and goals as animals', especially the apes', man's supposed closest relative. But if that is the case then something went terribly wrong, or rather terribly right, in man's history because the extended order, as Hayek explains, stands in stark contrast and in absolute discontinuity with such an evolutionary inheritance. Hayek's own explanation for this is predictable: the extended order enhanced survivability. Those groups that began practicing its precepts experienced greater success in the struggle for life than did those groups that did not. Yet this explanation does not convince. It seems to beg the question where these precepts came from in the first place. About <10> one thing Hayek is adamant: no one thought them up. They are in this sense non-rational, or as he puts it, between instinct and reason. The precepts of the extended order are passed down from generation to generation, are interweaved in custom and tradition. But how did they ever get off the ground if they are so counter-instinctive? Hayek offers no substantive explanation for this other than to say it just happened and it worked.

But it is this explanation that simply won't do if one is to defend the institutions of the extended order in the face of social engineering, as Hayek is

---

[9] Hayek, *The Fatal Conceit,* p. 64.
[10] Hayek, *The Fatal Conceit,* p. 12.

attempting to do. For the great motivation behind the constructivist, social engineer approach to dealing with social order is to get a leg up on the blind process of evolution which supposedly underlies the historical process. If ultimate reality is impersonal and ruled by chance, then man's best hope for survival is to use his reason to try to bend that process to his own ends. It is then that he reverts to the collectivist strategy, for it is this strategy which finds its legitimation in the mentality of a cosmic struggle for survival as opposed to the benign ultimate reality of a personal God seriously involved in creation and providence. For in the latter case mankind is not abandoned and alone, but working within a framework suffused with meaning and purpose. He therefore need not "take control," as it were, but rather learn to submit to the order within which he was created. And this mentality indeed provides a far better fit with the extended order than the blind-evolution mentality. For to accept tradition and work within it, one needs *pietas*, reverence, reverence for one's forebears who bequeathed it, a reverence born of the conviction that this order is willed by God and given to us as His gift.

What then are we to make of Hayek's approach? One thing is certain, he provided the definitive explanation of the basic contradiction of modern society. We are indeed confronted with a "head versus heart" incongruity which reaches deep down into our very souls. The extended <11> order of which we are a part runs contrary to deep-seated paternal/maternal instincts which rise up in revolt. Is there, then, a better explanation for this predicament?

---

The alternative explanation which follows is developed during the course of the book. Patriarchalism is indeed superseded by the extended order; how this occurred is explored in detail below. But the basic point that the family order is essentially collectivistic needs to be kept in mind at all times. Much of modern socialism finds its attraction in the promise to restore a familistic communitarianism to replace traditional family structures which have broken down. At bottom, it is the desire to go home again.

---

# Chapter 2

# The Gift of Liberty

THE IDEA that human society originally was organized on patriarchal lines is of course anything but new. But it is an idea that has had to struggle with a certain opposite number, the so-called social contract theory popularized by John Locke and Jean-Jacques Rousseau. Only in the 19$^{th}$ century did the "Patriarchal Theory," as one of its prime exponents Sir Henry Sumner Maine termed it, gain any ground. One reason for its grudging acceptance was proffered by Maine in his classic work *Ancient Law*:

> The effect of the evidence derived from comparative jurisprudence is to establish that view of the primeval condition of the human race which is known as the Patriarchal Theory. There is no doubt, of course, that this theory was originally based on the Scriptural history of the Hebrew patriarchs in Lower Asia; but, as has been explained already, its connexion with Scripture rather militated than otherwise against its reception as a complete theory, since the majority of the inquirers who till recently addressed themselves with most earnestness to the colligation of social phenomena, were either influenced by the strongest prejudice against Hebrew antiquities or by the strongest desire to construct their system without the assistance of religious records. Even now there is perhaps a disposition to undervalue these accounts, or rather to decline generalising from them, as forming part of the traditions of a Semitic people.[11]

If 19$^{th}$-century scholars had a problem accepting the biblical account as valid reference material, how much the more modern scholars? Be that as it may, the Bible offers its own version of an original patriarchal <**13**> condition, one which gives solutions to the questions generated by Hayek's exposition.

---

[11] Sir Henry Sumner Maine, *Ancient Law* (a series of lectures delivered in 1861), ch. 5.

We transition here from patriarchalism as an explanation for socialism to patriarchalism as an explanation of the origins of civilization. Likewise, we shift from prehistorical patriarchalism to historical patriarchalism. In this, we wish to take seriously the Biblical account of origins. Scientific? No less than putative, imagined evolutionary accounts of origins. The proof of the pudding is in the eating.

The Book of Genesis also begins with human society characterized by collective organization and the primacy of solidarity. But this condition is not spoken of as an evolved inheritance. Much rather it is explained as both the result of and remedy for the primordial Fall of Adam. The Fall is the Bible's explanation for that peculiar condition of man, the conflict arising from his double nature. Man is at the same time a participant in things of the spirit and things of the flesh, partaking of two worlds, combining them in his own soul. In his original state these things were ordered; in his fallen state, they came into conflict. "For the flesh lusteth against the Spirit, and the Spirit against the flesh: and these are contrary the one to the other: so that ye cannot do the things that ye would" (Galatians 5:17). The classic explanation was given by Augustine : "For the soul, revelling in its own liberty, and scorning to serve God, was itself deprived of the command it had formerly maintained over the body. And because it had wilfully deserted its superior Lord, it no longer held its own inferior servant; neither could it hold the flesh subject, as it would always have been able to do had it remained itself subject to God. Then began the flesh to lust against the Spirit, in which strife we are born, deriving from the first transgression a seed of death, and bearing in our members, and in our vitiated nature, the contest or even victory of the flesh" (*The City of God*, bk. XIII, ch. 13). The Bible goes on to report the result: unbridled anarchy and corruption, with a Lamech boasting of the victims of his vengeance, with "all flesh" corrupting itself on the earth, filling it with violence, to the degree that God determined to wipe it out and start anew with the Flood, the Ark, and the patriarch Noah. All this resulted in a social order established to counter the unbridled corruption of mankind in complete subjection to "the lusts of the flesh, the lust of the eyes, and the pride of life" (1 John 2:16).

Patriarchal society was thus the solution to the original universal corruption of society.

First the [*sic*]came the confusion of language, and following upon that (in fact <14> resulting from it) the division of mankind according to family. From then on men were determined by their language and ethnicity, parceled into groups standing over against one another and antagonistic to each other, a hostility only overcome with difficulty and through a long course of development.

From this point on, mankind has been afflicted with xenophobia, the effect of which is to keep him from joining forces to build another Tower of Babel. The tower-builders wished to make a name for themselves, in order to keep everyone from dispersing. God confounded this desire through the contrary impulse of xenophobia. The globalist temptation is here exposed as precisely that – a temptation, the temptation to join forces in the name of man, in disregard of God. The dialectic of xenophobia and cosmopolitanism finds its origin here.
By the way, we speak of the human race here as "men" and as "mankind," not because women do not matter, but because that is the way the Bible speaks – cf. Genesis 5: 2.

These familial groupings were the original "nations," organized patriarchally in terms of community and solidarity (Genesis chapter 10). The community of goods held primacy of place, in particular with regard to land. For the original title of ownership was simply occupation, and occupation not by individuals, as the social contract school thought, but by groups, by families and nations. The land, the basic resource, was held in common. It was shared out among group members but ultimate ownership remained in the hands of the collective. The product of labor was likewise shared rather than exchanged. An autarchical regime was maintained. All these developments helped to restrain the outbursts of anarchy which plagued original mankind.

The primacy of closed communities also explains that other less savory aspect of ancient society, conquest and slavery. The lack of exchange relations and the autarchical economic arrangement meant that the only form "international communication" could take was that of warfare. Conquest enabled the appropriation of property held by foreign groups, while slavery was the alternative to death proffered to those defeated in war. Augustine argued that slavery was the fruit of man's fall and the punishment for his sin. It was also the only alternative to death in an age of national isolationism.

The above should not be viewed as an absolute explanation of the arrangements of ancient societies, but rather as a description of their leading characteristics. Never is human society so absolute as to be entirely autarchic at the expense of an exchange orientation, nor is it ever so totally market-oriented as to completely exclude any form of societal solidarity. But ancient societies can be viewed as primarily autarchical, <15> just as modern Western societies are justifiably seen as primarily market-oriented.

---

This summary account can be augmented by consulting the treatments in *Common Law & Natural Rights*, *Investing in the New Normal*, and *Follow the Money*.

---

This explanation of the origins of human society serves better to explain the source of the extended order than does Hayek's evolutionary hypothesis because it shows from whence the impetus for the extended order came. For if mankind originally practiced only closed communitarianism, any explanation for the extended order has to be of the order of a *Deus ex machina*, parachuted in as it where, because the evolutionary system itself has no place for it. Survival value is not enough, for closed groups could have kept on surviving quite well enough without being integrated into a heterogenous framework such as the extended order. But if the Biblical explanation is valid, then we have a straightforward explanation for the existence both of closed communities and the extended order. They are both remedies for man's fallen condition, instituted by God to serve the higher purpose of establishing His Kingdom among men.

---

This explanation also enables us to see more clearly the attraction of collectivism as an escape from the rigors of responsibility and risk-taking, which are embodied in the extended order. See further *Investing in the New Normal*, "Collapsing Walls."

---

The Biblical narrative therefore does not stop with the provisional arrangement of nationhood. It goes on to describe the establishment of a "peculiar" nation in the midst of the sea of nations scattered about the ancient world.[12] On the heels of His establishing the new regime of separate nations, God called a man through whom He would initiate the subsequent phase of His plan and purpose, in fact nothing less than the initial installment of a new world order. "The Call of Abram" is the name theologians have given this development, described in Genesis ch. 12 (vv 1-3): "Now the LORD had said unto Abram, Get thee out of thy country, and from thy kindred, and from thy father's house, unto a land that I will shew thee: And I will make of thee a great nation, and I will bless thee, and make thy name great; and thou shalt be a blessing: And I will bless them that bless thee, and curse him that curseth thee: and in thee shall all <16> families of the earth be blessed." Two main things are to be noted here: the promise to make of Abram a "great nation," and the promise that through him "all the families" and by extension, as Genesis 18:18 states, "all the nations" would be blessed through him. With the establishment of nations God also provided the means through which the all-embracing rule of nations, of clans, of blood relationship, would be superseded.

---

The call of Abram stands in precise contrast to the Tower of Babel. There, men would make a name for themselves; here, God would make Abram's name great. Through Abram and the blessing that would come through him, the nations would be blessed, the curse would be reversed – precisely what the tower builders were trying to achieve.

---

The nation founded by Abram, later Abraham ("father of many nations"), was of course Israel. Clearly Israel was meant to stand in antithesis to the nations surrounding it even as it shared their basic tribal framework. It was to be both a model they would seek to imitate and a testimony through which they would be judged.

Israel's laws, its religion, indeed its divine mandate were geared toward the supersession of the closed community and monolithic national/religious barriers. Israel was not out for itself; it was rather a "kingdom of priests," God's ambassador nation in the world. It thus had a mission: to channel God's blessing to a cursed world (cf. Genesis 12:3).

Its main means of doing so was living out the break with itself as total community. Israel was a nation called to stand against itself: the natural

---

[12] Exodus 19:5; Deuteronomy 14:2, 26:18.

tendency of fallen mankind to deify itself in the group. Israel stood against group idolatry; it needed to watch over its own heart to see that it did not fashion or adopt gods to serve its interests, but rather that it was ready and able to serve God's interests. By embodying this mandate Israel made a decisive intervention in the lives of the nations, breaking the grip of the closed community, making possible progress toward true civilization: culture which outwardly transcends national boundaries and inwardly breaks the hold of the collective on individuals.

Paradoxically, it was the family itself which was the first to gain from the release from familistic totalism. The boundaries of family jurisdiction were pushed back in the direction of the nuclear household, freeing spouses and parents from the oppressive domination of senior members of the family/tribe. For within the total familistic community, the rulers <17> are fathers and the subjects are dependent minors. No one ever attains to a majority. Everyone is provided for, no one has to provide for himself. By the same token, everyone is dependent, and no one can make decisions for himself.

Freedom from benevolent despotism was attained first in ancient Israel. What enabled freedom to flourish was the establishment of the rule of law, which broke the monopoly of thought generated by tribal self-deification. Though imposed by divine mandate, the rule of law was offered in terms of covenant. Israel was in fact a junior partner with God in His rule. Israel participated in its own government: the essence of political liberty. But it did not do so autonomously, for it accepted God's offer that He be its king.

Israel thus clearly realized two great principles of liberty: the triumph of laws over men, and participation of the ruled in government. Here lay the basis of all future progress toward free society, as was noted by no less a historian than the great German 19th-century master, Leopold von Ranke:

> Under God's direct protection the life of the individual thus advanced together with the rights contained in the Decalogue, upon which all civil constitutions are based. Did not everything which modern states include in their constitutions develop from the concept and requirement of security of life and property [as mandated by the Decalogue]? The Mosaic state stands in opposition to kingship claiming to be a divine emanation – precisely in the fullest and sharpest contrast to Egypt. A more elevated inauguration of moral life in human society could not be conceived. Egypt is also significant

in that it evoked the opposite of its character and manners in the Israelite emigrants. No history of the human race could have come forth through the simple continuation of a national nature-religion. Such history first gains solid ground through Monotheism, which <18> frees itself root and branch of nature-worship. It founds a civil society that distances itself from every form of violation.[13]

Israel's laws established the necessary boundaries within which earthly life and culture could develop.[14] This is the purpose of biblical theocracy – not to realize heaven on earth, but to make room for heaven on earth, to ensure that, in Francis Schaeffer's words, nature does not swallow up grace.[15]

The rites established by Moses exemplify the break with the organic community. At every turn the "natural man" is bounded, warned off, put in his place. Right at the beginning the Israelite is circumcised, signifying that fertility, rather than worthy of stimulation and worship, is rather to be seen as a corrupted source of life. Life as it springs from the womb is fundamentally perverted; man is tainted by "original sin," as the theologians call it, something which, as Chesterton put it, is "the only part of Christian theology which can really be proved."[16]

---

[13] Leopold von Ranke, *Weltgeschichte* [World History], vol. I, p. 43.

[14] Gary North, *Leviticus: The Book of Boundaries* (Tyler, TX: Institute for Christian Economics, 1994).

[15] See in particular his *Escape from Reason* (Downers Grove, IL: InterVarsity Press, 1968).

[16] "Certain new theologians dispute original sin, which is the only part of Christian theology which can really be proved. Some followers of the Reverend R.J. Campbell, in their almost too fastidious spirituality, admit divine sinlessness, which they cannot see even in their dreams. But they essentially deny human sin, which they can see in the street. The strongest saints and the strongest sceptics alike took positive evil as the starting-point of their argument. If it be true (as it certainly is) that a man can feel exquisite happiness in skinning a cat, then the religious philosopher can only draw one of two deductions. He must either deny the existence of God, as all atheists do; or he must deny the present union between God and man, as all Christians do. The new theologians seem to think it a highly rationalistic solution to deny the cat." G.K. Chesterton, *Orthodoxy*, ch. II, "The Maniac."

The institution of sacrifice likewise symbolizes the shortcomings and corruption of the flesh and the need for its purification. That animals <19>
could be used as substitutes for human beings is testimony to the depth to
which man had fallen in his rebellion against God, namely, to the level of an
animal; such is the life lived after the flesh rather than the Spirit (cf. e.g., 2
Peter 2:10–12, Jude).

The priesthood itself, in its separation from the people, symbolized the
inadequacy of the organic community to approach God. Israel was called by
God to be His "holy nation" and "royal priesthood" (Exodus 19:6); nevertheless, when called to Mount Sinai the people were not allowed to approach
the mountain (v. 12, 21ff.); only Moses and Aaron were allowed to. God's
holiness was too much for them. God Himself established the tabernacle and
its accompanying priesthood as the indispensable precondition for His resi-
dence in the nation. A direct relation was out of the question; Moses and the
priesthood had to mediate the relation between Israel and Jehovah.

The Aaronic/Levitical priesthood also represented a break with the familistic priesthood model in use prior to the establishment of the tabernacle.
That priesthood was insufficiently holy, insufficiently set apart to mediate the
deeper, closer relationship God established with Israel at Sinai. It too, therefore, was not allowed to approach the mountain (Ex. 19: 22, 24). The priesthood and the sacrifices were removed from the families, centralized and
bounded, and the older mode of familistic worship – on "the high places" –
was banned (cf. Deuteronomy 12:5ff.).

Finally, the establishment of kingship sealed the judgment of God over
the natural community. Israel failed to attend to the tabernacle worship God
established and instead sought after the gods of the Canaanites: it thus re-
verted to the old-time religion of naturalist nationalism. God therefore delivered the nation into its enemies' hands, the most fearsome of which were
the Philistines. Israel then turned and asked for a king: "but we will have a
king over us; that we also may be like all the nations; and that our king may
judge us, and go out before us, and fight our battles" (I Samuel 8: 19–20) – a
clear rejection of God's <20> transcendent kingship in favor of nature-god
nationalist kingship. God gave them a king, but not the kind they asked for;
he give them a king after his own heart, who would honor Him and fulfill the
covenant in the place of the people; a king who was also a priest after the
order of Melchizedek (cf. Psalm 110), who thus stood above the nation both

in terms of his lineage – not being descended from Abraham, "without father, without mother, without descent, having neither beginning of days, nor end of life; but made like unto the Son of God" (Hebrews 7: 3) – and in terms of his ministry, a priesthood over the nations, empowered to judge between the nations and bless the righteous victor (see p. 33 below).

Israel fell short of its calling. In fact, one might say that it was fated – predestined – to do so. The career of the nation Israel is testimony to the inability of the natural community to exhibit true justice and true holiness. Its failure is an example to the ages not to seek salvation in the earthly community. Israel's positive legacy was nevertheless rich in every way. Israel was the first truly free republic. Its laws were and would remain the model for all human communities (cf. Deuteronomy 4: 5–8). And it gave birth to the spiritual community through which these laws and the worship of the one true God would spread to all the world.

Thus came the breakout. "I am the LORD thy God, which have brought thee out of the land of Egypt, out of the house of bondage" (Exodus 20:2). Truly this was mankind's declaration of independence. Liberty was a gift, not a right; by rights man was a slave. God offered; man must accept. Liberty would come as slavery was renounced. But the fleshpots of Egypt held their own charms, and slavery in its many guises would continue to hold its appeal to the sons of Adam.

---

Among other things, the covenant order established in Israel brought the objective aspect of liberty, the rule of law, into the foreground. This lies in the nature of the case: God made a covenant with Israel by virtue of the claim He had over it, gained by His victory over the Egyptians, by His action to free the Israelites from the house of bondage; in exchange, Israel became His possession. On this basis, He handed down His laws and ordinances and commanded obedience: the objective foundation of liberty. While the subjective, participatory aspect of liberty was included in this arrangement, it did not take the foreground. That would change with the advent of nations bringing the subjective aspect of liberty into prominence, making human action primary. This will be highlighted in the next chapter.

# Chapter 3

# The Subject of Liberty: The Citizen

THE LEGACY of Israel was picked up by a civilization which was in its infancy at the time the sons of Jacob were working out their covenant destiny. What is significant is that just at this time, when incipient Greek civilization was at its most plastic and most receptive, the missionary influence of Israel was at its height, in the form of the reign of Solomon. Solomon's influence extended throughout the inhabited world, and one conduit of that influence was the Phoenicians, through Tyre and its king, Hiram. Archaeologists and historians agree that Phoenicia had a massive impact on Greece; for one thing, the Greek alphabet was derived from the Phoenician. The Greeks followed the Phoenician pattern, settling in city-states and pursuing seaborne trade. With the growth of Greek civilization the center of gravity of the ancient world shifted westward, away from Egypt and Mesopotamia and toward the "Great Sea," the Mediterranean.

Like Israel, Hellas rejected the idea of human sacrifice to appease bloodthirsty gods. The legend of Theseus symbolizes Hellas's definitive break with the east: the beast with the body of a man and the head of a bull, demanding Athenian children on which to gorge – the very embodiment of the eastern god Moloch – is once and for all destroyed.[17]

The Greeks thus approached life more rationally than did the Asians. From the start it is clear that they wish to put everything in a certain uniquely human perspective.[18] The absence of divine kingship provided the Greeks the freedom to develop a "lay" culture. And of course the self-sufficient city provided the Greeks the environment in which to produce such a culture.

The major difference between Greece and the east lay in the system of government; in contrast to royal/national despotisms, Greek government was massively decentralized to the level of the city, with citizen <22> participation, in varying degrees, the norm. For this reason Greeks called

---

[17] cf. von Ranke, *Weltgeschichte*, vol. I, p. 119.

[18] Werner Jaeger, *Paideia*, vol. I, introduction.

themselves free, to contrast themselves with the "barbarians" of the east, whom they called slaves.

The center of Greek life was the agora, the market place/town center, the focus of both political and economic life. From the eastern perspective this testified to misplaced priorities, as witness the Persian king Cyrus's judgement, recorded by Herodotus:

> Cyrus is said, on hearing the speech of the herald, to have asked some Greeks who were standing by, "Who these Lacedaemonians were, and what was their number, that they dared to send him such a notice?" When he had received their reply, he turned to the Spartan herald and said, "I have never yet been afraid of any men, who have a set place in the middle of their city, where they come together to cheat each other and forswear themselves. If I live, the Spartans shall have troubles enough of their own to talk of, without concerning themselves about the Ionians." Cyrus intended these words as a reproach against all the Greeks, because of their having market-places where they buy and sell, which is a custom unknown to the Persians, who never make purchases in open marts, and indeed have not in their whole country a single market-place.[19]

Whether the story is apocryphal or not is secondary; it nicely expresses the gap between Greece and the east.

At the heart of the Greek *polis* is the break with the family as the total community. For this reason Greece was the first community to bring to the fore the citizen ideal. Aristotle's work contains the best discussion of this shift, to city-based as opposed to tribal society. In his *Politics*, he makes a sharp distinction between family and city government. The family he described as monarchical, which is the reason why all "primi- <23> tive" societies are monarchical: they are extensions of the family. Patriarchal government is monarchical government exercised over a familistic community. But the familistic community was superseded when men decided they wanted more from society than simply to live: they wanted to live well. For this purpose the city was called into existence. "When several villages are united in a

---

[19] *The History of Herodotus*, Book I.

single complete community, large enough to be nearly or quite self-sufficing, the state [*polis* – thus city – RCA] comes into existence, originating in the bare needs of life, and continuing in existence for the sake of a good life."[20] Though in its infancy city government was also monarchical, in time citizen rule came to be the norm.

What the city provides that the extended family does not is the *good* life, that is, a life consisting in more than bare existence. Thanks to the division of labor it has culture to offer. The good life is possible in a community which enjoys the provision of a diversity of goods and services. The means through which such a division of labor is coordinated is the market mechanism and money.

This means the supersession of the community of goods. The market functions according to a different standard than the family. In the market-place, one does not have the right to the fruit of another's labor, the way he does as the member of a family. He instead must offer something in exchange; otherwise he cannot obtain what he wants.

This is the secret of, and the key to, the freedom offered by the city. Freedom requires the supersession of the community of goods and the reintegration of economic activity via the market. While the community of goods requires a central distributing authority, an exchange economy makes such superfluous. Voluntary exchange of goods and services ensures that distribution occurs in terms of reciprocity: no one gets more than what he gives. This equilibrium of giving and receiving is the <24> epitome of economic justice; any other system imposes forced labor.

The key to the mechanism is the principle of reciprocity: no one gets who does not also give. Aristotle recognized the importance of this principle, going so far as to see in it "the salvation of cities."[21]

> For it is by reciprocity that the city holds together. Men seek to return either evil for evil – and if they cannot do so, think their position mere slavery – or good for good – and if they cannot do so there is no exchange, but it is by exchange that they hold together.[22]

---

[20] Aristotle, *Politics*, I:2.

[21] *Politics*, II:2.

[22] *Nicomachean Ethics*, V:5.

In economic terms, reciprocity means that goods and services are exchanged in such a way that an essential accounting balance is maintained between what is exchanged. The balance is maintained when the value of exchanged goods and services cancel each other out, leaving no further debt or claim.

But how does one know the proper value of varied and disparate goods and services? A house has a different value than a shoe has a different value than food. This is the rationale for the institution of money: it serves as a common mediator of value. It mediates value because, by common consent, it is a store of value. If one exchanges something for money, one can be sure that one can exchange that money for something of roughly equal value on a future day. This then enables exchanges to take more complicated shape than simple one-for-one barter. Multilateral exchange becomes possible, obviating the need for a central distributing authority.

> It is for this end that money has been introduced, and it becomes in a sense
> an intermediate; for it measures all things, and <25> therefore the surplus
> and the shortfall – how many shoes are equal to a house or to a given amount
> of food. The number of shoes exchanged for a house (or for a given amount
> of food) must therefore correspond to the ratio of builder to shoemaker. For
> if this be not so, there will be no exchange and no intercourse. And this proportion
> will not be effected unless the goods are somehow equal. All goods
> must therefore be measured by some one thing, as we said before. Now this
> unit is in truth demand, which holds all things together (for if men did not
> need one another's goods at all, or did not need them equally, there would
> be either no exchange or not the same exchange); but money has become by
> convention a sort of representative of demand; and this is why it has the
> name 'money' [*nomisma*] – because it exists not by nature but by law [*nomos*].... There will, then, be reciprocity when the terms have been equated so
> that as farmer is to shoemaker, the amount of the shoemaker's work is to that
> of the farmer's work for which it exchanges.[23]

---

[23] *Nicomachean Ethics*, V:5.

If this balance is upset, the system is forced out of equilibrium, meaning that somewhere somebody got more than his fair share while someone else got less. In the case of free exchange, this can happen only in the case of theft, or alternatively in gift-giving. Accounting ensures equity.

The upshot of this arrangement is the citizen ideal, the cornerstone of the free society. The citizen ideal combines three institutions: the nuclear family, the market, and participatory politics. The family, far from being eliminated in the shift from communal to city life, is accorded a place of honor as the seedbed of the prosperity of the city. Its role as a community of goods and unit of economic activity is necessary to the city. For only by deriving their basic sustenance from the family can citizens act in the independent, uncoerced manner required in the marketplace and in <26> politics.

Participatory politics is the corollary of self-sufficient economic activity. As the householder on his own account engages in exchange in the marketplace, he also on his own account engages in political activity as a citizen. Politics is the business of citizens, heads of economically independent households. This puts the city's constitution on a sound basis, for citizens do not subvert the political process for private economic gain, precipitating a return to dependency and authoritarianism as existed in patriarchal society. Rather, citizens are zealous to ensure that the political process is kept pure of the authority/dependency nexus. They strive to pass and uphold laws which answer to the city's basic bond, reciprocity.

Historically the city as described by Aristotle also functioned as a sovereign state – the city-state. This brought additional burdens to bear which its simple political apparatus could not stand up to without being deformed beyond recognition. Pressure came from outside. There was the need to deal with other sovereign states, many of which were powerful and predatory. There was also trade, the main connecting link between states. Not only did citizens trade among themselves, they traded with foreigners, and this required special arrangements as well.

If states abided by rules of peaceful exchange the maintenance of a decentralized city-based civilization would not have been problematic. But the need to defend against foreign aggression brought with it the need to establish military institutions which in themselves carried the seeds of the destruction of liberty, since they provide certain citizens with the means to subject their fellow citizens by force. Even more sinister was the need to use military means to achieve commercial ends, made necessary because foreign trade often encountered artificial and unfair restrictions and obstructions from traders of other states bent on preserving by military means their own market shares. By combining military and commercial ends the separation of economic and political action is ended: <27> politics becomes the struggle to have this citizen's economic interests advanced at the expense of that citizen's, because it is impossible to advance all interests equally.

Under these pressures the maintenance of freedom became, to say the least, problematic. Rather than maintain the bond of the city – the commitment to reciprocity and the renunciation of the pursuit of private gain through the political process – citizens resigned themselves to the unpleasant reality and worked to ensure that their interests were not forgotten within the power machine that the state had become. This predicament has been labeled "the Machiavellian Moment" by the eminent contemporary historian J.G.A. Pocock. Pocock saw this as the major theme of Machiavelli's political works.[24] Machiavelli wrestled with the problem of how to preserve liberty while striving to overcome external threats. His solution boiled down to a freeholding armed citizenry, an idea which later became highly influential in the English and American traditions of political liberty. Land ownership made the citizenry economically independent and thus preserved them from political corruption – selling out politically for economic gain – while arms and militias protected the citizenry from subjugation by a standing army and its military leaders.

Aristotle never made the connection that Machiavelli did. He never brought the problems of foreign and domestic policy together. He viewed things strictly from the perspective of the internal constitution. But he certainly recognized the problem of the aggrandizing state, and he cast far and wide for a solution to it. In his view this was the crucial problem to solve if a city was to maintain its existence. The invasion of economic interests in the political arena led to the formation of two basic parties, the propertied – the oligarchs – and the property-less – the democrats. Each <28> sought to ground the constitution on a particular principle which reflected their economic interest: oligarchs on restricted citizenship with a property

---

[24] J. G. A. Pocock, *The Machiavellian Moment*.

qualification, and democrats with unrestricted citizenship, without qualification. The strife between these two parties tears cities apart from the inside.

> Democracy... arises out of the notion that those who are equal in any respect are equal in all respects; because men are equally free, they claim to be absolutely equal. Oligarchy is based on the notion that those who are unequal in one respect are in all respects unequal; being unequal, that is, in property, they suppose themselves to be unequal absolutely. The democrats think that as they are equal they ought to be equal in all things; while the oligarchs, under the idea that they are unequal, claim too much, which is one form of inequality. All these forms of government have a kind of justice, but, tried by an absolute standard, they are faulty; and, therefore, both parties, whenever their share in the government does not accord with their preconceived ideas, stir up revolution.[25]

The solution to this problem lies in fostering and conserving the middle class. "This is the class of citizens which is most secure in a state, for they do not, like the poor, covet their neighbors' goods; nor do others covet theirs, as the poor covet the goods of the rich; and as they neither plot against others, nor are themselves plotted against, they pass through life safely."[26] Middle-class citizens therefore are not tempted to subvert the political process to economic ends, either to obtain that which is someone else's or to keep others from tampering with their vested interests.

Aristotle's solution and Machiavelli's meet in the doctrine of the economically independent citizen, uncorrupted by private interests and <29> so able to devote himself to the public good.[27] The question is, would that be enough?

---

We saw first, that the covenant with God furnished Israel with the objective aspect of liberty. Then, that with its citizen ideal, Greece provided the subjective aspect. These two aspects now merge in the further development of history. We turn to the process of this interaction.

---

[25] *Politics*, V.1.

[26] Aristotle, *Politics*, IV.11.

[27] Pocock, *The Machiavellian Moment*, p. 203.

# Chapter 4

# After the Order of Melchizedek

ARISTOTLE'S ANALYSIS of the problems facing the city is critically important, because he puts his finger on the major problem – the relationship between property and politics – and goes a long way toward a solution, in his delineation of the citizen ideal. Nevertheless his solution is lacking in a critical area. This is characteristic not only of his politics but his philosophy as a whole. His solutions are to be found in reconciling interests, a reflection of his immanental approach. Aristotle does not really believe in the rule of law; rather, he does believe in it, but he does not really trust that it will provide a lasting solution. And for good reason: Aristotle was a keen student of reality, and he saw clearly that interests play the deciding role in every conflict, and that if the rule of law was to be given a fighting chance, it would have to be grounded in a favorable balance of interests.

Thus for all the attention Aristotle gives to the mechanics of the constitution, he gives rather short shrift to the very idea of the source of a constitution. His constitution is grounded in justice, certainly, and is maintained by virtue, undoubtedly; but what is the source of justice and of virtue? Here more than anywhere else, Aristotle fell short of his teacher, Plato.

Plato diagnosed the disease of the city as civil war, just as did Aristotle, but he proposed another solution. Not the balancing of interests, but their transcendence – that was the way forward. Plato did not want to give an inch to appetite, which for him was the source of all the city's problems. He wanted to find out how mankind could realize its higher destiny, the destiny to which each individual's eternal soul testified, that man does not live on bread alone, but on every word that proceeds from the mouth of God. Only that word could have the authority and wisdom to put a stop to conflict and lead to peaceful social life.

Plato assuredly was one of those Athenians who worshiped at the altar <31> to the unknown God (cf. Acts 17:23). His writings are filled with the yearning to know the truth, the goodness, and the beauty whose only real home could be heaven. On earth was nothing but illusion, deception, violence. Men fought and killed for what? Passing, perishable things like wealth, influence, pleasure! Idiotic! Why is man so sick? Plato was sure it is because he does not know any better. Someone needed to come down from heaven and teach him the eternal truth; otherwise, he was condemned to pursue his lusts. And such a wise man not only needed to teach, but he needed the power to have his teaching enforced. The wise man must also be a king.

Distilling Plato's policy prescriptions, one may arrive at two core components. On the one hand monarchy, an institution which transcends the political process and is capable of imposing the rule of law on the factions of interest groups. On the other the philosopher, the lover of wisdom, the lover of truth, the one who has ascended into heaven and peered into the secrets of God, who can return with this knowledge to society and use this knowledge as his standard and measure for assessing the behavior of men. Early in his career Plato saw these offices combined; later he distinguished between them, and supposed that the philosopher would initially create a constitution, and this constitution would be implemented and maintained by the ruler. Then, and only then, would the city find peace.

But had not Plato's prescriptions already been fulfilled in ancient Israel? Was not Solomon such a king that ruled with utter justice, because he had been given wisdom from above, from God Himself? Did not Solomon write of wisdom in as fervent terms as Plato ever did? Who else but a philosopher-king could have written this paean:

> I wisdom dwell with prudence, and find out knowledge of witty inventions. The fear of the LORD is to hate evil: pride, and arrogancy, and the evil way, and the froward mouth, do I hate. <32> Counsel is mine, and sound wisdom: I am understanding; I have strength. By me kings reign, and princes decree justice. By me princes rule, and nobles, even all the judges of the earth. I love them that love me; and those that seek me early shall find me. Riches and honour are with me; yea, durable riches and righteousness. My fruit is better than gold, yea, than fine gold; and my revenue than choice silver. I lead in the way of righteousness, in the midst of the paths of judgment: That I may cause those that love me to inherit substance; and I will fill their treasures (Proverbs 8:12–21).

The first king of Israel, the Benjamite Saul, was a man of great stature and with all the outward appearance of a king, but whose heart was not right with

God. Upon his encroachment of the priestly dignity – standard fare for the divine kings of the nations round about – the kingdom was taken from him and given to David, the man after God's own heart. David understood the boundaries between the sacred and the profane; he recognized his calling as a servant under God for the people. He realized that God had established his throne, not man, and that this was something which was not simply a favor to him but of monumental significance for mankind. "And this was yet a small thing in thy sight, O Lord GOD; but thou hast spoken also of thy servant's house for a great while to come" (II Samuel 7:19a) – and then comes a very mysterious phrase, literally "this is the torah of mankind, Lord GOD" (v. 19b). It is a phrase the translation of which has stumped generations of exegetes. But the meaning seems to be this:[28] the Davidic monarchy carried with it the destiny of the human race.

Intimately connected with the ascension of David was his conquest of a city-stronghold still held by the Jebusites in the midst of the territory of <33> the tribe of Benjamin. Of old the city was called Salem, "Peace." It was here that the legendary figure Melchizedek, "king of righteousness," ruled as both king and priest. It was Melchizedek who blessed the patriarch Abraham for restoring justice to the international community of Palestine; Melchizedek was thus the type of moral authority which could sanction the use of arms even between sovereign powers, and in recognition of this Abraham paid him a tithe. It was therefore no empty gesture that David established his throne there, as well as, in time, the tabernacle service of God, on Mount Zion. This was Jerusalem, the city of peace, the city of God: "glorious things are spoken of thee, O city of God" (Psalm 87:3).

The prophecies regarding this throne began to take on majestic dimensions. David himself perceived the significance, in seeing that his son would sit at God's right hand, ruling his enemies with a rod of iron, elevated to the status of priesthood, "after the order of Melchizedek"(v. 4). This was empire – rule over the nations round about – Melchizedekian empire, the empire of righteousness and peace. Kings would submit to this empire, or be broken, as another psalm of David made clear: "Kiss the son, lest he be angry, and you

---

[28] Following Dumbrell, who follows Walter Kaiser: William J. Dumbrell, *Covenant and Creation*, pp.151–152.

perish from the way, when His wrath is kindled in but a little time. Blessed are all who put their trust in him" (Psalm 2: 12).

The initial fulfillment of the prophecies and the promises came already in the reign of David's immediate son, Solomon. The empire Solomon established was the high-water mark for the nation Israel. Solomon was not only blessed with rest from his enemies and with material prosperity ("And all king Solomon's drinking vessels were of gold, and all the vessels of the house of the forest of Lebanon were of pure gold; none were of silver: it was nothing accounted of in the days of Solomon" I Kings 10:21), he was renowned for his *wisdom*, and in particular his application of wisdom in judging the people. His decision regarding the two prostitutes and the child became a byword for his judicial acumen; his proverbs, his court, his wealth, the prosperity of his <34> people, the peace he brought to the entire region, made him an object of awe and reverence among foreign princes, such as the Queen of Sheba (cf. I Kings 10, II Chronicles 9). For [*sic:* read, "From"] his court the idea of wisdom and justice as the standard of government emanated throughout the world. It was this influence which, through the Phoenician conduit, took root in the incipient Hellenistic culture of "the isles" as the Bible calls them: the Mediterranean coastlands ("and the isles shall wait for his law," Isaiah 42:4), which would come full circle in Plato's vision of the philosopher-king.

But the Solomonic dispensation was only a down payment on the promises, not their exhaustion. In fact, Solomon ended his days in abject backsliding, even having joined his myriad foreign wives in worshiping their accursed idols. While his kingdom was the blessing of Israelites, the epitome of peace and security – "And Judah and Israel dwelt safely, every man under his vine and under his fig tree, from Dan even to Beersheba, all the days of Solomon" (I Kings 4:25) – in the end it became top-heavy from foreign wives and accompanying pomp & circumstance, and began to burden Israelite pocketbooks. When Solomon's son Rehoboam was set to ascend the throne, the elders put the matter succinctly: "Thy father made our yoke grievous: now therefore make thou the grievous service of thy father, and his heavy yoke which he put upon us, lighter, and we will serve thee" (I Kings 12: 4).

Still, Solomon's reign was exemplary for its respect of Israelite liberties. The superstructure of government and military Solomon erected over Israel supplemented rather than replaced traditional local and tribal forms of government. And the forced labor he required to build his palaces and cities, not

to mention the temple of the Lord, he obtained not among his brother Israelites but among subject peoples (cf. I Kings 9: 20-22). It is therefore likely
that the backsliding in his old age led to abuse of these liberties and increased
the weight of the royal edifice, to the point that the people could stone to
death the royal officer in charge of forced <35> labor (cf. I Kings 12: 18).

Upon Solomon's death the kingdom was split in two, and the northern
kingdom, which kept the name Israel, gained a monarchy which sported all
the characteristics of proper tyranny, mainly because it lost the independent
counterweight of the temple service and substituted a state-sponsored sa-
cred-calf religion in its stead. The kingdom of Judah, on the other hand, retained the religious institution of Moses, and was favored with not a few
faithful kings for it. Still, the trend in the period of the kings is clearly downward. This was the time of the great prophets, for the sins of kings and people,
public and private, were great. It became ever clearer that the covenant history of Israel could not be fulfilled in this trajectory, and in fact was not even
meant to be fulfilled in it. Old Testament Israel pointed beyond herself to
something greater.

That something was, in the first place, universal. It involved a universal
kingdom, extending over all the peoples and nations of the earth. It centered
on a royal city, seat of the throne of this universal emperor, king of kings.
This royal city had at its heart the temple of the LORD God, who Himself
would reign over the nations. And this universal kingdom would impose a
universal law.

The prophet Isaiah most beautifully captured the promise of the coming
kingdom.

> And it shall come to pass in the last days, that the mountain of the LORD's
> house shall be established in the top of the mountains, and shall be exalted
> above the hills; and all nations shall flow unto it. And many people shall go
> and say, Come ye, and let us go up to the mountain of the LORD, to the house
> of the God of Jacob; and he will teach us of his ways, and we will walk in his
> paths: for out of Zion shall go forth the law, and the word of the LORD from
> Jerusalem. And he shall judge among the nations, and shall rebuke many peo-
> ple: and they shall beat their <37> swords into plowshares, and their spears
> into pruninghooks: nation shall not lift up sword against nation, neither
> shall they learn war any more (Isaiah 2: 2–4).

All the more remarkable that Isaiah should entertain such felicitous visions, seeing as how the northern kingdom had already been carried off into exile and Judah was hanging on by its fingernails. To Isaiah it was given to see extraordinary things; he looked beyond the bare political prospects of national Israel to the prospect of a universal kingdom of peace.

Whatever that entailed, the hope of national Israel seemed to be dashed with her defeat and exile at the hands of Babylon. The temple was destroyed, the people carried off, the flower of Israel put to the service of Nebuchadnezzar. But something of profound significance occurred in this service. Nebuchadnezzar took four young Judeans and put them in charge of Babylonian imperial administration; one of these rose to become second only to the king in power and authority. Daniel, the one who achieved this, himself was also a prophet. What he was given to see was enough to curdle his blood and make him fall down dumbstruck. He saw the rise and fall of four successive terrifying empires, of which his master's was only the first; only after these empires had accomplished their dreadful work would come the final establishment of the kingdom of God.

---

With the coming of the Kingdom, the curse is reversed and the centripetal force in effect since Babel is overcome. The nations find their "center of gravity" in this fulfillment of prophecy. This falls under the Magnalia Dei, the great works of God, not human achievement. The four empires usher in this eschatological reality. Human attempts to "immanentize the eschaton" (Eric Voegelin) will meet the same fate as Babel.

---

# Chapter 5

# The End of the Beginning

DANIEL'S FOUR EMPIRES raised themselves on the crushed remains of the ancient east and its patchwork of nations. The ancient world was no more; a new age was upon mankind. One by one these independent kingdoms were snatched up and amalgamated. Even once-proud Egypt was impotent to stem the oncoming tide.

Daniel saw that the empire he served, Babylon, would be succeeded by the Medes and Persians, with the illustrious Cyrus at their head. Remarkably, Cyrus would rebuild what Nebuchadnezzar had smashed. "Thus saith the LORD, thy redeemer, and he that formed thee from the womb, I am the LORD... that saith of Cyrus, He is my shepherd, and shall perform all my pleasure: even saying to Jerusalem, Thou shalt be built; and to the temple, Thy foundation shall be laid" (Isaiah 44: 24, 28). For this Cyrus was God's chosen instrument, to further the work He had begun through Israel.

> Thus saith the LORD to his anointed, to Cyrus, whose right hand I have holden, to subdue nations before him; and I will loose the loins of kings, to open before him the two leaved gates; and the gates shall not be shut; I will go before thee, and make the crooked places straight: I will break in pieces the gates of brass, and cut in sunder the bars of iron: And I will give thee the treasures of darkness, and hidden riches of secret places, that thou mayest know that I, the LORD, which call thee by thy name, am the God of Israel. For Jacob my servant's sake, and Israel mine elect, I have even called thee by thy name: I have surnamed thee, though thou hast not known me. I am the LORD, and there is none else, there is no God beside me: I girded thee, though thou hast not known me: That they may know from the rising of the sun, and from the west, that there is none beside me. I am the LORD, and there is none else. I form <38> the light, and create darkness: I make peace, and create evil: I the LORD do all these things (Isaiah 45: 1–7).

This Persian empire constituted a new departure in history. Through it, the purpose of Israel – the spread of the knowledge of the true God to the nations, to the destruction of their national idolatries – moved to a new level. The destruction of Jerusalem by the Babylonians actually promoted this plan, as did the conquest of Babylon by Persia. For it was through the command and good will of Cyrus and his followers on the Persian throne that Jerusalem was rebuilt and the temple was restored. What was accomplished in the rise of the empires and the conquest of those nations was the destruction of their faith in their gods, and thus the destruction of their belief in the exclusivity of their national interests, the seedbed of organicist totalism. The favor shown the religion of Israel by the empire allowed *it* to fill the resulting religious vacuum.

While these events were taking place in the area of the Fertile Crescent, Hellas was taking root on the shores of the Mediterranean Sea. Split into a multitude of individual, autonomous cities, Greece had no political center, no overarching kingship. The clash with Persia was inevitable. Persia had a divine mission, to subdue all nations under its feet; Greece likewise had a mission, to preserve the liberty of the city-state. Thanks to its two leading representatives Sparta and Athens, Greece withstood the onslaught of the King of Kings and thus preserved the tradition of liberty for future generations.

Being spared that fate, however, another awaited the Greeks, that of exhausting the possibilities offered by the city-state. The Athenian democracy represented the end of the road, the rise of the Sophists the seed-time of the *polis*. As Plato realized, Persia and Athens represented the two great possibilities of organized human community. Persia exemplified monarchy, and under Cyrus it was a model monarchy. Athens exemplified democracy, and during the Persian War it was a model democracy. <**39**> Both polities degenerated from their original healthy state, each to exaggerate the basic characteristic underlying its polity: Persia exaggerated authority, Athens exaggerated liberty.[29] What lay beyond these two, each exhausted by conflict with the other and by conflict within itself? Daniel's prophecy held the answer – and only its first two stages had played out.

The rise of the Macedonian empire, first with Philip and then Alexander, represented the next stage in Daniel's prophecy and the logical next step in Plato's line of thought. For this empire consciously utilized the *polis*. The

---

[29] *Laws,* Book III.

*polis* became the tool of Macedonian dominion. For the first time the either/or – monarchy *or* city – was overcome; under the aegis of Hellenistic monarchical dominion cities blossomed throughout the east.

Nor was this stage the fulfillment. The fourth beast was loosed, anxious to take the course of history a step further. Rome arose, a republic – that is, a *polis*, a city-state like the Greek city-states – but a republic with a difference. Rome reigned, not by crushing its rivals, but by coopting them. It joined with its sister republics in a federal union. In developing the federal principle Rome enabled the rule of law to gain universal validity and universal application. Roman law bound cities and nations into a single civilization, something Hellenism never accomplished due to its union based in divine kingship rather than the rule of law.

Paradoxical though it may seem, as long as Rome remained a republic this honor lay beyond its grasp. The republican period of its empire was a period of naked exploitation of conquered provinces (as opposed to federated allies) in the name of republican liberty. Factions in Rome fought over the spoils; no one cared for the plight of the conquered. Only citizens mattered; citizens could fight back, citizens had political clout. Rome the city was the center of empire, and the internal politics of that city determined all else. Never have politics been so corrupt, the effects so <40> devastating.

Though the defenders of republican liberty wailed and gnashed their teeth, the transformation from republic to empire came as a relief to the subject peoples of Rome.[30] Augustus freed himself from subjection to the Senate and people of Rome, and thus, consciously or unconsciously, did something for the good of everyone who was not a Roman. City politics no longer ruled the destiny of the empire; instead, a monarchy transcending the political process brought a semblance of uniform justice. Virgil realized this, and wrote his *Aeneid* to proclaim it.

---

[30] "The Caesarean system gave an unprecedented freedom to the dependencies, and raised them to a civil equality which put an end to the dominion of race over race and of class over class. The monarchy was hailed as a refuge from the pride and cupidity of the Roman people; and the love of equality, the hatred of nobility, and the tolerance of despotism implanted by Rome became, at least in Gaul, the chief feature of the national character." Lord Acton, "Nationality," in *Essays in the History of Liberty*, Volume I, p. 422.

Let others better mould the running mass
Of metals, and inform the breathing brass,
And soften into flesh a marble face:
Plead better at the bar; describe the skies,
And when the stars descend, and when they rise.
But Rome, 'tis thine alone, with awful sway,
To rule the world and make mankind obey,
Disposing peace and war thy own majestic way.
To tame the proud, the fettered slave to free –
These are imperial arts, and worthy thee.[31]

Daniel's prophecy still had yet another stage to go. The statue had not yet been crushed by the stone taken out of the mountain (cf. Daniel 2:34). But the day was drawing near. Caesar hastened the day by arrogating to himself the same divine status his predecessors had in the east. He was <41> not yet the servant of the Most High God; far from it. But there was born in the reign of Augustus the long-awaited Son of David who would rule the Gentiles, yea even Caesar, with a rod of iron (Revelation 12:5; cf. Psalm 2:7). His kingdom would be an everlasting kingdom, which would crush the kingdom of the fourth beast (Daniel 7: 26–27). He it was who was "prince of the kings of the earth" (Revelation 1: 5). Even so, his kingdom was not of this world, for He could say, "Render unto Caesar the things that are Caesar's, and to God the things that are God's" (Mark 12: 17). Nevertheless, the hierarchy was clear: as Jesus said to Pontius Pilate, "Thou couldest have no power at all against me, except it were given thee from above" (John 19: 11). And as Paul would later put it, "For he [the Roman magistrate] is the minister of God to thee for good.... He is the minister of God, a revenger to execute wrath upon him that doeth evil.... For this cause pay ye tribute also: for they are God's ministers" (Romans 13: 4, 6).

Constantine would be the Caesar who would finally admit to, and submit to, this state of affairs, as would, in his own way, Julian "the Apostate," though entirely against his will: "Thou hast conquered, O Galilean." Rome was crushed into powder by this stone cut without hands (Daniel 2:35) –

---

[31] Dryden translation, Book VI.

but better by far to be pulverized by that stone than to stumble over it and be broken (Matthew 21: 44), than to discover in it a stumbling block and a stone of offense (I Peter 2: 8).

The heavenly kingdom had arrived, had been proclaimed, had triumphed. This kingdom too had a capital city, the heavenly Jerusalem; and it had its own citizenry, who shared in the rule with their King: this was the *ekklesia*,[32] the Church. The leading members of this heavenly citizens' assembly were the bishops, who by the time of Constantine headed worshiping *ekklesiai* throughout the empire. These bishops joined with the emperor to shore up the tottering reign of justice in his domin- <42> ions. They admonished the emperor to remember that he had submitted to the rule of the heavenly King of Kings. He was that king's servant, he was a member of the heavenly Jerusalem, his rule was rule entirely dependent on the things above. The emperor ruled by divine right, but not with divine power. And so he must rule according to the will of Him who called him. So was forged the alliance that would create Western civilization.

The institution of empire arose in response to the need to establish an authority over and above the organic community. Such a community found its focus in nature-god sacral kingship. The sacred king was bound up with polytheistic nature gods; pure immanentalism simply reified the people's interests, reflecting their own image back upon themselves. It enslaved them to the environment and caused them to fear everything outside their particular nature/culture continuum. Vicissitudinous acts of nature – floods, famines, pestilence – called forth bloody sacrifices to appease the gods embodying those forces and supposedly capable of withholding such punishments.

Bondage to sacral kingship was broken by the nation Israel. Greece, born downstream of that feat, therefore escaped its clutches, but in its own way also needed to be released from the shackles of the immanent. City life blossomed in Greece, most fully so in Athens; such a culture gloried in its release from tradition, from authority, from religion. The Sophists expressed the new reality: man is the measure of all things; absolute right does not exist; what matters is interests and the attainment of a balanced realization of those interests, and tough luck to whoever falls out of the boat. The result was class warfare revolving around property, the haves vs. the have-nots, government

---

[32] In the *polis,* the *ekklesia* was the citizens' assembly.

swinging between oligarchy and democracy. Aristotle postulated a mixed constitution in which these elements were balanced against each other, with a strong middle class the guarantee of continuity and peace. Brilliant, as far as it went: but as Plato realized, no final solution would be found in terms of the immanent; the process, the <43> situation, the praxis must be transcended in order to be restored.

The key to that transcendence was the establishment of the rule of law. Aristotle's citizen ideal needed to be established and defended in terms of an explicit law-order if it was to survive. The Romans provided that law; the Church harnessed it to the principles of universal justice.

---

The objective and the subjective aspect of liberty were finally brought together in symbiotic unity. The catalyst was the church. Further deliberations on the resultant constitutionalism are contained in *Calvin and the Whigs* and *Follow the Money*.

---

The Roman law has often been characterized as an instrument of absolute sovereignty, with maxims like *princeps legibus solutus*, "the prince is free of the laws," and *quod principi placuit legis vigorem habet*, "what pleases the prince has the force of law." But, as McIlwain has pointed out,[33] the essence of the Roman law lay not in such statements so much as in the priority of private law to public law, no matter how conceived. Roman law derives public law from private law; the citizen is antecedent to the state; the state serves to preserve and protect the citizen in his rights, and not vice versa. The pillars of Roman law are the household, private property, and market exchange, the very elements which make up the Aristotelian citizen ideal. Roman law establishes and regulates human relations in terms of these basic categories. Rome was able to establish and maintain its empire over diverse and numerous peoples and territories because its law was received as an advance over what was there before it. By it, the peoples were net gainers; its universality and simplicity likewise enabled their integration into a common civilization.

The triumph of Christianity in the Roman empire formed the final stage of this historical process and the fulfillment of ancient history. The Church took up the elements of Israelite and classical civilization and transformed them into a patrimony capable of being passed on to a new carrier. The great

---

[33] Charles Howard McIlwain, *Constitutionalism: Ancient and Modern*, esp. ch. III.

church father Augustine stood at the parting of the ways, in his great work *The City of God* subsuming the fullness of that dying civilization, capturing its essence in the light of universal and salvation history, bringing it to a new level of maturity by integrating the <44> two great movements contained in it: the citizen ideal and the kingdom of God.

In his doctrine of the earthly city, the subject of the crucially important 19th book of *The City of God*, Augustine confirms and establishes the citizen ideal in terms of the kingdom, the higher end of man. As a result, his doctrine makes for a radical break with both the total organic community and the Sophists' relativism. His comprehensive critique of Roman idolatry is a decisive rejection of the right of the community to impose ultimacy on its individual members. The earthly community is a limited-goal society. It cannot claim ultimacy because that is not its purpose. It is meant to provide earthly peace, within which individuals can live out their higher destinies on their own account, without being kept in minority status, in child-like irresponsibility. The ungodly make use of earthly peace to satisfy their appetites – the peace becomes an end in itself. For its part, the Church makes use of this earthly peace, utilizing the things of this life with reference to the life hereafter, adapting to the conditions imposed by life in the earthly city, understanding its limited purpose. In the light of the eternal end, church members perform good works, ruling with an eye to the good of the ruled in household, city and empire, obeying as if serving God and not man. The earthly city is only established to secure a degree of peace, a degree of security, within which the city of God and the city of man can coexist and come to fruition, not to realize human destiny.

It follows that the goal of Christian politics is to ensure that the earthly city remains in this condition without being subverted by any pretension to total community. The citizen ideal is thus made to serve the higher end of eternal life. The citizen ideal, in which men are free from the dominion of other men and responsible for their own livelihoods, turns out to be the goal of Christian politics because it provides the freedom to live out one's own destiny on one's own account. The time would come when the earthly city would revert to its status as the city of Man, when Antichrist <45> would arise and man once again would elevate himself to the throne of ultimacy. But hard on his heels would come the final judgement; in the meantime, the Church and the saints reign on earth, as they have been since the resurrection of Christ. Their reign consists in having destroyed idolatry and in keeping the nations from reverting to the bondage of false worship.[34]

---

This understanding is expanded upon in *Common Law & Natural Rights*, "The Quest for Atonement."

---

It was this message which the Church carried into the new age, beyond the classical world. When classical civilization finally disintegrated, the Church, in particular the papacy, maintained and transmitted the burden of Christian-Roman empire. The bishops remained to represent Roman civilization in the face of Germanic conquerors. The monasteries held forth the ideal of heavenly peace beyond the vicissitudes and temptations of earthly life. But would they be sufficient against the wave of barbarism which engulfed them?

---

[34] *City of God*, bk. XX, chs. 7–12.

# Chapter 6

# The Infrastructure of Liberty

THE GERMANIC TRIBES which infiltrated and eventually conquered the Western empire originally were bound to the nature worship characteristic of tribal societies; many, however, had been converted to that "low-priced"[35] version of Christianity, Arianism. The Roman population remained Catholic, the bishops staunchly so, despite persecution. Arian rulers and Catholic subjects developed a live-and-let-live relationship, as for example in the reign of the Lombard Theoderic, who counted in his service the orthodox Catholics Boethius and Cassiodorus.

The Arian tribes considered Catholicism the religion of the weak and vanquished. The Franks alone somehow managed to escape the mainstream religious currents, instead remaining mired in their polytheism. Precisely because of this, the church of Gaul viewed their Frankish overlords much more favorably than they did the Arian tribes: while the Arian Goths were impervious to conversion, the Franks were still open. Then came one of the turning points of Western history, when in the words of one historian "the future of the West [was] decided"[36]: the baptism of Clovis, king of the Franks, into the Catholic faith. The bishops of Gaul hereby swung behind the Frankish power, creating an alliance of mutual benefit to both sides. With the support of the bishops Clovis was able to extend the dominions of the Franks across half of Gaul. The unity of faith also eliminated what had been the chief barrier to the assimilation of Goth and Roman, opening the way for a new civilization to arise out the rubble of the Western empire.

Not only in Gaul did the Catholic church gain the allegiance of the monarch; in England as well, the vision of Gregory the Great paid rich dividends as King Ethelbert paid heed to the papal emissary Augustine and bowed the knee to Christ; in the same year the archbishopric of Canterbury <47> was founded with Augustine its first occupant (597). Just prior to these events

---

[35] H. Daniel-Rops, *The Church in the Dark Ages*, p. 182.

[36] Daniel-Rops, p. 190.

the Visigoths of Spain joined the ranks of the Catholic faithful as King Rec-
cared renounced Arianism and embraced orthodoxy (589). With the establishment of these Catholic monarchies arose the prospect of a unified Western civilization, of many kingdoms joined in a common faith. The religious
fervor of these new converts – like Clovis, "who, on hearing the account of
the Passion, cried impetuously: 'Oh, if only I had been there with my
Franks!'"[37] – could not help but reinvigorate the near-moribund project of
Christian civilization.

With conversion came discipleship for both king and people. Christian-
theocratic kingship involved two basic principles: the de-divinization of the
king with respect to pagan nature-worship, resulting in his elevation above
the people; and the education of the king in just government, his demotion
under God and under law.

Anointment most succinctly symbolized the new kind of kingship, the
visible testimony of the status of the ruler, cleansing him of the defilement of
the organicist principle. Modeled on the Old Testament, anointment lifted
the king out of the reach of his subjects, so that, as David asked, "who can
stretch forth his hand against the LORD's anointed, and be guiltless?" (I Samuel 26: 9). Thus the king gained a new office and a new charge, for he no
longer represented the interests of the conquering tribe but of all the peoples
of his territory. Impartiality in administering justice was his calling.

Release from submission to the divinized people also meant release from
bare custom and folkways in favor of the transcendent law-order. As Pope
Gregory VII would put it, "Christ did not say, I am the custom; Christ said,
I am the Truth." The truth, even over the will of the people. Initially only
religion and ecclesiastical government were affected by the imperial claims of
Christianity, but in time all areas of culture, especially <48> law and education, were permeated by the transcendent idea of justice promoted by these
institutions of government.

Conversion therefore brought with it a top-down law-order which allowed the concept of justice to permeate, slowly but surely, into every nook
and cranny of Germanic culture.[38] The Church successfully pressed the

---

[37] Daniel-Rops, p. 189.

[38] Harold Berman details the shift from pagan to Christian justice in the Germanic
tribes in his seminal work *Law and Revolution*, especially ch. 1.

claims of the gospel on these nations, by first laying claim to the conscience of their kings, and then with the sanction and blessing of these kings by working to convert and disciple the populace. The "state," therefore, proved indispensable to the mission work of the Church. Using the example of the Roman empire, German historian Leopold von Ranke elevated this idea to the level of principle:

> One might say that, humanly speaking, the Roman Empire supremely promoted the idea of Christendom. A great complex of peoples had first to be created, with a certain level of unity, to enable the idea of world-religion to progress; if the peoples remained apart as various individual entities with diverse religions, only national gods would have been possible. *My idea of church and state is that the state must first exist before the church makes her appearance.* The state makes the church possible, as is fully demonstrated in the appearance of the church in the [pre-existing] Roman state. Without it the Christian religion would have had a difficult time spreading.[39]

The same principle applies to the conversion of the Frankish (and Anglo-Saxon and Visigoth) kings. The objection is often raised that on the part of the people such conversions were nominal only, since they had <49> no choice in the matter. Of course, this is in a certain sense true; but it must be remembered that the people never would have been reached for the gospel if the kings had not first opened the door to it. And it was Christianity that brought the idea of individuality to these peoples, so that prior to Christianity the concept of "choice" with regard to religion never would have entered their minds.

It has also been objected that Christianity's elevation of the king above the people put him out of touch with the people, creating a despotism where once the people were sovereign and possessed the right of resistance over against their kings.[40] Besides the question of whether this characterization is

---

[39] Leopold von Ranke, *Über die Epochen der Neueren Geschichte*, [On the Epochs of Modern History], p. 24. Emphasis is mine.

[40] For example: Walter Ullmann, *The Carolingian Renaissance and the Idea of Kingship*, pp. 13ff.

historically accurate,[41] it is likewise based on a misunderstanding. The top-down law-order imposed by the theocratic king did not stand in the way of bottom-up participation; even the framework of Roman church government, which served as a model for secular governments, contained strong elements of such participation, not to mention the fact that in establishing kings the Church allowed election and hereditary succession to continue, even as she plumped for her right to pass judgment on the choice in terms of her own criteria. To view top-down government as an inevitable impediment to bottom-up participation is to misconstrue the issue. These two forms of public organization are not mutually exclusive: in fact, rightly understood they complement each other. The one provided the necessary preliminary infrastructure for the establishment of the other.

The objective and the subjective aspects of liberty function in coordination. Where the underlying socioeconomic condition of society is weak, the objective aspect will be predominant, establishing the conditions for growth; the subjective aspect grows under the spreading branches of the objective. Here, the rule of law, the idea of justice as an overarching precondition of society, had first to be established, before the subjective aspect of personal responsibility and citizenship could develop.

The great medievalist of the previous generation Walter Ullmann, was one who promulgated a negative view of the transformation of Germanic kingship. For Ullmann, the transition from pagan to Christian government was retrograde, a regretful interlude before the return of "ascending" <50> government with the revival of Aristotle. As one of its retrograde characteristics, Ullmann singled out the principle of concession, in which "the king conced[ed] to his subjects, as a matter of royal grace, offices and rights which they otherwise would not have had." This stemmed from the Pauline "descending" concept of right, in which all legitimate power derived from God, thence to the king and finally to the subjects. According to this principle "subjects received offices, functions, rights, etc., as a matter of royal

[41] In particular, see the article by P. D. King, "The Barbarian Kingdoms," in J. H. Burns (editor), *The Cambridge History of Medieval Political Thought c. 350–c. 1450,* pp. 123–153.

concession, as an effluence of royal favour."[42] For Ullmann, this only underlined the subjection of the people, where once they fully shared in the governmental process. Christianity stripped them of their accustomed liberty, and put them in a position of wardship, permanent minority, under the king, their legal guardian.

Such a characterization does not take into account the context in which this transformation took place. The early middle ages are not called "Dark Ages" for nothing: this was a period of tumult, uproar, unsettlement, instability, and full-blown cultural decline. Royal government was desired by the weak for the peace it would bring them from the depredations and oppressions of robber barons, and the protection it would provide from foreign raiders. Concession was the indispensable means by which lawful authority was able to replace the raw use of force.

The principle of concession also assured the return of "ascending" government, after the long night of the Dark Ages. For it was this principle by which rights, liberties, and privileges were granted which served as the basis for a new civilization. The Church did not elevate kings just so they could enjoy an absolute dominion over their subjects; she did so in order to establish a framework of authority within which liberty could be revived. This pattern accompanied the rise of theocratic kingship from the beginning. Charlemagne was the first Western king to enjoy the kind of undisputed, legally sanctioned authority the Church was <51> claiming for legitimate rulers. He was also the one who introduced the feudal bond as the instrument by which to govern his territories. The feudal bond accomplished two things: it established rights and responsibilities between lord and vassal, so restricting arbitrary rule; and it established vassals as lords over a given territory, as rulers in the place of the king. Since the feudal system interposed the authority of lesser rulers between the king and his subjects, it could and often did backfire against royal authority, creating overweening vassals who could act as sovereigns in their own right and simply stand in the way of the exertion of royal authority. On balance, however, this system served to maintain a system of authority during times of intense disruption and disintegration, and it served to underline the constitutional basis of authority, precisely by decentralizing

---

[42] Ullmann, *A History of Political Thought: The Middle Ages*, p. 55.

power. In fact, it paved the way for the further progress of incipient Western civilization.[43]

---

This process is elaborated upon in *Calvin and the Whigs*, "Establishment," and *Follow the Money*, "Reorientation."

---

Charlemagne also presided over the renewal of Christian classical culture – a development of crucial importance to the recovery of the citizen ideal in the West. The study of classical letters kept alive the concept of citizenship in an age of rulers and subjects. The Augustinian dualism of the earthly and the heavenly city, granting the earthly city a position of relative importance in subordination to the ultimacy of the eternal city, dominated among the thinkers of the Dark Ages, providing a justification for the pursuit of culture as a legitimate and necessary goal on the road to eternity.

Another rebirth took place in the reign of Charlemagne – that of the Roman empire in the West. The empire had been split between West and East upon the death of Theodosius in 395 A.D., but since 476 the Western throne had lain unoccupied. In the meantime, the emperor on [*sic:* read, "in"] Constantinople exercised a nominal hegemony over the erstwhile Roman <52> provinces in the West, but de facto rule was in the hands of the barbarian chieftains. Nevertheless, the papacy kept alive the memory of a truly Roman empire, and with the auspicious conversion of the Franks to Catholicism, the Roman church gained not only a warrior people to deliver it from the grip of the Arian Lombards but also a bulwark against the inroads of Byzantium in Italy. The emperor in Constantinople claimed sovereignty over all the Church, including that in Rome. During their period of relative powerlessness, popes combined an overt attitude of subjection with covert independence. In the Franks, the papacy gained a champion through which it could make its independence a reality.

This was Leo III's primary motivation for crowning Charlemagne emperor on Christmas day of 800 A.D. The Frankish king, already an imperial power by virtue of his conquest of the disparate tribes of Western and Central Europe, now received the incalculably important seal of legitimacy on his

---

[43] A concise exposition of this is provided by R. van Caenegem, "Government, Law and Society," in Burns, *The Cambridge History of Medieval Political Thought*, pp. 174–210.

conquests. Charlemagne accepted the Roman-Christian imperial mission, to protect and promote the Roman church and to bring civilization where barbarism once held sway, with gusto.

Almost since its inception, however, the imperial dignity and the reality it was supposed to represent began to diverge. The territories over which the imperial scepter held sway refused to submit to direct imperial dominion, as the future France went one way and what would become Germany went the other, with the intervening territories along the Rhine and into Italy forming an unsettled boundary between them. The imperial crown came to rest on the head of the German king, who thus retained a nominal overlordship over the original Carolingian domains, an overlordship which in practical terms remained a dead letter, as France was entirely out of his reach.

Nevertheless, the imperial dignity retained major concrete significance, in the connection it established between Germany and Italy. The emperor was the lawful king of Italy as well Germany, and his interference in internal Italian affairs was one of the major recurring elements of <53> medieval history. Of supreme importance was his relationship with the papacy. It was the emperor who lifted the papacy out of the cesspool of Roman politics in the tenth century and promoted the spiritual reforms which saved the Church from certain disaster. These reforms in the end backfired on the emperor, however, because they led to the Papal Revolution of Gregory VII, in which the papacy claimed to be free of all political relations of dependence, even regarding the emperor. The Church and its officers needed to be free of carnal entanglements, devoted fully to the things of the spirit. This meant that the emperor and other secular rulers could no longer dispose of church offices and livings, but that full control over them should be in the hands of the pope's army of celibate clerics.

In the struggle between pope and emperor, the estates of the empire – princes and cities – were able to gain freedoms just as elsewhere, as in France and England, these freedoms were being curtailed. The pope supported the German princes in their rebellions against the emperor, and he also supported the cities of northern Italy in their struggles against imperial domination. In the end the emperor could not make his authority stick; the German princes gained essential control of the German constitution, while the Italian cities gained a fitful independence which would last until the onslaught of

France, Spain and a rejuvenated empire in the late 15<sup>th</sup> and early 16<sup>th</sup> centuries.

The imperial dream of universal domination came to an end with the interregnum which followed the death of Frederick II in 1250. But this by no means spelled the end of the imperial ideal. In fact, it was the necessary condition for the appearance of something entirely new, a resurrected, redeemed imperial ideal, an ideal of a *respublica Christiana*, a unified body of Christian republics sharing one law, one faith, one <54> civilization.[44] The law of that empire, the Roman law, was subjected to the same process of regeneration, enabling it to become something other and greater than it had ever been before. From being the law of a single sovereign, it was transformed into a universal law-order which set boundaries to all sovereigns and established a framework for mutual exchange and communication, the ligaments binding them together.

---

It is at this point, not in 1648 with the Peace of Westphalia, that we see the rise of the order of nation-states in Europe. This of course contradicts the received wisdom of our day, which seeks to paint nation-states as late-historical artificial constructs of empire-builders. Nothing could be further from the truth.

---

The election of Rudolph of Hapsburg to the imperial throne in 1273 reflected this transformation, and turned a new leaf in the history of the Empire. No longer was the focus put on Italy to the neglect of affairs in Germany. No longer was the emphasis on fighting the papacy for supremacy and plumping for recognition as King of Kings. Italy Rudolph left to the pope, so as to concentrate on bolstering the position of his family in its patrimonial lands and gaining the cooperation of the German princes. All the while Rudolph never lost sight of the imperial ideal, nor of his place in the scheme of things as represented by that ideal. By following his example his heirs would consolidate the family's hold on the imperial crown, and would eventually restore it to a position of primacy in the affairs of nations.

---

[44] Though still making use of the imagery of a literal Roman Empire, Dante anticipated the empire's transformation into an ideal community of Christian nations as a single civilization: see his *De Monarchia*.

What happened to the Roman law is best described as a shift in emphasis from civil law to common law, *jus civile* to *jus commune* (also known as *jus gentium*, "law of nations"). Civil law, *jus civile*, refers to Roman law as the law of Rome the city/state/empire – and, by extension, Roman law as the internal law of a sovereign polity. Common law, *jus commune*, refers by contrast to Roman law as a framework for a universal law-order, a law *between* sovereigns.

---

This is the "common law" referred to in the title of the book – the constitutional framework of nationhood. In it was comprehended the synthesis of objective and subjective aspects of liberty.

---

The common law had always been something of the poor relation in the Roman-legal structure, because it dealt with cases on the periphery of the Roman-legal horizon. Developed on an ad-hoc basis, it the law applied in Roman law courts to cases involving foreigners or between Roman citizens and foreigners. Its main concern therefore was private law. Its basis was the emerging conviction that a universal law-order actually existed. Not a speculative conviction of the Stoic variety, though, but a conviction arising from concrete experience. "Because one realized that purchase and work agreements, agreements to borrow money and contract out work and suchlike were also made and carried out by other peoples, one assumed that the obligations stemming from such agreements rested on juridical principles valid everywhere in the same way."[45] Using a hard-nosed, inductive approach to the demands brought by the administration of their burgeoning empire, Roman judges and jurists gradually developed the body of legal principles known originally as the *jus gentium* and eventually as the *jus commune*. What they did was to apply the Roman-legal principles of the civil law to the changed circumstances brought on by an intercultural situation. "In the form of the *jus gentium*, Roman law emerged from its restricted area of validity, the community of Roman citizens."[46] By the latter half of the second century Roman jurists had developed a comprehensive definition:

---

[45] Wolfgang Kunkel, *Römische Rechtsgeschichte* [The History of Roman Law], § 5.1.
[46] Kunkel, § 5.2.

All peoples with laws and customs apply law which is partly theirs alone and partly shared by all mankind. The law which each people makes for itself is special to its own state. It is called 'state law' [*jus civile*], the law peculiar to that state. But the law which natural reason makes for all mankind is applied the same everywhere. It is called 'the law of all peoples' [*jus gentium*] because it is common to every nation.[47]

The knowledge of the existence of this law was carried into the middle <56> ages by the seventh-century churchman Isidore of Seville, who included the Roman-law trichotomy of natural law, civil law, and the law of nations in his compendium *Etymologiarum sive Originum Libri XX*. Its Roman-legal content regained importance with the revival of Roman-law teaching in the 11th century. It became a basic category of canon law and also, through Thomas Aquinas, moral law. It began to gain ascendancy among Roman lawyers after the collapse of imperial power and consequent lack of the ability to enforce the *jus civile* strictly speaking. Roman law henceforth began to be interpreted along the lines of *jus gentium* or *jus commune*, as the common law of Christendom, rather than as the law of an imperial state.

It was in Italy, the cradle of imperial legal science, that jurists in the early 14th century began to reinterpret Roman law in terms of *jus commune* rather than *jus civile*. They did so because the Italian cities had in effect thrown off imperial sovereignty, but nevertheless acknowledged a vague imperial supremacy. The leading figure in this reinterpretive effort was Bartolus of Saxoferrato (1314-1357). Bartolus maintained the idea of the empire as a theoretical construct; this justified his adherence to Roman law as binding law. But his intention was different: the adaptation of that law to actual Italian conditions. Using Roman public-law concepts of sovereignty, he fashioned a theory which recognized the rights of self-government of the Italian cities, attributing to them a relative sovereignty, while retaining nominal allegiance to the emperor as overlord. The result was a theory of a "hierarchy of sovereignty,"[48] a budding federalism in which lower levels of government

---

[47] Gaius, *Institutes*, § 1.1. Quoted in *Justinian's Institutes*, p. 37.

[48] J. P. Canning, "Law, sovereignty and corporation theory, 1300–1450", in J. H. Burns (editor), *The Cambridge History of Medieval Political Thought c. 350–c. 1450*, p. 471.

were recognized as having legitimacy in their own right rather than as mere creatures of a sovereign overlord.

What then was the source of this legitimacy? As the Roman lawyers began to claim, it was the *jus gentium* itself: "According to [Bartolus's <57> student] Baldus natural reason in the form of its product, the *ius gentium*, not only brought city-*populi* into existence, but endowed them with autonomous powers of self-government without the need for the authorisation of a superior: the foundation upon which the argument for their sovereignty could be built."[49] The common law was emerging from the shadows of the civil law and taking on the shape of constitutional law, a law which defined and established public authority and private rights. The common law was replacing the civil law as the law-order expressive of the imperial ideal; the emperor was becoming a guarantor of a universal law-order embracing and restricting sovereigns, rather than an overlord of tribute-paying subjects.

Did not this constitute the reversal, indeed the overthrow of the foundations of government as described earlier? Ullmann attributed to Bartolus's doctrine of popular sovereignty precisely such a significance: "Authority stemmed from the people, and not from a 'superior' authority.... It was no longer the superior insight of the Ruler which determined what was in the interests of the people, but the people itself was recognized as perfectly capable of forming its own judgement on what was in its interests.... Once again we meet the concession principle, though in an inverted sense...."[50] But Bartolus had in mind an incipient federalism, a "hierarchy of sovereignty" whose ground rules were laid up in a universal law-order, the common law. Within this law-order room existed for both bottom-up, popular civil government and top-down, divine-right royal government. Such a system would require a delicate balance, a balance which, as it happened, was actually struck as the tradition of imperial common-law jurisprudence came to maturity. For no jurisdiction was certain which was not recognized by the sovereign power; it was the primary function of the emperor not to establish jurisdiction but to recognize it, to grant through the instrument of <58> chartered liberties the legitimacy lower jurisdictions needed in the face of the world at large. This was the security and stability provided by the emperor to Germany in a

---

[49] Canning, "Law, sovereignty and corporation theory," p. 473.

[50] Ullmann, *A History of Political Thought*, pp. 216–217.

period when it otherwise would have collapsed into its member components, as in fact happened in Italy.

---

Chartered liberties were an essential element of the development of institutions of freedom. They formed the warp and woof of the Western constitutional order. They arose out of the historical give-and-take between ruler and subject. They are thus the product of the historical process generated by the interaction of the objective and subjective aspects of freedom. They are also therefore the fruit of Christian civilization. With the elimination of public Christianity came likewise the transformation of rights, as we shall see.

---

The opposite course was taken in medieval France, where a school of jurisprudence took root whose center of gravity lay in establishing the juridical foundations for an independent, supreme monarchy, over against the emperor, the pope, and feudal barons. The jurists' key formula was *rex in regno suo est imperator regni sui*: "The king is the emperor in his kingdom." Thus the French king was the equal of the emperor, occupying the same position within the Roman law as the emperor. In this manner the French king and his jurists appropriated the interpretive tradition of the civil law, just as that tradition collapsed in the empire proper. It was France which would carry on the tradition of sovereign overlordship, with momentous consequences for the future.

---

Here dawns a divergence in the course of Western sociopolitical institutions, embodied in Germany on the one hand and France on the other: the prolegomena to the divergence between the common-law and the civil-law traditions.

# Chapter 7

# The Crisis of Liberty

CONFLICT between France and Germany, more specifically the kings of France and the occupants of the throne of the Holy Roman Empire, dominated the history of early modern Europe. The roots of this conflict lay in the diverging constitutional traditions each embodied, derived from the common law/civil law opposition. The German 19th century philosopher G. W. F. Hegel gave clear expression to this conflict. Writing of the Duc de Richelieu, who steered France's ship of state during the Thirty Years' War, Hegel had this to say:

> France as a state and Germany as a state had both of them the same two inherent principles of dissolution. In the one Richelieu completely annulled these principles and thus raised it to be one of the most powerful states; in the other he gave these principles full play and thus canceled its existence as a state. In both countries he brought completely to maturity the principle on which they were intimately grounded: in France the principle of monarchy, in Germany the principle of developing a multitude of individual states. Both principles had still to struggle against their opposite. Richelieu succeeded in bringing both countries to their fixed and mutually opposed systems.[51]

The conflict between these two countries and these two systems underlay the entire history of the Reformation; in fact, without taking it into consideration the Reformation itself becomes nearly unintelligible. Why could not the Church, which had displayed such unity throughout its history, of a sudden prove entirely unable to maintain that unity, despite the earnest, unceasing attempts of men (and women, for that matter) of good faith on both sides of the divide to heal the breach? <60> Certainly the split between Catholic and Protestant was deep; but nevertheless there remained broad areas of

---

[51] *Hegel's Political Writings*, p. 216. The quote is from "The German Constitution," written between 1799 and 1802.

fundamental agreement which could well have served to form the basis of a working relationship, over against those who opposed the basic creeds of Western Christendom as a whole. Why was such never attained? In a word: *politics*. It was not in the interest of certain states and leaders to see the Church restored in her unity and in its [*sic*: read, "her"] purity. And it is no accident that those whose interest lay in a splintered and warring church were precisely those who pursued the civil-law as opposed to the common-law form of constitutionalism. The major force opposing the establishment of the absolute state was, and is, a unified church.

---

The Reformation, as fundamental as it was, was also a reflection of an even deeper underlying conflict. For more on this, see the relevant sections in *Calvin and the Whigs* and *The Debate that Changed the West*. The importance of a unified church and the crippling effect of its absence are emphasized in *Reformed Ecclesiology in an Age of Denominationalism*.

---

Though there was underlying agreement, it must also be affirmed that there were clear areas of difference between the warring factions in the Church, so deep as to make the Reformation a necessity. The man who first and foremost brought these disagreements to the fore was Martin Luther.

Luther's attack went to the heart of Latin Christianity, where a certain ambiguity had been left unresolved by Augustine, the father of Latin theology. Augustine's theology revolved around two poles. One, the absolute sovereignty of God, made God the Ordainer and Predestinator of all that comes to pass, even salvation: the saved were elected from all eternity to be saved, so that even their choice in the matter was subordinate to God's. God saved man through grace; thus man could not really resist that grace – otherwise God could not bring to pass what He had ordained from all eternity.

The other pole was the Church, and here lay the rub. In Augustine's view, the Church dispensed the sacraments which mediated the grace of Christ and thus brought salvation to man. Augustine enthusiastically repeated Cyprian's dictum, *extra ecclesia nulla salus*, "no one is saved outside the Church;" thus man, in the form of the ministers of the Church, had a hand in the dispensing of grace, grace which, however, was irresistible, and which alone could save him from his sin.

Augustinian theology therefore synthesizes two points of view regarding grace. Together, they spell paradox: grace does not depend on man – it depends purely on the election of Christ who obtained it – but yet it does depend on man – because Christ has given its administration into the hands of the ministry of the Church who dispenses this grace. Thus the dispensation of grace is, at one and the same time, both independent of the will of man and dependent on that very same will.

Luther drove a wedge between these two poles of Augustinian theology.[52] Following Wycliff and Huss, he set predestination in opposition to a ministry which stood between God and believer. Predestination meant that no man could administer the grace of Christ, that this was a direct act of the Holy Spirit, from the perspective of man unpredictable and uncontrollable. This teaching undercut the position of the ministry in the Catholic church, which conceived itself as a priesthood which mediated the sacrifice of Christ to the faithful. With the elimination of a separate, elevated priesthood came the demise of the entire concept of a hierarchy of lifestyles reflecting closeness to God. The monastic life was rejected: one could come close to God in any way of life not sinful in itself; the priesthood of believers meant that every calling is a holy calling. Works did not get one any closer to God, either; no matter what one did, it was what he believed that mattered. The important thing was one's faith; faith saved, not works.

The Reformers had no desire to strip the leaven of Christian teaching from the public life of peoples and nations. They were working to restore <62> the pristine purity of the primitive church as they saw it. From a modern perspective it is apparent that their efforts were one aspect of a peculiar conjunction of historical forces, reflected also in the French power play and Italy's Machiavellian Moment (see above, p. 27, original numbering). These developments were not accidental. They expressed the underlying, all-embracing confrontation between civil law and common law, between absolutism and constitutionalism.

---

[52] "For the Reformation, inwardly considered, was just the ultimate triumph of Augustine's doctrine of grace over Augustine's doctrine of the Church." Benjamin B. Warfield, *Calvin and Augustine*, p. 322. Pelikan considers this judgment "an exaggeration but... not a total distortion"; cf. Jaroslav Pelikan, *The Christian Tradition: A History of the Development of Doctrine. Volume 4: Reformation of Church and Dogma (1300 –1700)*, p. 9. Pelikan's work also follows closely the career of this bipolar Augustinianism.

The Reformation in its purest form was the attempt to restore proper order to the Church, not to gut her. It was an attempt to give the Church a
constitution based on laws not men. The Bible was the divine lawbook, and
no human institution could take its place. The pope had made himself an
absolute monarch in the Church, whose will was law, and who could promote and sanction, even personally pursue, the most corrupt aggrandizing
practices with impunity. Reformation meant removing this parasitic arrangement in favor of a constitutional one, restoring the Church to her biblical basis, enabling her to fulfill her divine mission, to dutifully carry out her
ministerial and diaconal tasks and to play her proper constitutional role in
the public life of the nations, so that she not overreach herself and, in her zeal
to dethrone would-be absolutists in the state, turn around and herself arro-
gate absolute power.

The best of the Reformers thus held up before themselves the ideal of the
Church as God's City in God's Kingdom, the seat of divine order spreading
the grace of God to the far reaches of earthly civilization. No man and no
institution could encompass this City; at best, human, institutional representatives witness to this divine reality, through the pure preaching of the
Word and the administration of the sacraments. The church of Rome had
gone much too far; she had seen the gospel ministry as the means and herself
the end; the Reformers wished to make the institutional church merely a
means to the great end of seeing the pure gospel preached and believed.

At a deeper level, opposition to the papacy was more than only what
<**63**> Luther stood for, which was the purification of the Church. For a long
time a movement had been building which aimed at overthrowing church
authority altogether. To greater or lesser extent, nominalism, conciliarism,
the Renaissance, all were expressions of this underlying movement. It thus
preceded the Reformation; in fact, in many ways one might argue that both
the Protestant Reformation and Catholic Counter-reformation were not
simply movements in opposition to each other, but a common response of
the collective church[53] to a nearly invisible threat, which one scholar has
dubbed "the third force"[54] and another, the "major reformation."[55] This

---

[53] Kenneth Scott Latourette, *A History of the Christian Church,* vol. II.

[54] Paul Johnson, *A History of Christianity,* part V.

[55] H. A. Enno van Gelder, *The Two Reformations of the Sixteenth Century.*

movement grew out of Renaissance humanism. Beyond a commitment to restore the sources of classical literature as accurately and completely as possible, humanism was a world-and-life-view entailing the rejection of Augustinian doctrines such as the sovereignty of God and the depravity of man in favor of ideas placing man at the center, with his powers and accomplishments the orientation point. Contrary to what contemporary prejudice would have us believe, those who favored such ideas also tended in practice to favor a civil-law approach to civil government. The paradigm case is France, where the libertine strand of humanism took much stronger root than the ethical strand, as represented in a figure such as Erasmus. Libertine as opposed to Erasmian humanism had a more restricted impact in the realms of the imperial orbit, especially Germany and the Low Countries. There, renewed forms of piety gained a good deal of ground, as represented in the Brothers of the Common Life, leading figures of which were Geert Grote and Thomas a' Kempis. Thus, ferment in Germany was characterized by zeal to restore the church's purity; in France it was fueled by the desire to throw off spirituality altogether. <64>

---

So then, there was another movement afoot in the 16th century besides the Reformation: this was humanism, likewise angling for emancipation. For more on this subject, see *Calvin and the Whigs* and *The Debate that Changed the West*.

---

The constitutional order of the Holy Roman Empire enabled the Reformation to get off the ground. Constitutionalism had taken root in the empire to the degree that central government could not simply dictate religious conformity. At the same time, however, imperial allegiance demanded a degree of cooperation among the estates of the realm, even after the establishment of Protestantism. If the Reformation had simply been a matter of some countries going Protestant and others remaining Catholic, the pressure to pursue common ground would not have been nearly as strong, and Western Christendom might have fractured in even greater degree than proved to be the case. In Germany, the Reformation was an ongoing proposition.

The weight of the Reformation thus fell on the shoulders of Germany to a degree not experienced by any other nation. This burden weighed especially heavily on the emperor. The ideal of the Holy Roman Empire was the very embodiment of medieval theocratic monarchy. The emperor was the protector of the Church, not only in Germany but wherever the Church might be found; he was the guardian of universal justice and the patron of universal Christian culture. He set the example for the other Christian rulers, by submitting to the teaching and discipline of the Church. This calling was at the center of the conflict between emperor and pope. It was the Hohenstaufen desire to lord it over the Church and over Christendom which brought the united opposition, led by the pope, which permanently derailed the imperial quest for hegemony. The Hohenstaufens did not realize that the imperial throne was never meant to be a throne of direct universal rule over Christendom. The ideal set before the imperial dignity was to be the first prince in Christendom, an example of Christian rule in Germany, and the leader of united efforts to conquer the heathen and the infidel.

As such the German emperor lived a double life. Not only must he rule Germany in the best interests of Germany, but he must have an eye for the universal interest of Christendom. It was this double identity and <65> double burden which weighed so heavily on the emperor, and on Germany as well.[56] The German nation recognized that her role as seat of the imperial dignity made her special among the nations of Europe. It was Germany's burden to care not only for Germany but for the interests of Christendom as a whole. It is this destiny which makes Germany's history so tragic, for her failures have meant the failure of Christendom, her apostasy the devastation and ruin of Europe.

The defeat of the Hohenstaufens in the thirteenth century spelled the end of the dream of universal monarchy. But for constitutional government it was only the beginning. The emperor's loss was the imperial constitution's gain; the constitution became grounded in the idea of liberty rather than authority. Recognizing this, later emperors sought only to retain the emperor's position as *primus inter pares* while allowing the establishment and growth of a legal order whose center of gravity lay in the estates, the members of the realm.

The document ratifying this state of affairs is the Golden Bull, signed by Charles IV in 1356 and permanently establishing the electoral college of seven electors, a majority vote among which would be required to elect a new

---

[56] Could this be the hidden meaning behind the imperial symbol: the double-headed eagle?

emperor. The Golden Bull established a dual rule in the empire between the emperor and the electors. In effect it dispersed the center of gravity among the constituent parts of the empire, at the level of the territorial lords. But the emperor retained that chief element of theocratic government: the power of concession, the power to legitimate authority. Far from being the kind of absolute centralist force feared by Ullmann (see above, p. 50 [**original pagination**]), concession served as the legitimating ground of the German constitutional order, the recognized source of authority lifting the princes, estates, and cities above the level of civil war. As Ranke noted, "the imperial dignity, stripped of all direct executive power, had indeed no other significancy than that which results from opinion. It gave to law <66> and order their living sanction; to justice its highest authority; to the sovereignties of Germany their position in the world. It had properties which, for that period, were indispensable and sacred."[57]

It was in this constitutional environment, with the center of gravity resting with the seven electors, that the Reformation, almost overnight, exploded on the scene to become the primary factor in European life. When Martin Luther challenged the papal establishment, thus incurring its wrath, it was his territorial prince, the elector of Saxony Frederick "the Wise," who took the upstart monk under his wing and preserved him from certain execution.

The rise of Protestantism guaranteed the continued development of the empire along constitutionalist rather than absolutist lines. Charles struggled mightily to reestablish church unity on the basis of the received Roman tradition (though not necessarily under the headship of the pope) and thus solidify a power base and restore the imperial authority, but his efforts came to nought. With the Peace of Augsburg in 1555, the ecclesiastical split was put on a legal basis, thus granting the estates the kind of authority which was being snuffed out by strong rulers elsewhere in Europe.

But the German constitution was not out of the woods yet. The combination of petty Lutheran self-interest and a resurgent Catholicism's will to conquer led to one of the greatest catastrophes in Germany's history – the Thirty Years' War. This war, which had such a promising beginning for the emperor insofar as reestablishing monarchical hegemony was concerned, in

---

[57] Ranke, *History of the Reformation in Germany,* I, pp. 57–58.

the end led to the definitive shipwreck of any such monarchical pretensions. Never again would the empire fall under the shadow of a strong central government. From the time of the Peace of Westphalia (1648) forward, the emperor assumed the role of the leading prince in the empire, in effect renouncing any pretension to a kingship <67> above the other leading princes. The emperor led a body of equals in joint actions agreed to by all; he did not command a body of vassals.

The period of history between the Peace of Westphalia and the French Revolution is often viewed as "the age of Absolutism," during which time the nations of Europe established strong central governments over their dominions and a balance of power between themselves. There is of course much truth in this perspective, but it nevertheless is fatally flawed. It does not take into account the continued existence of the Holy Roman Empire as a viable entity in its own right, and of a continued underlying community of interests binding the empire with its "natural" allies, the same allies as prior to the Reformation.

The pre-modern German tradition of liberty was known as "Die Deutsche Freiheit," German Freedom. Modern scholarship has rediscovered this tradition. Its most illustrious historian is perhaps Otto von Gierke, whose *Die Deutsche Genossenschaftsrecht* memorialized the tradition of bottom-up government. See also pp. 114ff. below.

These alliances were determined by the division spoken of at the beginning of this chapter: common-law constitutionalism versus civil-law absolutism. Prior to the Reformation, this division found expression in the confrontation of the two powers representing these two traditions: the Hapsburgs on the imperial throne and the Valois on the throne of France. Beginning with in the fifteenth century with Frederick III, then with his son Maximilian and finally with Maximilian's grandson Charles V, the emperors pursued a strategy of containment vis-à-vis France which found surprising success. The famed Austrian policy of marriage as a political tool – the truth in the dictum *Bela gerant alii, tu felix Austria nube,* "let others make war, you, happy Austria, marry!" – bore undreamed-of fruit in the accession of Charles to the thrones of Spain, the Netherlands, northern Italy and the empire itself. Thus were the individual natural antagonists of France brought together in a formal political alliance in the person of the emperor. Though not joined in this political bond, England also allied against France – at least until Henry VIII broke with the pope.

The Reformation threw this state of affairs into hopeless confusion. The simple common law/civil law opposition was compounded by the division between Catholic and Protestant. <68> Adherents to the two opposing political traditions could be found among both Catholic and Protestant, belying the simplistic view associated with the so-called Whig Interpretation of History (see p. 2 above [**original pagination**]) aligning Catholicism with absolutism and Protestantism with constitutionalism. Spanish Catholicism, for example, was Thomist *via antiqua* Catholicism, which in the School of Salamanca boasted a tradition of constitutionalism fundamentally important to the constitutional tradition as a whole (see chapter 8 below). On the other hand, there were no lack of Protestants advocating absolutist government. The premier exponent of this approach would be Prussia, as shall be seen.

It was not until after the Thirty Years' War that the "pure" state of affairs was restored, as the emperor forswore the attempt to impose Catholic unity on the imperial estates, rather turning to a policy of cooperation with the same group of allies as before: England, Holland, Spain, and Italy.[58] Thus began the period of Grand Alliances, spearheaded by William III of Orange, grandson of Hapsburg antagonist William the Silent, which led not only to the defeat of Louis XIV but also to the final elimination of that perennial threat from the east, the Ottoman Empire.

---

These key events, the monumental effort undertaken to stave off absolutism, are memorialized in "What We Are Up Against," which is included in this volume.

---

The achievements of this period are hidden in the shadow of the Sun King and the "pattern nation" which was France under his reign. France boasted the consummate absolute monarchy, the envy of the other principalities of Europe, great and small. Petty German courts patterned themselves after it, appearing not a little ludicrous in the process. It would certainly seem that

---

[58] The figure who best exemplifies the new state of affairs is probably Gottfried Wilhelm Leibniz (1646–1716), who, as a Protestant, championed the common-law tradition as embodied in the Holy Roman Empire over against the French model.

this was the Age of Absolutism, and modern historiography in general has been cast in this mold. But this view essentially follows the French version of events, whose major conduit was Voltaire, from whom it flowed into Anglo-American historiography. According to this version of history, France and England played the leading role in <**69**> European history, while the empire was a nonentity. But this is not the way things were viewed then. Far from being something to be imitated, many recognized in France a common despotism and upheld the imperial constitution as the embodiment of German liberties and the much preferable political order.

An example of this kind of thinking is found in the German jurist Nicolaus Hieronymus Gundling (1671-1729). In the empire, said Gundling, the laws are sacred and cannot be forcibly changed; the empire enjoys a firm, stable, enduring legal order which engenders respect for law and secure legal relations. In France, by contrast, strong centralization with an exclusive focus on the will of the king makes for an unsettled legal situation. In France, subjects realize that the king can change their rights and introduce new ones, something impossible in the empire due to its structure and its constitution. No absolute rulers exist in the empire and none could. The plethora of territories create a situation of balanced legal relations and contractual bonds. The fundamental laws of the empire are marked by the fact that they apply not only to the people but to the princes. Because in the empire it is law that reigns, freedom is preserved and the law is able to fulfill its function, *conservatio libertatis*, the conservation of liberty.[59]

Thus there was in the time of the Age of Absolutism an alternative tradition of law and government, carrying on the classical and medieval tradition of law and liberty. This tradition lived on in the Holy Roman Empire as well as in the countries in its orbit: England, Holland, Switzerland. It is now time to take stock of this tradition before turning to its antagonist.

---

Burke's "common law of nations," the tradition of constitutionalism and limited government, indeed lived on, even during the "Age of Absolutism." And it was shared in greater or lesser degree by a host of countries. How it further developed, but then became restricted to the Anglo-American orbit, is the subject of the following chapters.

---

[59] Notker Hammerstein, *Jus und Historie* [Right/Law and History], pp. 223–224.

# Chapter 8

# The Constitution of Liberty

THE CHIEF early contribution to common-law constitutionalism was made by the university of Salamanca in Old Castile. This was no coincidence: the acquisition of territories in the New World brought the need to both justify their conquest and legally integrate them in the domains of the Holy Roman Emperor. The common law, specifically the law of nations (*jus gentium*) provided the necessary framework.

The task was taken up by the occupant of the first chair of theology at the university, Father Francisco de Vitoria, the illustrious founder of what historians would dub the School of Salamanca. Vitoria initiated a Thomist renaissance in Spain, a renaissance which recovered for the Church her divine mission as moral arbiter among kings and nations and advocate of the poor and oppressed in the face of the powerful.

The Spanish church distinguished herself by functioning as the conscience of the conquistadores and the champion of the Indians. The Dominican father and bishop Bartolomeo de las Casas gained the attention of all Christendom, and the ear of his sovereign, through his passionate pleas in favor of the benighted natives. Las Casas's vehement protestations against the ravages of the Spaniards were translated into Vitoria's solemn and measured judgements as given in his famed lectures on the Indies delivered in the late 1530s. These lectures are considered to be the first to present a truly modern law of nations. With Vitoria the common law took a decisive leap from the medieval to the modern world. Vitoria's exposition brings these developing principles to a new level, circumscribing the rights and duties of nations as nations; the *jus gentium* finally breaks out of the restrictive framework of a putative Roman Empire to view the nations as potentially a great community under law.

Vitoria's lectures on the Indies attempt to demonstrate that the relationship between Spaniards and Indians is essentially a relationship of equals. The Spaniards cannot presume that they can legitimately <71> conquer the Indians by virtue of a supposed superior level of civilization. Even if that were the case, it would give no just cause. But it cannot even be proved that the Indians are entirely lacking in the arts of civilization:

> ...they have some order in their affairs: they have properly organized cities, proper marriages, magistrates and overlords, laws, industries, and commerce, all of which require the use of reason. They likewise have a form of religion, and they correctly apprehend things which are evident to other men, which indicates the use of reason.... Thus if they seem to us insensate and slowwitted, I put it down mainly to their evil and barbarous education. Even amongst ourselves we see many peasants who are little different from brute animals.[60]

Though he later significantly qualifies this judgement, even going as far as to cast into doubt the Indians' actual ability to govern themselves,[61] it forms the basis for a series of far-reaching conclusions.

Because the Indians form self-governing societies, they must be treated as full-fledged nations, enjoying the benefits and immunities accruing to nations as set forth in the *jus gentium*. The logical corollary is that they also must adhere to the criteria set forth in the *jus gentium*. Vitoria lists them: freedom of trade; freedom of movement – open borders, freedom of the seas, freedom of domicile; freedom to spread the Gospel; all subsumed under the category, communication. If the Indians were to infringe these so-called "rights of communication," the Spaniards would have the right to wage war on them. Vitoria leaves open the question of whether Spain's conquests were justified on these terms or not; for him, <72> conquest is not a very good way of establishing a relationship anyway. His main point is to highlight the basic rules which bind nations to each other and which they cannot get out from under, which establish peaceful communication, the indispensable condition for civil society lived for the sake of citizens and not rulers or state or government. For this purpose conquest is unnecessary, as the example of the

---

[60] Francisco de Vitoria, "On the American Indians," in *Political Writings*, p. 250. The authors note that Vitoria closely adheres to the criteria of civil life set forth by Aristotle in his *Politics*.

[61] Vitoria, "On the American Indians," pp. 290–291.

Portuguese shows, "who carry on a great and profitable trade with similar sorts of peoples without conquering them."[62]

---

It should also be mentioned that in Vitoria's scheme, these rights of communication were restricted if they were to have an adverse impact on indigenous populations. Obviously, this was the case with Spanish colonization, which is the reason why Vitoria brought up the issue in the first place.

---

Vitoria's work on the *jus gentium* had an immense influence on 16th century political and legal thought. His pupil Domingo de Soto, who succeeded Vitoria to the first chair in theology at Salamanca, produced a ten-volume treatise *Of Justice and Law*, advancing the Vitorian agenda in what Pagden and Lawrance see as "probably the most influential treatise on jurisprudence written during the sixteenth century."[63] Vitoria's and De Soto's moral theology bore fruit in the world of jurisprudence proper through the work of Diego de Covarruvias, a canon and civil lawyer who was held in such esteem internationally that he gained the nickname the Spanish Bartolus. Covarruvias applied Vitoria's principles to current questions in Roman-legal studies, in particular the increasingly urgent question of state sovereignty. Covarruvias rejected the advancing notion of absolute sovereignty; in fact, he rejected the idea of state sovereignty altogether, arguing that sovereignty rested with the people and that all state power was derived from the community. Covarruvias made popular sovereignty an explicit principle of the *jus gentium*: all nations had the right to establish their own government and all just governments were those established by the people. Thus in a sense kings were elected by the people even when hereditary succession determined who would ascend the throne, for in that case the people chose a family line, not an individual alone, and agreed to accept the descendants. A corollary of <73> popular sovereignty was that kings must rule by the advice and consent of their subjects, as represented in a council of "optimates;" the example Covarruvias gives is the Holy Roman Empire and its seven electors.

Covarruvias made the decisive move from moral theology to jurisprudence; his colleague Fernando Vasquez de Menchaca sealed that move by developing a full-blown legal system putting in concrete legal terms the lofty

---

[62] Vitoria, "On the American Indians," pp. 291–292.

[63] Vitoria, *Political Writings*, p. 366.

moral principles of the *jus gentium*. Vasquez draws a clear line – far clearer than anyone before him – between society, the social dimension of life, and the state, the apparatus of coercive authority set over society. All of human life needs to be seen first and foremost as people in their private capacities living and working together for each other's benefit. Private, social life cuts across all particular human societies; it is the common fabric of greater civilization. The locus of this common life is the city, where people gather to pursue private interests for common benefits, to share a life whose goal is happiness. Everyone shares this calling, the necessary conditions for which are freedom and equality, where none is set over another, lording it over another.

This is the backdrop of the *jus gentium*. In it, private property comes first, then comes the state. Private property is an institution of the *jus gentium*, it is not the creature of the *jus civile*. It enables people to fulfill their callings as mutual benefactors in common society. The state exists to protect this institution. This *ratio* for state power also contains its limitations. For state power to be justified it must be exercised to restrict lawlessness, and no more. Citizens accept the restrictions on their freedom which the introduction of state power makes necessary, but only those restrictions which are necessary for the state to fulfill this limited goal. If the state goes beyond that, it is acting unjustly. In the jargon of the lawyers, the *dominium* of the state is *dominium jurisdictionis*, a limited jurisdiction to punish crime, not *dominium proprietatis*, a form of ownership. [*] Sovereignty does not entail ownership of subjects' goods. Citizens' private ownership is inviolable. <74>

In consequence, Vasquez insists that the law of the state, *jus civile*, is strictly subordinate to the *jus gentium*. The *jus gentium*, postulating a universal "private-sector" human community, cannot suffer usurpation by the *jus civile*: state power cannot absorb the original powers of citizens. The sovereignty exercised by the state is a limited sovereignty, different in kind than ownership.

Is sovereignty then derived from citizens? Is it then a creature of individuals or groups joining together to form a state, as the social contract theory would have it? If so, then the theory of popular sovereignty propounded by

---

[*] "Dominium proprietatis – dominium jurisdictionis": the title of a chapter in Reibstein, *Johannes Althusius* (note 68).

the School of Salamanca would deny the theory of concession, which, as we have seen, was formative to the development of constitutionalism. But this is not the case. Sovereignty and property are of a different order and cannot be subsumed one to the other. Hence, private actors as bearers of *dominium* cannot establish any form of *imperium*. Sovereignty is the power to enforce law and justice, not to create it. By extension, it grants rights in terms of law and justice, by so doing establishing rights as the concrete outworking of law and justice in society. Rights-bearing individuals are not the constituent elements of sovereignty but rather its products, for rights are nothing apart from an authority confirming them in terms of higher principles.

The historical development of rights and liberties confirms this analysis. Mankind did not begin as isolated individuals or families joining forces to form a political community; mankind began in the form of established political communities, sovereignty-bearing communities, by virtue of divine ordination. As we have seen (pp. 12ff. [**original pagination**]), this was the basic form of social order, out of which developed the institutions of civil society.

Vasquez provided the theoretical reconciliation of sovereignty and liberty in his theory of rights as forms of property. Vasquez recognized the primacy of the "the private sector" and the purpose of sovereignty as simply the guarantor of this private order. But he also understood that <75> sovereignty historically came before property, that the community came before the individual. His achievement was to perceive how sovereignty, while preceding property in history, nevertheless remained its subordinate. Sovereignty existed for the sake of property.

Vasquez made this connection by applying the Christian conception of the nature of man, as made in the image of God, to legal theory. By virtue of his being made in God's image, man possessed dominion as an inherent aspect of his nature. The command to pursue dominion, made by God in Genesis ch. 1, was thus a command to live out the image of God. It was also the way in which man expressed his freedom. Freedom is gained through the exercise of dominion. The freedom of the will is the dominion of Spirit over flesh, the subjection of the passions to reason. Dominion and freedom therefore are correlative expressions of the image of God. Man exercises dominion as a proper expression of his freedom. True freedom is dominion carried out in obedience to God's will.

One of the ways in which this freedom/dominion principle becomes concrete is through the institution of private property. Man expresses dominion through taking possession of parts of the creation; when he works on these parts, he adds value to them. The sum of his works comprise culture. His works are his property; private property therefore is essential to culture.

But with the fall of man, men began to envy their neighbors and then to usurp their goods. Warfare was the result. This brought another form of dominion – that of man over man – to offset the inability of men to restrain their appetites. God subjected men to the coercive authority of other men both as punishment for sin and to mitigate the effects of sin.

The lordship/subjection relationship, so alien to man's original condition, found institutional expression in the state. Given the reason for its institution – to restrain man's attacks on his fellow man – its primary purpose lay in the preservation of the institution of private property, since the root cause of warfare was envy. <76>

From here Vasquez innovated in attributing the status of *dominium*, of property, to all specific legal positions held by citizens. As a result, rights were vested with the same protections and privileges as property in the strict sense. The state existed to establish citizens in their acquired rights. Thus, not only did the state exist in the interest of property owners in the narrow sense, but also in the interest of property-owners in the broad sense: all rights-bearing citizens were protected in their "property" by the state.

In Vasquez's system, the full recognition of both man's status as a being created in the image of God and fallen away from God comes to fruition. Man's dominion is the expression of this image; dominion is also placed over man, to mitigate his rebellion. Man's exercise of dominion is greatly restricted by the establishment of institutionalized dominion of man over man – the state – yet dominion remains an essential aspect of his nature, a potential waiting to be actualized. Within the framework of the rule of law and progress in the virtues, his dominion-potential can be actualized; this actualization finds expression in rights granted by the state, which once granted are irrevocable. The state, through the principle of concession, is the efficient cause of liberty through this rights granting and maintaining ministry.[64]

---

Further discussion of the constitutionalism of the School of Salamanca and its influence on Althusius and Grotius can be found in *The Debate that Changed the West.*

---

The School of Salamanca thusly developed a theory of popular sovereignty as the basis for all legitimate government, in so doing establishing the theoretical basis of the common-law tradition. This theory restricted state sovereignty by recalling its rationale as a power to preserve society, not commandeer it. Society and civilization have an <77> inherent sustaining power not derived from the state but only realized through its ministry; a power based in the citizen ideal, property rights, household inviolability, and rights of communication/exchange. This doctrine of popular sovereignty also restricts peoples themselves as collective organisms. In the separation of state and society, the organic community is itself disarmed, reduced in significance to one among many cultural factors rather than an all-embracing, total allegiance-demanding collective.

While the common-law tradition was proving so fruitful in Spanish jurisprudence, its counterpart, the civil law, began bearing bitter fruit in France. The contagion of religious conflict had spread there from Geneva through the efforts of an exiled French constitutionalist, John Calvin. For a major – perhaps *the* major – source of discontent in France was the dispute over the powers of government. Was the French monarchy an absolute monarchy, as its propagandists argued, or was it limited, constitutional, as claimed its opponents? This conflict preceded the religious one.

The priority, at least chronological, of the constitutional conflict can be seen even in the work of John Calvin himself. Before going over to the side

---

[64] The first historian to call attention to the importance of Fernando Vasquez was Ernst Reibstein: cf. his *Die Anfänge des Neueren Natur- und Völkerrechts* [The Start of the Modern Law of Nature and Nations]. Other works of importance regarding Vasquez include Reibstein's *Johannes Althusius* (see note 68) and Kurt Seelmann, *Die Lehre des Fernando Vazquez de Menchaca vom Dominium* [Vasquez's Doctrine of Dominium].

of the Reformation, Calvin penned a learned commentary on Seneca's *De Clementia*, a work which gave clear expression to his constitutionalism. Calvin directed his arrows against the juristic school of Toulouse, which "even more than the legists of the thirteenth century [see above] interpreted Roman law in an absolutist sense," and against its "theoretical support for the centralist-absolutist state of Francis I."[65] In Bohatec's words, "[Calvin's] Seneca commentary signals the young humanist's open war against the absolutist claims of the government of his homeland."[66] <77>

Not that Calvin rejected Roman law. He found himself on the other side of the great divide in Roman-legal interpretation; he was a common-law man. "When [Calvin] lashes out against the contempt shown for the *communes leges gentium* [i.e., common law of nations] by its opponents, judging such contempt to be folly, he doubtless had the Roman law in mind, since at the time this law enjoyed the status of universal law over against the civil laws of particular territories."[67] His comments in favor of the common law are to be found in the famed 20th chapter of the fourth book of his *Institutes of the Christian Religion*, which deals with civil government, and appeared in the first edition of 1536 as well as every subsequent edition.

France's constitutional conflict simmered under the surface all the while that Francis attempted to extend his dominions abroad; it did not break into the open until the death of Henry II in 1559. Henry's three young sons were next in line to the throne. The under-age Francis II succeeded but lived only a year. He was succeeded by his even younger brother Charles IX. A regency was established, headed by the queen mother Catherine de Medici. The power behind the throne was the house of Guise, fiercely Catholic and anxious to stamp out the spreading Genevan contagion.

The efforts of the Guise party brought open conflict with the French Protestants, generally followers of Calvin, for obscure reasons dubbed the Huguenots. The rebels were led by the prince of Condé, himself a prince of the blood. Like the other Reformers, Calvin was quite reluctant to countenance rebellion against the lawful sovereign. He certainly did not rule it out; the very same chapter on civil government in his *Institutes* mentioned above

---

[65] Josef Bohatec, *Calvins Lehre von Staat und Kirche,* p. 43.

[66] Bohatec, *Calvins Lehre,* p. 43.

[67] Bohatec, *Calvins Lehre,* p. 32.

also contains the famed exposition of the power of the so-called ephors, lesser magistrates constitutionally charged with keeping the king in line. Calvin saw the three estates of France as filling this role. Whether lesser magistrates – individual nobles and city regents – could likewise defy the king with armed might was another question. In this case Calvin argued purely along ancient-constitutional lines. The prince had the right to defend his position within the French court against the usurpations of the house of Guise.

Calvin refused to base his constitutionalism on the idea of popular sovereignty. Like Luther, he viewed the authority of the king to be divinely-established and above second-guessing by subjects, unless subjects had obtained such rights by covenant. Thus the right of resistance in Calvin's teaching remained within the realm of positive law, that is, it was an acquired not a natural right. Calvin's position was shared by Lutheran theologians and jurists, who grounded their right to resist the emperor in the German constitution and the explicit rights granted to lesser magistrates, especially the electors.

It is here that the work of the School of Salamanca, in particular through Vasquez, made its mark in the struggle between absolutism and constitutionalism. The arguments from constitutional history were helpful, but they could always be countered by the argument from prescription. That may have been the way it was then, the absolutist would say, but this is the way it is now, and you, the constitutionalist, are inciting revolution by opposing it. The constitutionalist might counter by pointing out that the "rise of absolutism" was marked by a string of broken promises, oaths reneged in violation of the common-law principle *pacta sunt servanda*, "agreements must be kept." Yes, the absolutist would reply, in normal situations that principle does apply, but reason of state precludes that the king always keep faith with his subjects; *salus populi suprema lex esto*, the well-being of the people is the highest law; where that well-being requires a dispensation, even from oath-bound covenant, then so be it.

Constitutional arguments thus ran into a dead end; they were always trumped by reason of state. There followed the most horrendous <80> expression of that infernal principle to date: the St. Bartholomew's Day massacre of August 1572, which saw thousands of Huguenots wiped out in a matter of days. Reason of state itself, it was clear, had to be slain: from this time forward, constitutional arguments would be buttressed, undergirded, and eventually refounded upon the principles of the *jus gentium* as expounded by Vasquez.[68]

Calvin's protégée Theodore Beza was the first to take this step. His treatise *On the Rights of Magistrates* (1574) grounded the claims of French constitutionalists regarding the estates and lesser magistrates on popular sovereignty as a universal principle of the *jus gentium*. The king exists for the benefit of the people, not the people for the king; peoples establish kings for the common good, and through the instrumentality of lesser magistrates and constituted ephors may keep kings within those bounds. Every people has this right by virtue of the *jus gentium*, which conditions and restricts all constitutions and all governments.

Beza's exposition was influential, though not nearly so much as the pseudonymous treatise published a few years later in 1579, the famed *Vindiciae contra Tyrannos*, "Defence of Liberty Against Tyrants." The *Vindiciae* carries Beza's incompletely developed train of thought to a new level of consistency and conclusiveness. The principle of popular sovereignty is developed in detail as the God-ordained basis of legitimate government. "We have already shown that it is God who makes kings, gives kingdoms, and selects rulers. And now we say that it is the people that establishes kings, gives them kingdoms, and approves their selection by its vote. For God willed that every bit of authority held by kings should come from the people, after Him, so that kings would concentrate all their <81> care, energy, and thought upon the people's interests."[69] The authority of kings is "from God, but by the people, and for the people's sake."[70] The estates are the people's representatives over against the king, to ensure that he rules according to his mandate.

This was the gateway through which the synthesis of moral theology and Roman law, achieved by the School of Salamanca and summarized in the *jus gentium*, found its way into Protestant political thought, putting the right of

---

[68] This matter forms the thesis of the monumental work by Ernst Reibstein, *Johannes Althusius als Fortsetzer der Schule von Salamanca* [Althusius as Continuator of the School of Salamanca]. My debt to this book will become evident to any who peruse it.

[69] Stephanus Junius Brutus, *Vindiciae contra Tyrannos,* in *Constitutionalism and Resistance in the Sixteenth Century: Three Treatises by Hotman, Beza, & Mornay,* p. 158.

[70] Still Waters edition, p. 55.

resistance on a universal basis. The linchpin was the idea of popular sovereignty – peoples, not states, are sovereign. The state is subordinate to peoples and nations. It exists to rectify injustices arising from the abuse of freedom, it does not exist to create freedom. It exists to restore, or at least mitigate, the disturbances produced in the course of social life, it does not exist to create social life.

This line of thinking reached its culmination in the work of the German Calvinist jurist Johannes Althusius. Althusius provided an all-embracing theory of society synthesizing the juridical formulations of Vasquez *et al.* and the constitutional/political conclusions of the Huguenots. Althusius provides a theory of the *nature* of popular sovereignty, and makes quite clear that he has no intention of promoting either a democratic or an aristocratic form of government, contrary to his opponents who labeled him (as they had the Huguenots before him) a "monarchomach," a king-killer. Kingship plays an essential role in Althusius's political theory. Althusius integrates it with the other elements of society; the result is a comprehensive theory justifying and restricting political power in terms of the needs of civil society itself.

Of fundamental importance to the idea of popular sovereignty is the idea of "people" which underlies it. Say that it is the people that is <**82**> sovereign: what in fact is the people? Althusius advances two definitions. Firstly, simply a conglomeration: *turba* [crowd], *coetus* [gathering], *multitudo* [assemblage], *congregatio* [throng].[71] This is a people in their pre-juridical state, not bound together by a *jus symbioticum*, a constitutional law-order. Without such a constitution a people also lacks sovereignty, because it lacks the ordered unity which accompanies sovereignty. For Althusius, therefore, this is actually a theoretical rather than an actual condition, for as he points out elsewhere, if a people loses sovereignty it altogether ceases to be a people.[72] It is a people as a *corpus consociatum*, an associated body, that is sovereign.

The associated body is something more than a simple assemblage of individuals: it is an integrated composite of members of one body, just as a

---

[71] Following Carney's translation of Althusius's *Politica Methodice Digesta*: *The Politics of Johannes Althusius* (London: Eyre & Spottiswoode, 1964), p. 34 [39]. This work was recently reprinted by Liberty Fund (Indianapolis: 1995). Page references to this, more accessible version will appear in brackets.

[72] Preface to third edition: Carney, pp. 9, 10 [12, 13].

human body is an integrated composition of corporal members. And like human members, these members are more than the individual cells of which they are composed. Althusius uses a different analogy:

> It can be said that individual citizens, families, and collegia are not members of a realm, just as boards, nails, and pegs are not considered parts of a ship, nor rocks, beams, and cement parts of a house. On the other hand, cities, urban communities, and provinces are members of a realm, just as prow, stern, and keel are members of a ship, and roof, walls, and floor are essential parts of a house.[73]

Not a people as a multitude, but a people as an association of lesser associations, as a federal union of integral units of government. <83>

Is this a return to organicism? At first sight it might appear so. But not when one examines the different nature and purpose of the various associations which go to make up the whole. The basic distinction is that between private and public. Private associations – the family and the corporation – are formed for the pursuit of substantive economic goals, while public associations – the city, the province, the republic – are formed to foster the activities pursued by private associations. From this simple distinction flows the purpose of government, which is to promote and encourage private activity, not subsume it.

Each association is based on the principle of consent by way of covenant. All associations are formed by covenant, a *pactum* or *vinculum* by which the members of the association agree, either explicitly or implicitly, to share the burdens and benefits of the association. The principle of hierarchy comes into play in that every association must have some form of government, and that requires the establishment of rulers and subjects. Rule is established to promote the well-being of the association and is restricted to what is necessary to attain that end. Members bind themselves by covenant to submit to the ruler; rulers agree by covenant to rule according to the laws of the association.

These two principles, consent and hierarchy, also come into play in the building of greater out of lesser associations. Families and private associations

---

[73] Carney, p. 62 [67].

form towns and cities; these in turn form provinces; leading cities and provinces form republics. In forming greater associations lesser associations do not lose their identity nor give up their right of self-government; what they do give up is the sovereignty they exercised when they had to "go it alone." This process is "confederation;" by it, "a foreign realm, province, or any other universal association, together with its inhabitants, are fully and integrally coopted and admitted into the right and communion of the realm, by a communicating of its fundamental laws and right of sovereignty. To the extent that they coalesce and are united into one and the same body they become members of that one and <84> same body."[74]

The universal association is thus an associated body of members, each of which is itself composed of associations: this, then, is a people in the fullest sense of the word. It is this entity to which the *jus gentium* ascribes sovereignty. In fact, as Althusius shows, a people and the power of sovereignty are two sides of the same coin: a people is a body possessing sovereignty, and sovereignty is the power which creates and sustains a people.

This sovereignty is therefore something entirely different from the power exercised by the state. How could it be otherwise if "a people can exist without a magistrate, but a magistrate cannot exist without a people"?[75] It is also far removed from the modern concept of popular sovereignty, not only because it does *not* serve to justify a supposed transfer of sovereignty to the state but because it is not based on individuals but associations. And it is restricted to what is required by "the purpose and scope of the universal association, namely, ... the utility and necessity of human social life.... [T]he nature and character of imperium and power [is] that they regard and care for the genuine utility and advantage of subjects."[76]

Government exists for the sake of the people; public authority is established for the benefit of private activity. The tradition of the *jus gentium* comes to fruition in the comprehensive ordering of public power to private well-being. The state exists for the sake of society, i.e., the lesser associations out of which it is built. The state "does not execute or perform [private]

---

[74] Carney, p. 84 [89–90].

[75] Carney, p. 117 [122].

[76] Carney, p. 68 [73].

functions, but only establishes, orders, and directs them, which it does by ruling, commanding, forbidding, and impeding."[77] These private functions – industrial, agricultural, and commercial <85> occupations – "inclin[e] princi-
pally to the utility of those who perform them, and consequently to the public utility of the city or of all the citizens collectively;" they are brought together through the operations of the market.[78]

The entire purpose of social life, in Althusius's view, is communication,
distribution, exchange. This is how people come together; it is also why they
come together, because none can live entirely on his own. The law-order
which binds them together, the *jus symbioticum*, is nothing other than "a
plan and manner for communicating things and services"[79] for the advantage
of all, both collectively and individually. This *jus symbioticum* is the essence
of sovereignty, as we have seen, and the reason for which state power is established. In establishing communication as the supreme bond and purpose of
society and the rationale of sovereignty, Althusius incorporates the basic
theme of the *jus gentium* as formulated by Vitoria: the state exists to conserve
and promote communication. It is precisely this communication which
binds not only a people but all peoples, at least in principle, and it is this
transnational, civilizational level of communication which the state exists to
further.

---

[77] Carney, p. 87 [92].

[78] Carney, p. 42 [47].

[79] Carney, p. 14 [19].

# Chapter 9

# The Cooptation of Liberty

THE LEADING IDEA of the common law is the circumscription and limitation of sovereignty. This means that the common law stands over the civil law – state law must measure up to universal standards. As Reibstein summarizes, "*jus gentium*... is everything that is not *jus civile*.... the *jus gentium* is independent of individual sovereigns and binds those sovereigns."[80] The common law was developed in direct opposition to civil law-oriented Roman jurisprudence.

As we have seen, the civil-law orientation was pursued most vigorously in France. It reached its height in response to the wars of religion which shook France to her core and threatened irreparably to weaken her governmental institutions. As time wore on and the religious conflict proved utterly irreconcilable, many began turning to absolutist theories of government to overcome that conflict. The king must be vested with unrestricted authority, in their view, and elevated over the divided church.

---

Hence, absolutism was called upon to solve the problem absolutism created....

---

This so-called *politique* strategy was carried to its logical conclusion by the polymath scholar Jean Bodin. Originally Bodin was counted among the constitutionalists, those who wished to restrict royal power. But the experience of civil war gradually wrought a change of heart; the experience of the St. Bartholomew's Day massacre and its aftermath generated in him the same fever of scholarly application as worked in Beza, François Hotman, and Mornay, though in the opposite direction. In 1576 Bodin published the results of his labor, his *Six Books of a Commonwealth*, a landmark in political theory

---

[80] Reibstein, *Die Anfänge*, p. 72. See also Althusius's description of the common law and its relation to civil law (which he calls *jus proprium*, proper law), in ch. 21 of his *Politica Methodice Digesta*.

because the first work to attempt a comprehensive and conclusive definition of sovereignty.

Bodin's doctrine contained two key elements which militated against *jus gentium* constitutionalism. First, he put forward a doctrine of indivisible sovereignty and placed such sovereignty in one determinate <87> institution. Indivisibility means that sovereignty cannot be divided up and parceled out among, for example, branches of government. Thus Bodin held that sovereignty must be lodged in a specific single location. Sovereignty had to be institutionalized, he held; the alternative to indivisibility was anarchy, because no one would have final responsibility and final authority. The buck would stop nowhere.

This principle rules out the idea of a mixed constitution and therefore federalism, especially as developed in Althusius's constitutional theory. The interesting thing is, Althusius accepted Bodin's concept of indivisible sovereignty, though attributing it, as we have seen, not to any institution but to the associated body of the people as a whole, i.e., to society, not government. By so doing Althusius could maintain the concept of a mixed constitution, in which powers of government are divided among different institutions. In fact, he held that every government inescapably incorporates a mixture of the three basic forms, monarchy, aristocracy, and democracy. These powers are not the essence of sovereignty but are only derivative of the true sovereignty which is possessed by the collective realm. In this way Althusius maintained the ideal of the rule of laws, not men.

This in Bodin's view was an invitation to institutionalized anarchy. Against it he marshalled the Roman-law dictum *princeps legibus solutus est*, "the prince is not bound by the laws," perhaps the chief vehicle of civil-law absolutism in the Roman-legal tradition.[81] Adherents of this view felt that if the prince was held accountable to the civil law he would come under the jurisdiction of his subjects, which meant that he could no longer act as a sovereign. Therefore, the prince should not legally be bound to the civil law, though he should still remain morally bound to it – in other words, accountable to God, not man. Nevertheless, Bodin did <88> maintain that the

---

[81] For an overview of this doctrine and its influence, see Dr. Dieter Wyduckel, *Princeps Legibus Solutus.*

prince was restricted both by the *jus gentium* and by purported fundamental laws of the realm, i.e., constitutional law.

What determines the restrictions on state power, therefore, is the scope given to the *jus gentium* and fundamental laws. This is where Bodin made his move. He defined the *jus gentium* not as the received tradition of Roman-Christian universal jurisprudence but as a comparative science of the laws of the various nations. In such a scheme the civil law of each nation comes to the fore, and becomes paramount. The idea of an overarching law-order circumscribing each nation's laws is lost in favor of the idea that general legal principles are to be derived from the actual practice of each nation as expressed in its own laws, averaged out to discover least common denominators.

Bodin's minimalist method reflected the rising nationalism most visibly represented in sixteenth-century France. A range of French jurists appealed to the superiority of French political and legal institutions to set their country apart from the rest of Europe. Such an approach was promoted by the crown as a means to strengthening its own position atop the social order. It was also pursued by certain constitutionalists who felt that adherence to the authority of Roman law would lead to absolutist government, since Roman law was seen by them to be an instrument of despotism. The latter approach was comparable to the course taken by the common lawyers in England.

The contrast with Spanish jurisprudence is instructive. In Spain the devotees of the School of Salamanca were quite keen on the independence and even superiority of Castilian and Spanish political and legal institutions. Nevertheless they admitted that these were bound by the *jus gentium*. Spanish jurists put forward a relatively objective and unprejudiced view of the historical development of their country's and other countries' institutions, in stark contrast to French jurists, for whom historical accuracy ran a distant second to propaganda value.

Bodin thus entirely denatured the *jus gentium*, just as constitutionalists <89> were developing it to a pitch of perfection. Jurisprudence had developed to the point that it could present Europe with two options – the path of absolute sovereignty in closed communities, or the path of limited sovereignty in a greater community of peoples.

That choice was bound up with the degree to which religious unity transcended nationalist fervor in Latin Europe. The idea of a universal community was based on the idea of the Holy Roman Empire, at least in a figurative sense.

But the wars of religion upset that unity and opened the door to the absolutist alternative. National monarchs increasingly moved into the void, claiming the prerogatives of total sovereignty as the only way out of chaos. The churches were coopted in the effort to impose peace. The bands which tied the various polities of Europe together were loosened in favor of bands joining domestic factions, with the effect of reducing the interdependence and intercommunication championed by the *jus gentium*.

Despite the trends the unified *corpus Christianum* remained a viable alternative right up into the seventeenth century. The final blow did not come until the Thirty-Years' War, which brought a definitive end to the conflict in Germany raging since the time of Luther and Charles V. The war changed the face of Europe: prior to it, Europe was still recognizably medieval in many ways; after it, the closed absolute state enjoyed pride of place. Its triumph was gained by the once-and-for-all elimination of a common religion as the basis of, and restraint on, state power. By failing to agree, the churches had essentially removed themselves from the independent constitutional position they had enjoyed since the inception of Western civilization. The *jus gentium* was part and parcel of the theocratic constitution of Western Christendom. Thus its fate was linked with that of the Church. The loss of the constitutional position of the churches spelled the end of the common law as the dominant force of Western civilization.

---

Thus, while nationhood was a part of Western civilization from early on, the absolutist understanding of nationhood – a function of the doctrine of sovereignty – was now triumphant, at least theoretically. The loss of transnational community accompanied the fragmentation of the church. Now the nation functioned as vehicle of absolutism.

---

Nevertheless, the tradition of constitutionalism continued, albeit in <90> transmogrified form, due largely to the efforts of one man, who at the height of the Thirty-Years' War rescued the *jus gentium* by refounding it on updated, recognizably modern principles. The effort involved stripping out the discredited theocratic basis, leaving intact a basic constitutional, limited government superstructure. The overhaul was carried out by Hugo Grotius, the Dutch jurist, politician, and statesman.

Grotius deftly combined a confluence of trends and traditions to produce his epoch-making work. The scion of a leading regent family, he was brought up in the heady milieu of the infant Dutch Republic and so imbibed that country's tradition of constitutionalism and liberty. The Dutch constitutional tradition was a branch of the *jus gentium* tradition. For a long time a Hapsburg possession, the United Provinces were imbued with *jus gentium* teaching as propagated by the School of Salamanca. Grotius leaned heavily on the teaching of the Salamancans in formulating his own theory.

But Grotius also shared the conviction that the removal of the Church as an independent constitutional player was of paramount importance to the furtherance of peace and order. As a leading political figure during the struggle between Calvinist and Arminian in the first two decades of the seventeenth century, Grotius championed the idea of the sovereign state vis-à-vis the Church. He advocated a broad latitudinarian church establishment embracing all citizens but exercising no independent judicial or constitutional authority. The triumph of the Calvinist party under Maurice, son of William the Silent, the leader of the Dutch revolt, put an end to Grotius's Dutch political career. He was imprisoned but later escaped to France, where he was received at court, though at arms' length.

Exile provided Grotius the leisure and perspective to formulate a new theory of the *jus gentium*, embracing constitutionalism and an open community of nations but rejecting theocracy. Against the background of the mounting devastation of the Thirty-Years' War, he sought to <91> formulate universal principles to which all peoples and nations could agree in a supposed post-theocratic environment.

His approach centered on a reevaluation of the source of authority. What made authority legitimate? How could authority be established so as to maintain peace and restrain anarchy? The relevance of the question is clear: a new basis of authority was needed now that theocracy had been rejected.

It might seem that a solution to this problem was already at hand in the received tradition of the *jus gentium*. Was it not clear that sovereignty lay with the people, and that all legitimate authority was derived from the consent of the people? There was a hitch to this supposed solution, however, one which has escaped modern historians of political thought: the theory of popular sovereignty as put forward in the *jus gentium* was conceived within a theocratic framework. The upholders of popular sovereignty were invariably either Catholics or Calvinists, both champions of the public right of the church. The *jus gentium* theory of popular sovereignty upheld the idea of a

restricted state within the framework of a structure of loci of authority outside the state, independent of the state. Popular sovereignty meant the sovereignty of the entire constellation of authority structures taken together, so
that none could claim an absolute position outside of and superior to the
others. In essence, the legitimacy of each and every authority was based in
divine right. Divine right was thus not exclusive to the state or the king but
to all legitimate authorities in society, including lesser magistrates, but also
including the Church and the family, the local community, voluntary associations, even occupations in agriculture, industry, commerce. Every group
and every activity functioned in terms of a *jus symbioticum*, a law-order particularly its own, prescribed by its purpose to enable it to fulfill that purpose.
Althusius most fully articulated this idea of popular sovereignty. In it, divine
right is not done away with but much rather multiplied. Popular sovereignty
is itself an expression of divine right and ultimately an unshakable belief
<92> in the sovereignty of God.

Thus popular sovereignty as then understood depended upon a notion of
divine right in which authority receives its legitimacy from a divinely-or-
dained law-order. This is the point at which Grotius went to work. Grotius
introduced a far-reaching distinction in the concept of justice which enabled
him to overthrow the notion of divine right altogether. In accordance with
the Aristotelian-Thomistic tradition, Grotius understood justice to be divided into the categories distributive and commutative. The ruling principle
of distributive justice is divine right, that of commutative justice, contract.
The received theory of popular sovereignty therefore obviously incorporated
a great deal of distributive justice. Grotius, however, denied that law should
be based on distributive justice. Distributive justice is a moral, not a legal,
category; it depends on subjective, not objective criteria. To be applied, distributive justice requires agreement as to absolutes; Grotius, recognizing the
signs of the times, saw the need for a standard of justice that recognized and
accepted disagreement as to ultimates. Such justice was the kind prescribed
in the category commutative justice, which presupposed a minimum of criteria, all of which on the horizontal, secular plane, regarding human nature
as such, not theology, not dogma.

Grotius thus advocated the restriction of legal justice to the realm of commutative justice, and spelled out the criteria: natural rights, rights which are
inherent to individual human beings. Such rights include power over oneself

– liberty – and over others within the household – fathers over children, masters over servants – as well as property, and credit – the right to receive back what one has lent.[82] The obligation to keep agreements also belongs to this category, as does the requirement to do restitution for damage and the right to mete out appropriate punishments.[83] Such rights do not depend upon a legitimating authority; they <**93**> are not bestowed by society; they belong to individuals as such, apart from what society adds.

From this strict category of justice flows the broader category which Grotius equates with distributive justice. This justice is based on the inborn ability of people to judge for themselves what lies in their own best interest, both short-term and long-term, and to act on that knowledge without being swayed by fear or temptation. Because people have this ability they can agree to establish ranks in society, to recognize the difference between rich and poor, wise and less wise, relative and stranger. This is the source of distinctions in society, and thus of hierarchy: people accept these because they realize that such an arrangement promotes their own best interest. Grotius takes pains to make clear that this authority is not a command of justice but rather an option, a voluntary arrangement resting on the decision of each individual. "For a long time many have considered this to be part of law in the actual and strict sense, even though the latter actual law is of an entirely different character, resting as it does on the notion that what is another's is left to him or transferred to him."[84]

Thus society is a collection of self-conscious individuals acting in their own best interest to establish a social order. They do this because they have a built-in *appetitus societatis*, literally an "appetite for society," which drives them to form a social order, and in fact – and Grotius is adamant about this – this community spirit is the actual source of justice in the strict sense; in other words, the point of natural rights and the pursuit of enlightened self-interest is the good of society. "One of the properties which characterizes people is their *appetitus societatis*; I mean by that their need for a social life with fellow human beings which is ordered, peaceful and geared to their

---

[82] *Law of War and Peace,* I.I. § 5; cf. Prologue, § 8.

[83] *Law of War and Peace,* Prologue, § 8.

[84] *Law of War and Peace,* Prologue, §§ 9–10.

intelligence, a property which the Stoics termed οἰκείωσις.... This solicitude for community... forms the source of law in the strict sense."[85] <94>

Thus the drive to live in society is the basis for strict law, contractual law, and contract is the means by which an ordered society which answers to that community spirit is established. Contract is the premier means by which people join together: "it was necessary that a means be found by which to bind people to each other, and another natural way of doing this cannot be devised."[86] Society is effectively a voluntary construct: individuals could conceivably remain separated if they wished, but since in isolation they are weak, relatively defenseless, and relatively poorly able to provide for themselves, they join together for their own individual benefit.[87]

The Grotian system therefore presupposes the fully self-conscious, order-seeking, community-spirited individual guided by enlightened self-interest, what the ancients considered to be the end-product of the difficult process of civilization, and this before society is even formed. Thus natural man answers to the citizen ideal. But more than this: as was noted above, man in this "state of nature" is also endowed with the power of judging in his own cause and inflicting corresponding punishments on those who commit crime. This goes far beyond the power of self-defense; it includes the power to judge and punish crimes committed against others, even strangers.

By drawing these conclusions Grotius took a giant leap into the unknown. He recognized their novelty, but was convinced that he was the first to uncover the true principles of natural law, of strict justice, and that his conclusions were therefore incontrovertible. And he was sure that in this he had trumped his predecessors, the Salamancans. "Vitoria, Vasquez, Azor, Molina and others... state that the authority to punish flows from the judicial power of the state, while we are of the opinion that this also flows from the natural law...."[88] "Covarruvias follows others in <95> the opinion that the authority

---

[85] *Law of War and Peace,* Prologue, §§ 6, 8.

[86] *Law of War and Peace,* Prologue, § 15.

[87] *Law of War and Peace,* Prologue, § 16.

[88] *Law of War and Peace,* II.XX. § XL.4.

to punish is unthinkable apart from jurisdiction in the strict sense, an opinion we have already rejected."[89]

Grotius's doctrine makes individuals sovereign states unto themselves. The power of the state properly speaking is a direct outgrowth of this power inherent in each individual. It is the source of both the civil law and the *jus gentium*.[90] This is the solution Grotius offered to solve the problem of reason of state. Individuals are prior to the state; they erect a state not because they have to but because they see in it a surer path to the same goal, an ordered, peaceful social life. If the power of the state is absolute, it is so only because the original contractors willed it; they have only themselves to blame.

By magnifying the individual Grotius limited the state. But, like Bodin though in a far different way, he also limited the *jus gentium*. Its decisive, transcendent, sovereignty-conditioning content as presented by the School of Salamanca was reduced to whatever contracting individuals agreed on, according to the principle of *pacta sunt servanda*.[91] Still, Grotius felt that he had discovered a sufficient basis for protecting society from the ravages of robber states and for ensuring that states pursue the interests of society at large: not only the nation, but all nations. For individuals also establish the *jus gentium* as a means for promoting the welfare of the entire human community. "Just as the laws of every state have at heart the interest of that state, so certain laws have been developed between all, or <96> at least most, states, and indeed through agreement – laws that do not have the interest of

---

[89] *Law of War and Peace,* II.XX. § XLIV.1.

[90] *Law of War and Peace,* Prologue, §§ 16, 17.

[91] "The developed account of the principles of justice found in the Aristotelian tradition, according to which even quite detailed provisions of contractual and commercial law were explicable as derivations from general and universal principles, was thus radically thinned down in Grotius' work, and the bulk of it pushed into the category of limited and local rules.... [Grotius' doctrine of] the law of nature... consists only of propositions which are absolutely obvious and will be denied by no one, whatever their religion. The traditional content of the law of nature had largely been abandoned." Richard Tuck, *Philosophy and Government 1572–1651*, pp. 175, 188.

separate communities at heart but much rather that of the great community of nations. This law is what men call the law of nations [*jus gentium*]."[92]

Grotius retained the essential elements of the *jus gentium*, the rights of communication, but in founding them upon a presumed contract, he undermined their obligatory character, reducing them to the level of customary law.[93] As such, states could modify them by treaty. This of course destroyed the nature of the *jus gentium* as a restriction on sovereignty. Grotius's exposition opens the curtain on the world of modern international law, in which states negotiate by treaty to establish laws which they otherwise are in no wise bound to respect. There is no authority over the state except the individuals which form the state, but these same individuals having formed the state become subject to it. This was the blueprint he provided a world faced with the collapse of the Holy Roman Empire and the devastation of the Thirty-Years' War. It would remain to be seen whether such a system could, as he hoped, truly deliver on the goals of limited government and the rights of communication.

---

We may conclude: Grotius was the first Whig.

---

[92] *The Law of War and Peace,* Prologue, 17.
[93] *The Law of War and Peace,* I.I. § 14.2.

# Chapter 10

# True Freedom

HUGO GROTIUS sent the *jus gentium* limping into the new age. His home-land, the Dutch Republic, maintained a living, albeit tenuous, connection with that tradition, an island of constitutionalism – however imperfect – in a world of would-be absolute monarchs, a champion of free trade – however self-serving – in a world of would-be autarchic national economies.

The transformation that on a theoretical plane took place in Hugo Gro-tius's head on a practical plane took place in the Dutch Republic. The fledg-ling confederation of supposedly sovereign provinces conducted the same kind of radical operation on late-medieval constitutional institutions that Grotius carried out on the *jus gentium*. It had to if it were to succeed in filling the vacuum left by the loss of its monarch. The success of the revolt left it headless, as it were, and threw it into the kind of situation about which state-of-nature political philosophers were only conjecturing. This was a major im-petus behind Grotius's work, and goes a long way toward explaining its rad-ical nature.

But this was only one part of the transformation affecting all of Europe during this age of "the rise of the modern state." The natural, multiple bands of communication that developed during the ages of ripening civilization, binding the nations of Europe in one body, were being forcibly severed, or at least rerouted, through the increasingly effective and far-reaching efforts of national rulers. War was only the most obvious method of disrupting these lines of communication. The main driving force was in fact the increasingly important science of "political economy" with its core idea of a self-con-tained national economy serving the national interest.

Recent scholarship has brought to the fore just how obsessed early- <98> modern states were with enhancing their ability effectively to wage war.[94] In ever-increasing degree states worked to marshal the nation's resources to the war effort. More and more the state viewed the resources of subjects as state

---

[94] By way of example: John Brewer, *The Sinews of Power: War, Money and the English State 1688–1783*.

resources, needing to be more efficiently organized so as to more effectively serve the needs of the state. This was one of the major sources of conflict between absolutists and constitutionalists: recall that a major plank of the *jus gentium* was the idea that the state in no way was the master of private property, but rather existed to preserve private property for the rightful owners. But reason of state came to outweigh the *jus gentium*. The upshot was mercantilism, a series of doctrines aimed at maximizing the utilization of a nation's resources in service of the state. Mercantilism worked under the assumption that the nation's interest was equivalent to the state's interest, and that nations were at war just like states were, with economic winners and losers just like military winners and losers. The state successfully propagated the notion that the nation needed to organize its economy at the national level under the leadership of the state to successfully defeat other nations equally bent on economic supremacy. Thus, the state harnessed the economy of the nation to its own ends – in fact, created the national economy – and passed off the result as economic progress, when in fact the nationalization of economies was economically disruptive and counterproductive, and in this sense not much better than all-out war.[95]

See below, "National Economy?" for the further development of this theme.

During this age of nation-building, the Dutch Republic maintained the *jus gentium* tradition nearly single-handedly. Alone among the Great Powers of the post-Thirty-Years' War era, the Dutch Republic championed the rights of communication, freedom of the seas, freedom of trade, the primacy of "the essential economic interests and aspirations of the <**99**> subjects" rather than of the rulers.[96] It had to: trade was its life-blood. The Dutch Republic in the seventeenth century rose to become the leading trading nation in Europe and served as the hub of the first truly global trading network, "the first and, for most of early modern times, the only true world entrepôt."[97]

---

[95] Jane Jacobs' book *Cities and the Wealth of Nations* contains much food for thought along these lines.

[96] J. C. Boogman, "The Raison d'Etat Politician Johan de Wit," in *The Low Countries History Yearbook*, 1978, p. 57.

[97] The title says it all: Jonathan I. Israel, *Dutch Primacy in World Trade 1585 –1740*.

The Dutch Republic maintained the institutions of the *jus gentium* in an attenuated form, analogous to the attenuated form in which Hugo Grotius maintained the doctrine of the *jus gentium*. For example, the hugely successful Vereenigde Oost-Indische Compagnie (VOC), otherwise known as the United East-India Company, established by its merchant capitalists to trade with friendly nations in the Indian Ocean and South Pacific, was put on a monopoly basis. The argument was that freedom of trade and freedom of the seas were in principle right and just, but the times demanded that certain areas of trade be organized so as to exclude foreign nations because those very nations would do the same if they could. Grotius formulated the legal doctrine to back up this approach. Since the *jus gentium* was the product of agreement, states as representatives of peoples could negotiate between themselves to modify it to establish exclusive trade links between the two nations represented by the states, leaving other nations out of the picture.

---

These trade treaties established trading relations between the VOC and the indigenous countries, to the exclusion of third parties (see, e.g., *Calvin and the Whigs*, pp. 90–91). The relations so established also tended to shift in the direction of lord and vassal: see the commentary in *The Debate that Changed the West*, pp. 83ff.

---

In its constitutional arrangement the new republic likewise adapted the *jus gentium* to the new realities. The keynote was decentralization. Each province was essentially sovereign: the Dutch Republic was really nothing more than a confederation, the United Provinces. The province of Holland, economically the strongest, likewise had the most to say about policy. But Holland itself had eighteen "members" or voting cities and each of these jealously regarded its own position. The upshot was a system <100> in which the cities retained the lion's share of power, delegating only as much as each thought necessary to the provincial and "national" level. A long tutelage in federalism under the houses of Burgundy and Hapsburg had taught these members enough about cooperation for mutual benefit to make the arrangement work.

Thus centralism remained a dead letter in the Dutch Republic. While monarchs in other nations were busy trying to implement their schemes of top-down economic policy, the Dutch confederacy adhered to its decentralized ways; economic policy remained the prerogative of individual cities. Most industries were left undisturbed by government; a few were promoted and regulated "virtually as much as in the typical mercantilist countries," but cities rather than central government did the promoting and regulating.[98] With the center of political gravity located in the cities, the Hollander mercantile aristocracy enjoyed the primacy in the constitution of the new republic. In Holland itself, the city regents enjoyed near-total control. This is where the Dutch Republic made constitutional history. The justification for the Dutch Revolt was grounded in the monarchomach literature produced during the French wars of religion. The justification of the primacy of the estates over the king, as representatives of the people, was applied to the estates of the provinces taken separately as well as to the combined States General of the confederation.

Interestingly, the viceroy under the prerevolution monarchy – the so-called *stadhouder* – was retained even after the monarchy was overthrown. After renouncing the authority of the king, the estates of each province assumed the sovereignty and thus the power to appoint its own *stadhouder*. But even though appointed by the estates, the office of *stadhouder* maintained prerogatives from the days when the *stadhouder* stood over the province and thus over the estates. This made for great confusion, which <101> in times of crisis could lead to open conflict between *stadhouder* and estates, as occurred in Holland in 1618 and again in 1650. But for the most part the *stadhouder* deferred to regent rule, and worried mainly about military matters.

The Church likewise occupied a novel position in the new republic. With the overthrow of Catholicism, the Reformed church took a leading position in all the provinces of the new republic, gaining official recognition from the civil authorities, though not a full, exclusive establishment. The difference is important: no one was forced to become a member of the Reformed church. Because church discipline extended only to members, the direct authority of the Church over society was restricted. This was beneficial because the Church could concentrate on what she conceived as her spiritual mission without having to engage in cheerleading for the state – the maintenance of civil religion – as the price for a state grant of coercive jurisdiction. The Church successfully strove to maintain her independence by keeping a tight grip on church discipline, not handing it over to the civil authorities as oc-

---

[98] J.G. van Dillen, *Van Rijkdom en Regenten* [Of Wealth and Regents], p. 487.

curred in other – Lutheran, Zwinglian, and to a degree Anglican – Protestant churches. Church authorities restricted membership to those who accepted the tenets of the Church. The only people who were required to become members, and thus – theoretically, at least – to submit to the spiritual discipline of the Church were the civil magistrates.

Hoedemaker argued that this requirement had a negative effect on the church, restricting rather than expanding its influence. We may surmise that such a mechanism, instead of helping the church influence the magistrates, helped magistrates influence the church.

But the Church actually had no position in five of the seven provincial estates, but only in Utrecht and Gelderland. The nobility's position was also severely restricted, saved only by the position of the *stadhouder* in the estates of Holland and Zealand, though in the other provinces it had a more substantial role. On the whole, the third estate had the primacy, and here it was only the merchant aristocracy, an exclusive group of moneyed oligarchs, who ran the show. It has been estimated that across the republic <**102**> this group numbered 2,000.[99] With such a preponderance it comes as no surprise that a certain "mercantile world-view" took hold across the republic to the detriment of a more balanced, full-orbed culture in which all the facets of material and spiritual life received harmonious expression. The Dutch Republic became noted for a focus on the "mercenary" side of life – money, accounting, contract. Thus its lopsided political constitution came to find expression in its social constitution.

Althusius well described the kind of full-orbed culture a well-balanced constitution nurtures. The various elements of life find expression in groupings, in estates. The harmonious interaction and mutual counsel of these orders lead to a unified, healthy body politic.

As the ecclesiastical order of the province will bring forth pious, learned, wise, and good men, so the political and secular order of the nobility will be concerned to bring forth for the province strong, militant, and brave men who

---

[99] Fockema Andreae, S.J., "De Nederlandse Staat onder de Republiek" [The Dutch State under the Republic], *Verhand. Kon. Ned. Akad. afd. Letterk.*, Nwe. reeks (XVIII no. 3), 1961, p. 37.

are ready with arms and counsel, and are experienced in military matters. So also the order of burghers and agrarians – the commons – will strive to produce and bring forth for the fatherland merchants, farmers, and workmen who are skilled, industrious and distinguished. By the services, labour, and industry of these orders, self-sufficiency can be obtained in association and symbiosis.[100]

In Althusius's view this balance was lacking in the Dutch provinces of Holland, Zealand, West Friesland, North Brabant and Groningen. They had only two orders, the nobility and the burghers; the clergy was left out, as were the yeoman farmers – in Althusius's view a mistake.[101]

The *stadhouder* and the Church provided counterweights – and no <103> more than that – to the predominance of the trading interest as represented by the regents and the province of Holland. With such a unique predominance it comes as no surprise that the regent class would come up with a unique ideology justifying its rule. Hugo Grotius was one of the pioneers of this genre. His doctrine was in large part an extended adaptation of the *jus gentium* tradition to the exigencies of regent rule. One example was his attitude toward free trade and monopolies – the state needed to represent the interests of trade even when in violation of the rights of communication as expressed in the *jus gentium*. Another was his reduction of sovereignty to the rights-bearing individual. Crucially, Grotius's rights were property rights. The rights-bearing individual was the propertied individual, now situated at the center of the social order, with all legitimate political authority extending outward from him.

In his *Law of War and Peace* Grotius did not take sides in the controversy between monarchy and republic. In fact, he dedicated the work to the French king Louis XIII, probably because of the favor shown him in allowing him to set up in Paris, even to the extent of granting him a pension. In his works as a Dutch patriot, however, Grotius expressed himself clearly. A republic was clearly preferable to a monarchy; the one was free, the other in subjection. Holland – the locus of his republicanism – had suffered long under the oppressions of the House of Burgundy; it had liberated itself from the tyranny

---

[100] Carney, p. 56 [61].

[101] Carney, p. 56 [61].

of the House of Hapsburg and the king of Spain, and had every right to stand up for itself in the world of princes and potentates.

This was the root of the regents' self-legitimation: *Ware Vryheid*, "True Freedom," freedom over against the tyranny of Church and state. The ideology of True Freedom was anti-clerical and anti-monarchical. Its proponents formed the States party over against the Orangists, the coalition of Reformed churchmen and supporters of the *stadhouder*, the Prince of Orange, who stood for the old order of church and state. In the eyes of the States party, regent rule provided salvation from the warmon- <104> gering, money-wasting ways of princes and from the moral and intellectual oppressions of the clergy. Both of these forms of oppression were the bane of trade, the life-blood of the young republic: wars used huge sums of money and accomplished little more than the requiting of the irrepressible appetite for glory; religious dogmatism drove out all those who could not split hairs the same way as the theologians, leaving a servile, superstitious populace driven hither and thither by the fanatical demagoguery of jealous, hidebound, power hungry preachers. To flourish, trade required liberation from these two age-old forms of tyranny. The regents provided that liberty, and the economic boom produced under their benign leadership was proof positive of the rightness of their viewpoint.

---

"Ware Vryheid" was the first iteration of Whig ideology.

---

Thus, while the *jus gentium* undoubtedly received shelter under the wings of the fledgling republic of the United Provinces of the Netherlands, it was forced into the mold of the trading interest of the dominant regent class. In politics, Grotius and his progeny removed the "sacred canopy" of Church and state, of priest and king; in jurisprudence, they removed the category of distributive justice, leaving only contract, ownership, property, as the source and legitimating criteria of all forms of authority.

In essence, Grotius and his many followers established the citizen ideal as a self-sufficient starting-point for the social order. The elements of that ideal – the household, private property, and market exchange – were assumed to be self-evident. Their basis was human nature itself. They therefore were natural rights. They required no legitimation in terms of a higher law, they *were* the higher law. Grotius thus severed the link between theocracy and the citizen ideal, the foundation of Western civilization. While seeming to free the citizen ideal from the clutches of theocracy, Grotius in fact delivered it into the hands of a new master: the religion of humanity. For if human nature itself is the source of law, then sovereign power resides in each and every individual; transcendence is <105> lost, humanity becomes its own guide and master. The age of Enlightenment was dawning. And there would prove to be more than one list of self-evident natural rights.

---

Grotius put all his eggs in one basket: the citizen ideal, abstracted from and stripped of all supporting institutions. For its part, the Dutch Republic served as the crucible of the coming Whig establishment. How this establishment took root, and how it came to form the "yin" to the "yang" of progressivism, will be explored in the coming chapters.

# Chapter 11

## The Apotheosis of Liberty

IN A SENSE the Dutch Republic was the beneficiary of the wars of religion that ripped apart the fabric of Christendom. It was able to pick up and carry forward the trading network that other countries no longer could maintain. And it made enormous profits from the wars, both directly and indirectly, in supplying armies and navies and in making up for the shortfalls generated by the privations of war. England was the only nation similarly advantaged, but domestic discord and outright civil war kept her from full participation.

France was the other main beneficiary of the tragedy of Europe. She arose from the ashes of the Thirty-Years' War as the leading nation of Europe. Her main enemies, the Hapsburgs of Austria and Spain, lay prostrate, the Holy Roman Empire devastated. Under the leadership of Cardinal Richelieu, France came out united, intact, and ready to make her own impression on the wax of Christendom.

While common-law, *jus gentium* constitutionalism soldiered on in one form or another, France and its civil-law absolutism now moved to the forefront. Its ascendancy also led to the ascendancy of a world-view, the keynote of which was struggle and conflict. At the heart of this position was a belief in an existential antagonism rooted in the cosmos itself. Life is ruled by the conflict of interests. The gain of one can only be at the expense of another. The environment is evil and needs to be brought under direct control. Life is a struggle for survival.

This viewpoint received vivid expression in the midst of religious warfare of late sixteenth-century France in the writings of, among others, the pioneer essayist Montaigne. A chapter of his *Essays* entitled "The Profit of One Man is the Dammage of Another" proffered this viewpoint:

The Merchant thrives not but by the licentiousnesse of youth; the Husband-man by dearth of corne; the Architect but by the <107> ruine of houses; the Lawyer by suits and controversies betweene men: Honour it selfe, and practice of religious Ministers, is drawne from our death and vices. *No Physitian delighteth in the health of his owne friend*, saith the ancient Greeke Comike:

*nor no souldier is pleased with the peace of his Citie, and so of the rest.* And
which is worse, let every man sound his owne conscience, hee shall finde, that
our inward desires are for the most part nourished and bred in us by the losse
and hurt of others; which when I considered, I began to thinke, how nature
doth not gainesay herselfe in this, concerning her generall policie: for Phy-
sitians hold, that *The birth, increase, and augmentation of every thing, is the
alteration and corruption of another.*[102]

This was a frontal attack on the *jus gentium* notion of an inherent harmony of interests in human society. Of themselves people sought their own
interest to the detriment of the public interest. The state needed to intervene
in social life to overcome this inherent conflict.

Such a belief formed the metaphysical basis for the doctrine of absolute
sovereignty inherent in the civil-law tradition and the engine behind
France's constitutional development. France's victory over her arch-rival, the
empire, sealed the victory of the proponents of absolute monarchy. By yielding absolute submission to the king, the nation had gained the victory. The
lesson was that the key to realizing national aspirations lay in accepting the
civil law approach to government, and rejecting that of the *jus gentium.*

Doctrines of economics and international relations developed as comple-
ments to divine-right absolutism. Rather than a community of nations
which needed to live in mutual harmony, respecting one another's legitimate
rights, international relations were conceived as a state of continual warfare
in which each nation needed to defend and expand its <108> own interests.
Reason of state lay at the heart of absolutism. Mercantilist doctrine replaced
the open-border, free-trade orientation of medieval theocracy in the realm of
economics. The notion of balance of trade came to be seen as a crucial deter-
minant of national well-being: if the balance of trade was negative, the nation
was being defeated by foreign nations; if the balance of trade was positive, the
nation was triumphing over foreign nations. The commercial and mercantile
interests of the nation needed to be favored and privileged through grants of
subsidy and monopoly in order to enable them to compete successfully
against foreign commercial and mercantile interests, thus fusing the interests
of the nation with the interests of its capitalist class. Domestic industry

---

[102] Michel de Montaigne, *Essays*, pp. 104–5.

needed to be protected by discriminatory tariffs. These measures were not conceived as exceptions to the rules under the pressure of extraordinary circumstances, but as a group of positive policy prescriptions good for all time.

This is quite an interesting passage in the light of recent developments. The key sentence is the last one. The freedom-oriented institutions of the *jus gentium* are the goal to which international arrangements ought to aim; but they cannot be pursued to the detriment of nationhood and the national interest. There is a balance that must be struck in each juncture, each period of history. See the articles under "National and Global Economy" below.

Thus the age of Baroque, the age of court and king, was also the age of the expansion of power of the nation-state and the development of political economy focused upon its advancement. For it was imperative that the resources of the nation be concentrated as effectively as possible, and directed against the external world of competing nations. The relative autonomy and independence of lesser associations and polities within the nation had to be broken down in favor of a direct bond between the king and citizenry, because such a direct link better served the national interest by removing distracting bonds of loyalty. Business and commercial interests were privileged and protected, brought under the direct shelter and control of the crown, in order to succeed in the omnicompetitive international arena.

In embodying such an approach to national and international affairs, France came face to face with its tiny neighbor to the north and its fundamentally opposed constitution. Conflict was inevitable between the two nations, embodying as they did two fundamentally antagonistic <109> ideals. Through the efforts of Louis XIV's finance minister Jean-Baptiste Colbert, France embarked on a campaign to displace Dutch preeminence in trade by pursuing a full-blown mercantilistic policy joining French commercial interests to the French monarchy. Eventually Louis even went so far as to invade the Republic in 1672, nearly defeating it, in order to subordinate its trading interest to that of France. But by the skin of her teeth the Republic escaped, helped by the skill of her young *stadhouder* William III and by her then-unmatched navy. The Dutch Republic henceforth maintained its place at the center of the world-economy until well into the eighteenth century.

Colbert based his policy directly upon the doctrine of conflict of interest. In his eyes there was "only a given quantity of money which circulates in

Europe," and "the trade of all Europe is carried on with about 20,000 ships of all sizes [whose] number cannot be increased, since the populations and the consumption of all the states remains the same." The conclusion was that France must increase its share at the expense of the other nations, especially Holland. "Commerce causes a perpetual battle in peace and war between the nations of Europe as to who will win the best part of it."[103] These kinds of views were staple elements of "new" monarchy's approach to the *jus gentium*. Given such a view, it comes as no surprise that the United Provinces should have been viewed as such an anachronism and with such distaste. If trade was carried on always at the expense of some victim or enemy, then a nation which made its living from trade must then be the embodiment of evil itself. This notion implanted itself in the minds of Baroque princes as the notion of a unified Christendom receded, contrary though it was to the *jus gentium* which had framed Christendom's original order.

The popularity of absolute monarchy and its attendant ideology, mercantilism, in the eighteenth century waned along with the defeat of <110> Louis XIV's pretension to universal dominion. The idea of a war of all against all and the idea that national wealth could only be increased at the expense of other nations lost currency as Louis's power play was thwarted by the efforts of the Allies, Holland, England, and the empire. With the victory of the "*jus gentium* powers," the *jus gentium* itself gained a new lease on life, albeit in a form even further removed from its original shape than that which Grotius had given it.

This was the project of the Enlightenment. It consisted in a reaction to the despotism and pessimism of reason of state as pursued by the princes of the sixteenth and seventeenth centuries. In a reversal of roles, the Dutch Republic and post-Glorious Revolution England became the pattern states, replacing the France of Colbert and Louis XIV. The ideology of *Ware Vryheid* was adopted and updated with the new metaphysic of Reason and Natural Religion. Kings and priests came to be seen as the root of all evil, while the cultured layman moved into their place as society's role model. Property and trade were fitted to a mechanistic framework which guaranteed the automatic good of all from the simple pursuit of profit. Peace among nations was inevitable, it was thought, as long as countries organized themselves as

[103] Quoted in A. Lloyd Moote, *The Seventeenth Century: Europe in Ferment*, p. 63.

republics rather than monarchies, for republics were inherently peace-loving, seeking to trade rather than to conquer. Nationalism itself moved far into the background, as enlightened thinkers began to embrace "the concept of a universal human community to which the rational man owed his highest terrestrial allegiance."[104]

---

The assimilation of the citizen ideal and the *jus gentium* to a nature-oriented, post-revelation framework was the great project of the Enlightenment, giving birth to full-blown Whiggery.

---

A key part of this project was the cooptation of the citizen ideal and the *jus gentium* in terms of autonomous Reason, the result being the so-called "System of Natural Liberty." Following the lead originally provided by Grotius, the proponents of Natural Liberty were convinced that if only the stultifying institutions of oppression and tyranny were taken out of the <111> way, people would respond by acting rationally, i.e., in terms of the principles inherent in their own human nature, and thus build for themselves a society of freedom. Theocracy, far from nurturing and promoting civil liberty, was the biggest stumbling block in the path of the triumph of civil liberty.

Of course, in reading history in this manner the thinkers of the Enlightenment proved to have lost the distinction between absolute monarchy and the theocratic constitutionalism which had come before it and which indeed had fought a death-struggle with it. For them, theocracy and absolutism were one and the same. Perhaps the influence of a Bossuet, the great French bishop, historian, and apologist for the reign of the Sun King, is to blame for this telescoping of history, for making it appear as if absolute monarchy were the only historic expression of Christian government. At any rate, liberty and citizenship came to demand the abolition of divine-right authority of any kind, even revealed religion itself. The enlightened citizen would automatically fill the gap.

As with the one, so with the many. Responsible citizens would sprout like mushrooms as the suffocating blanket of superstition and credulity lifted, automatically creating a society of justice and equality. Natural Law would take

---

[104] John U. Nef, *Western Civilization Since the Renaissance: Peace, War, Industry and the Arts*, p. 347.

care of that. The eighteenth century put into service a mechanistic concept of natural law to fill out this vision of the Heavenly City[105] on earth. Vitoria's rights of communication and Grotius's *pacta sunt servanda* were transformed into an automatic mechanism meeting everyone's needs simply by the workings of the market.

But there was a fly in this ointment, entirely invisible to this generation of naive optimists. Essentially it boiled down to this: citizenship is a privilege, not a right; it is the end-result of an educational process, not the starting point. Human beings are not born citizens, they simply have the potential to grow into citizens. Responsible citizenship requires discipline, <112> high standards of ethical conduct, and a commitment to the inviolability of the bond of the city, reciprocity.

The fact is, theocracy provided the necessary infrastructure to support the citizen ideal. The Church's educational program included a heavy dose of the liberal arts, in essence an education in citizenship. The Church also enjoined on people the requirements of the Ten Commandments, the principles of which are obligatory to the maintenance of ordered freedom. Through its diaconal ministry, the Church provided a safety net for those who were unable to sustain themselves in the free society and who had no family to take them in.

By eliminating the theocratic foundations, the Enlightenment also removed these supports for the free society. The result was predictable: ever-increasing numbers of displaced persons, unable to find their place in the free world, increasingly subject to exploitation by those who could bend the system to their own ends. The project of the Enlightenment thus had an unintended consequence of the most momentous kind: the desire for a social order of exactly the opposite sort, a resurgent communal organicism in which people, rather than being left to make their own decisions, have their decisions made for them, who rather than take care of themselves, become cared for by the community.[106]

With this development, the ideology of the civil law gained a new lease on life. The naively optimistic view of the naturalness of good citizenship gave way under the pressure of the overwhelming reality that citizenship does

---

[105] Carl Becker, *The Heavenly City of the Eighteenth-Century Philosophers*, 1932.
[106] On this point see Michael Oakeshott, *On Human Conduct*, pp. 274ff.

not grow on trees. Suddenly, sensitive souls became aware of the dregs which before they had scarcely noticed. In the age of aristocracy, the common man did not have much of a standing; increasingly, however, as the Enlightenment doctrine of human nature gained hold it became plausible that the man in the street, yea even the servants, were also human beings and thus also equals. "There was no rational <113> justification for perpetuating a social scum at a time when European thought manifested increasing confidence in the perfectibility of human nature under civilized conditions, and when Voltaire, Rousseau, and other influential men of letters attributed special virtues to man in a state of nature, without wealth or even schooling."[107]

This is where France, representing the tradition of the civil law, and England, representing the common law, experienced a parting of the ways. The English solution was to recognize that the citizen ideal would not simply be the product of a release from the institutions of Christendom. The first person to draw this conclusion and explore its ramifications was Edmund Burke. The French solution, on the other hand, was to go "the whole hog" and violently overthrow the institutions of the *ancien regime*, thus carrying to its logical conclusion the Enlightenment ideal of liberty and citizenship.

Having traced the genesis of the de-theocratized *jus gentium*, resulting in the Whig version of the common-law tradition, it is time to trace the genesis of a resurgent civil-law absolutism, this time cast in terms of natural equality. This movement filled the vacuum left by the "natural liberty" of Whiggish individualism with a renewed version of collectivism. This was given birth by the French Revolution.

What happened in France determined the entire further history of Western civilization. The inability to establish a working republic in essence rang the death-knell for the citizen ideal in France. According to Alexis de Tocqueville, who in his *The Old Regime and the French Revolution* made perhaps the definitive diagnosis of revolutionary France, the Revolution backfired because France's previous history had been determined by the civil-law tradition of absolute sovereignty rather than the common-law tradition of limited sovereignty. France's absolute monarchy had essentially kept its subjects in a condition of childhood, without the opportunity to exercise

[107] Nef, *Western Civilization*, p. 308.

responsibility in political life; when the time came that the people demanded
the opportunity, they didn't know what to do with it. "In no other country
in Europe had all political thought been so thoroughly and for so long stifled
as in France; in no other country had the private citizen become so completely out of touch with public affairs and so unused to studying the course
of events, so <114> much so that not only had the average Frenchmen no
experience of 'popular movements' but he hardly understood what 'the people' meant."[108]

The vacuum created by the incapacity of republican government was
eventually filled by a dictator, Napoleon. This was only the logical consequence of France's civil-law tradition. In effect, the Enlightenment in France
was the attempt to root the citizen ideal in the soil of absolutism, an attempt
which was doomed to failure. The citizen ideal could only blossom in the tradition of the *jus gentium*, not the civil law. France's institutions remained
those of the *jus civile* even after the Revolution – another, and perhaps the
most important, of de Tocqueville's conclusions. The centralized, paternal-
istic apparatus of government was maintained intact into the republican period and was assumed by Napoleon.

What happened next was that the citizen ideal itself was twisted almost
beyond recognition in order to make it serve the ends of civil-law absolutism.
Since France could not adapt to the citizen ideal, the citizen ideal would have
to adapt to France. The adaptation revolved around the priority of liberty
vis-à-vis equality. Increasingly it became clear that the latter rather than the
former would serve as the great end of civil society.

The new ideology of equality focused its attack on the institution of private property. The shift was portended in the conspiracy of Babeuf in 1796.
"Their slogan was the abolition of *property*. They believed that unless this root
of bitterness were destroyed the tree of liberty would not blossom."[109] Private
property was the source of all society's ills. Far from being a natural right, it
was an artificial convention which could be modified or abolished at the be-
hest of the community. "The perennial cause of the enslavement of nations
lies entirely in inequality," Babeuf's <115> followers affirmed; "so long as

---

[108] Alexis de Tocqueville, *The Old Regime and the French Revolution*, p. 205
[109] G. Groen van Prinsterer, *Lectures on Unbelief and Revolution*, p. 219.

inequality remains, the exercise of political rights will be little more than illusory for a host of men whom our civilization debases to a subhuman level."[110]

Here was dawning the prospect of an entirely new set of priorities, which spelled the destruction of the original Enlightenment ideal of liberty. Property rights were central to the Enlightenment program; even the celebrated *Declaration of the Rights of Man and Citizen* had emphasized property as "an inviolable and sacred right" (art. XVII). But now property was coming to be seen as the stumbling block, the reason for the failure of popular government, rather than the main pillar.

Jean-Jacques Rousseau made the initial and crucial contribution to the transformation of the citizen ideal in terms of civil-law absolutism. His work constituted a frontal attack on the received Enlightenment wisdom. He refuted the Enlightenment notion that man enters society already fully-formed – that citizenship is innate. Rather, society formed the individual and made him what he is. Rousseau also disputed the notion that man in civil society is superior to man outside of society, in the state of nature. For Rousseau, man in the state of nature is also in a state of innocence; it is society which corrupts him.

Rousseau saw the foundation of civil society in the institution of private property. "The first man who enclosed a plot of ground and thought of saying, 'This is mine,' and found others stupid enough to believe him, was the true founder of civil society" is the famous line with which he began the second part of his *Discourse on the Origin of Inequality* (1754). With property came agriculture, generating surplus production, enabling population to grow and necessitating a division of labor to distribute the fruits of surplus production. Specialization and leisure were the result, bringing idleness and social awareness – the desire to see and be seen. Then came envy, jealousy, manipulation, as each strove to be <116> greater, more proficient, more accomplished in others' eyes than he in fact was. The arts of civilization raised duplicity to an art form, and alienated man against himself. "The savage lives in himself; the man accustomed to the ways of society is always outside himself and knows

---

[110] Buonarrotti, *Conspiration de Babeuf*, I, 81, quoted in Van Prinsterer, *Lectures*, p. 219.

how to live only in the opinion of others. And it is, as it were, from their judgment alone that he draws the sentiment of his own existence."[111]

Such duplicity was also applied to labor relations. The rich tricked the poor into doing the work and appropriated the lion's share of the product to themselves. The poor responded by resorting to violence and brigandage, pillaging what they could not obtain fairly. The resulting lawlessness led to the establishment of a legal order, which in fact solidified the domination of the propertied and sealed the fate of the propertyless. "Such was... the origin of society and laws, which gave new fetters to the weak and new forces to the rich, irretrievably destroyed natural liberty, established forever the law of property and of inequality, changed adroit usurpation into an irrevocable right, and for the profit of a few ambitious men henceforth subjected the entire human race to labor, servitude and misery."[112]

Nevertheless, for Rousseau private property was less an evil in itself than the indispensable precondition for the rise of civil society and its discontents. In fact, in his *Discourse on Political Economy*, first published in 1755, Rousseau could say that "the right to property is the most sacred of all civil rights."[113] What Rousseau was after was the subordination of private property to the common good; and that could be attained only within the proper political framework, in which the community had the upper hand and property served the good of all. Naturally, the idea was to leave property in the hands of citizens, but the thrust was that the <117> proper use of that property had to be framed in the laws, and the laws had to be the expression of the General Will, the will of the community.

The upshot is that property rights are the creature of positive law, of the civil law. Rousseau rejected the tradition of the *jus gentium* which lifts property rights above state law, ostensibly because he confused it with the Enlightenment ideology which had coopted it; the rejection of the one for him entailed the rejection of the other. But his scheme bears all the hallmarks of the civil-law tradition stemming from Bodin and Montaigne, postulating a basic conflict of interests in civil society which has to be resolved by the

---

[111] Jean-Jacques Rousseau, *Discourse on the Origins of Inequality,* in *The Basic Political Writings*, p. 81.

[112] Rousseau, *Discourse on Inequality,* in *The Basic Political Writings*, p. 70.

[113] *The Basic Political Writings*, p. 127.

power of the community. Rousseau then took things a step further. Not only did material interests need to be harmonized by the community, but even spiritual conditions – the alienation afflicting every sensitive human being – had to be resolved, likewise through the power of the community. And no matter how hard he may have tried to keep from drawing this conclusion, the state was the only candidate for representative of the General Will. Certainly Rousseau's followers would see it that way.

Rousseau's criticisms of civil society and his vision of alienation must be seen against the background of the contemporary French society in which he formed his opinions. As Alexis de Tocqueville so tellingly described, France in the eighteenth century was a nation alienated against itself. It was the country in which men were most like each other, and at the same time the most split up into isolated little groups. Nobility and bourgeois in France enjoyed the same education, manners, and culture. Even in England the gap between classes was greater than in France, with class culture a distinguishing mark. But while in manners, thought, and outlook the classes in France were becoming more and more alike, in terms of social intercourse they were drawing farther and farther apart. Nobility withdrew from day-to-day affairs behind the screen of sham rights and privileges granted by the crown to compensate their dismissal from authority; the bourgeois purchased their crown offices and turned their backs upon their erstwhile <118> equals in favor of their newfound superior status; the peasantry, while enjoying property rights and prosperity in greater degree than ever before, suffered under the ignominy of being treated like inferior creatures. The cult of absolute monarchy culminated in the alienated society: "It is only government by a single man that in the long run irons out diversities and makes each member of a nation indifferent to his neighbor's lot."[114]

---

We see here how absolute monarchy corrupted the ancient constitution. It suppressed inherited rights and privileges, the fabric of that constitution, while granting a mélange of privileges which suffocated the nation and divided the country into mutually antagonistic factions, held together only by the crown. This is the so-called "royal mechanism," discussed in detail by

---

[114] Alexis de Tocqueville, *The Old Regime and the French Revolution*, pp. 77 –96; quote, p. 81.

Norbert Elias (*Power and Civility*). It is the early-modern analogue to modern-day identity politics.

---

Rousseau thus took the crucial, and logically indefensible, step of blaming the situation created by the civil-law tradition on the institutions of the *jus gentium*. By so doing he created a smokescreen behind which the civil law could gain a new legitimacy, by taking on the guise of popular sovereignty, pinning the responsibility for the mess it had created on the tradition which in fact would have guarded France from the disaster which in the end befell it.

From this point on, the so-called "social question" took up its position front and center as one of the primary considerations of public policy. As the new industrial order took shape, it created more wealth than had ever before been imagined, but left in its wake more, if not poverty, then dislocation and anomie, than had ever been experienced before either. The Enlightenment ideology increasingly appeared the threadbare, hopelessly inadequate little armchair philosophy that it in fact was, totally unable to provide answers to the real-world problems people could see springing up around them every day. Rousseau appeared to provide the basis for a philosophy which could address those conditions. His followers certainly thought so. "'The first man who enclosed a plot of ground and thought of saying, 'This is mine,' and found others stupid enough to believe him, was the true founder of civil society.' It is this famous sentence, and the arguments that sustain it, that fed the fervor of revolutionaries and socialists for a century."[115]

---

[115] Peter Gay, introduction to Rousseau, *Discourse on the Origins of Inequality*, in *The Basic Political Writings*, p. 25.

# Chapter 12

# The Eclipse of Liberty

THE FRENCH REVOLUTION accomplished what the Valois and the Bourbons never could: it established the hegemony of the civil-law tradition at the expense of the common-law tradition on the continent of Europe. First through the revolutionary armies and then through Napoleon, the Christian-historical institutions of Holland, Belgium, Spain, Italy, and most of Germany were swept away as if by a flood, to be replaced by the institutions of abstract jurisprudence emanating from the sovereign authority, the state.

For the states of Germany, the result was nothing less than a cultural catastrophe. No event since the Thirty-Years' War had weighed so heavily on the German soul as the defeat of the empire at the hands of Napoleon. That defeat shook patriotic Germans out of their lethargic provincialism. But it also sounded the death-knell of their noble spirit of universalism. Prior to Napoleon, Germans were of all peoples the least aggressively patriotic. After Napoleon, there was not a people more bent on clearing out a place for itself, literally and figuratively, among the nations of Europe and the world.

The blame for Germany's prostrate condition was placed squarely on the constitution of the empire. Its fragmentation had finally caught up with it; when Napoleon's armies crossed the Rhine, the princes of the various territories tripped over each other in their zeal to welcome the new Kaiser and join him in spoiling their homeland. Not even proud Prussia and Austria could stand up to the onslaught; instead, they received modest gifts of territory from Napoleon's hand in exchange for their groveling.

Hegel was one who mourned the collapse of Germany but not the passing of the Holy Roman Empire. He seconded Pufendorf's opinion that the empire was a monstrosity, and savaged the views of those who saw in the empire a bulwark of liberty. In his view, the old constitution <120> simply ratified the saying *Fiat justitia, pereat Germania*, "Let there be justice, though Germany perish." The old conflicts among jurists about the precise nature of the German constitution have now been put to rest, Hegel wryly affirmed; for what no longer exists is no longer worth debating. Hegel argued that the nation-state is the true end of civil society, an end against which the German constitution had perversely barred the way. By contrast, France, Spain, and England showed that power, wealth, and freedom were to be achieved through the rise of the nation-state.

Germany needed to unify, to itself become a nation-state; that was its only hope, and indeed the proper goal of it and of all nations. Here Hegel echoed the chief principle of German anti-Enlightenment thought: community realized in the nation-state. Rather than join in with the Enlightenment and celebrate the rights of man and citizen, German thinkers began to celebrate the joys of subordinating individuality to the common good as realized through central government, in the name of the nation. This too is popular sovereignty, but of another kind altogether; a sovereignty of the collective will, of which the individual is a subordinate part.

This teaching was, as we have seen, already present in Rousseau. In fact, despite its universalist pretensions the French Revolution itself provided the first expression of the new nationalism. This was inherent in the doctrine of the rights of man. "As soon as one sets out to formulate the rights of man, the state appears to be required as the framework for his society. Humanity could not be the vehicle of the liberty desired so ardently. Its domain was the fatherland, and its subject the people. Hence from the outset the French Revolution served pre-eminently to activate an enthusiastic patriotism and nationalism."[116] <**121**>

In fact, militant nationalism served as the glue to hold together the now-fractured post-Christian world. Entering the scene now were liberals, champions of the original Enlightenment version of the citizen ideal, and socialists, protagonists of the revised, egalitarian version of citizenship. What these two groups shared was a hatred for the received institutions of Christendom. What divided them was social class. The new bond would be nationality. "The few rich and the many poor found no basis for unity, except in the grim and transitory bond which joined the peoples of one nation against those of others in the marching armies."[117]

---

[116] Johan Huizinga, "Patriotism and Nationalism in European History," in *Men and Ideas: History, the Middle Ages, the Renaissance*, pp. 132–133.

[117] Nef, *Western Civilization*, p. 314.

In this new iteration, nationalism served as the vehicle of statism. Absolutism found its vehicle in the nation-state. Statism was the glue that held together the disparate factions in society. In our day, nationalism, having served its purpose, has been replaced by globalist ideology, the new, preferred vehicle of statism.

After a long and stormy period of transition, Germany most successfully achieved this higher synthesis. It could do so because it had the biggest vacuum to fill. The Holy Roman Empire ceased to exist in 1806. Hereby Germany lost its sense of mission as the leading nation of Christendom, and the sense of responsibility that went along with that position. Now it had to regain lost ground; the nation had to become a state. And the only way it could do so was by submitting to a strong central government which could override the myriad provincial particularisms which stood in the way of progress. As the century progressed, Germans proved increasingly willing to pay this price.

Now the Enlightenment doctrine came to be derided as an expression of the French spirit, abstract and mechanistic; the new German philosophy prided itself in being organic, mystical. The German nation had a destiny to fulfill which could not be subsumed in the categories of Reason and Rights. For Germans, the watchwords became obedience, blind respect for authority, individual sacrifice for the common cause.

Ranke summed up this sentiment in an essay entitled *Frankreich und Deutschland* published in the early 1830s. After describing how little, in his view, the French Revolution actually affected Germany, he concluded by writing: <122>

Shall we allows ourselves now to be overwhelmed by the French schools? I do not deprecate the French: let them be what they are, what they can become. However, when they wanted to transmit to us that eighteenth century philosophy, in part brought over from England, with its accompanying view of religion and nature, did we let them cajole us into accepting it? In fact it is in opposition to them that we, as they themselves now admit, have dug so much deeper and [in so doing have] approached the truth. In all branches of science – no one would deny it – their viewpoint has been defeated and pushed aside. Their poetry and art? Happily we have not followed their example since developing our own literature. All the intellectual pursuits of our fine age, all scientific achievements of our great men, everything that makes a name for the Germans, has been achieved in opposition to France. And the state, which the French came up with by contemplating strange forms but which in fact consists entirely in the nominal connection of ideas, in that mechanical view of things which comes so naturally to them – and which therefore threatens to collapse at any moment – we should imitate and introduce it here! After we have defeated them in each individual branch, after we, striding forward in that great movement of the spirit when we reached for our arms and defeated them in the field, should we, in the most important element of life, in the form of the state, join with them and imitate their barren inventions? Perish the thought! Everything that we live for and are, everything that we have acquired during our centuries of history, rebels against it.[118]

The history of German unification is recounted as the struggle between Prussia and Austria for supremacy within Germany and thus for control of Germany. Prior to Napoleon's flattening of Germany's ancient <123> constitution, however, German unification was seen in terms of the federal tradition of the Holy Roman Empire, as a decentralized legal union of a multiplicity of self-governing estates, both large and small. It was the smaller units, not the larger ones, who put the most stock in the constitution of the Holy Roman Empire and struggled the hardest to maintain its institutions. The ongoing struggle to maintain the institutions of the empire in their "weak," decentralized condition was mainly the work of the small estates, who dreaded the establishment of a strong central authority and who likewise dreaded the predominance of one of the major German powers in the empire, fearing that such dominance would come at the expense of their freedom within the constitutional order. "It was not the most territorially fractured areas of Germany that threatened to tear the Empire apart; support for the Empire was greatest of all in the bewilderingly entangled areas of the west and south, in Franconia and Swabia and along the Rhine, where the authority of Imperial institutions was most necessary for settling local issues....

---

[118] Leopold von Ranke, *Frankreich und Deutschland* [France and Germany], in *Geschichte und Politik* [History and Politics], p. 71.

Rather than the small estates, it was the more consolidated territories that posed the greatest threat to the Empire, for in these areas Imperial support seemed less necessary for the ongoing processes of political life."[119]

When France defeated the empire it wiped out all the institutions supporting the independent self-governing estates, replacing them with consolidated territories on the model of its own rationalized system. German princely allies eagerly accepted rule over these consolidated territories, seeing in them the opportunity for domination which had eluded them in the old constitutional order. When Napoleon was defeated and a new German federation established, it inherited the changed conditions, emerging as a totally different order than the old <124> empire. The new agenda was clear: "All [the rulers] aimed at unification and standardization of bureaucratic organization, at establishment of equal citizenship and abolition of the cogoverning privileges of the old local dignitaries, at erection of unified codes of law and, ultimately, rationalized written constitutions."[120]

Even so, it took a generation to wipe out the deep-rooted localism so characteristic of the German estates.[121] The smaller territories struggled to maintain an independent existence vis-à-vis the two Great Powers. The sentiment to maintain the old German tradition of liberty was alive even as late as 1870, as witness the following extract from a book published in that year, entitled *Für die Erhaltung der Süddeutschen Staaten* ("For the maintenance of the south-German states"):

> One may be of the opinion that it would be better if Germany were one single state. We do not share this opinion. On the contrary, we think that the total amount of culture, morality, and prosperity, the mass of civilizing and humanizing institutions (such as universities, art and professional schools), the closely woven net of communications and so many other advantages which Germany has over France and over other great empires, have their

---

[119] Carol M. Rose, "Empire and Territories at the End of the Old Reich," in *The Old Reich: Essays on German Political Institutions 1495–1806* ed. James W. Vann and Steven W. Rowan, p. 74. This article provides an excellent exposition of the constitutional framework of the empire.

[120] Rose, "Empire and Territories," p. 75.

[121] Rose, "Empire and Territories," p. 75.

origin in the number of centres from which they may take their beginning
and in the mutual competition of the individual German states. It is precisely
south Germany and Saxony that are very significant evidence of this. No
right-thinking person will deny that intellectual and political freedom would
have had a better home in a many-membered Germany than it has ever
found in a unitary monarchy. Who would dare to answer the question
whether the Reformation, for example, would have happened in Germany
had it been a unitary state or say whether it would not rather have been
<125>extirpated by Dragonades as in France? The variety of its political,
constitutional, and administrative arrangements has safeguarded Germany
from the one-sidedness of the whole cultural and educational system, which
characterizes France, and from its petrifaction, which characterizes England.
This variety has made the Germans the best educated people in the world.
This is the most noble blossoming of a nation's history. We grant that political unity has its advantages for a great nation, and we are not so prejudiced
as to be hostile to those who consider this standpoint conclusive and hon-
ourably speak in its favour. But he who knows from experience the waste and
neglect of so many important economic interests in the provinces of great
empires and compares that with the more concentrated vitality and the
quicker pulse of life in our south-German states will not, for very love of our
fine and happy principalities, counsel us to prefer a unitary state in Germany.[122]

Nevertheless, this was a last gasp. In 1871 Otto von Bismarck fulfilled the
promise of German unification by obtaining the ratification of a new German constitution firmly sealing the dependence of the German states (apart
from Austria) in a so-called federal union, actually "a Prussian Reich, shaped
to accord with Prussian interests, constructed in conformity with Prussian
traditions, ruled by the dynasty of Hohenzollern, and dominated by the
Prussian Junker class."[123]

---

[122] M. Mohl, *Für die Erhaltung der Süddeutschen Staaten*, excerpted in *The Foundation of the German Empire: Selected Documents,* ed. Helmut Böhme, p. 26.
[123] Geoffrey Barraclough, *Factors in German History*, p. 120–121.

For more on the pre-unification German constitution, see below, "What We Are Up Against." For more on the struggle against German unification, see my biography of F. J. Stahl: *Authority Not Majority*.

The roots of German unification lay firmly in the civil-law tradition. Customs union lay the basis for further political union: free trade was established within the customs union, tariff barriers between it and the rest of the world. Germany's smaller territories had little choice but to go <126> along, otherwise they would be shut out of their main markets. The economies of the German states of necessity became oriented toward Prussia, and the economic boom that followed lasted just long enough to finance unification.

In the common-law tradition, tariff barriers are removed between sovereign states; in the civil-law tradition, they are removed only within sovereign states. This is the economic expression of the world-views embodied in the two traditions (see above, pp. 106ff. [**original pagination**]). In the civil-law tradition, sovereignty establishes an area of order within a broader chaos; in the common-law tradition, sovereignty works to implement and secure a preexisting law-order: chaos is not pre-existing, but only the result of disobedience within that law-order. In the civil-law tradition, trade can only be securely established within an area controlled by the sovereign; the domestic economy is the only stable economy. In the common-law tradition, trade binds societies under law, a law which also binds sovereigns and commits them to enforce it. In the civil-law tradition, law is the servant of the sovereign; in the common-law tradition, the sovereign is the servant of law.

Economics was the driving force behind German unification, but it also created insoluble antagonisms within Bismarck's laboriously constructed edifice. Bismarck was only able to gain support for unification by shutting out the working classes from power; he in turn sought to buy off the working classes by establishing welfare-state provisions and enacting "social" legislation. Power was in the hands mainly of the industrialists and secondarily of the Junkers, the landowning aristocrats. These practiced a degree of paternalism unacceptable in countries with a higher degree of citizenship, thus maintaining the lower classes in a condition of political and economic childhood, ultimately paving the way for cultural radicalism, the rejection of all authority.

Thus the autocracy and absence of self-government which characterized pre-unification Prussia was imposed across the board in unified <**127**> Germany. The result was the kind of social unrest which characterized pre-revolutionary France, and accompanying it, the kind of alienation signaled by Rousseau and described in-depth by de Tocqueville (see above, p. 109 [**original pagination**]). "So long as the growing popular forces were excluded from government, there could be no stability for the Reich. But so long as political and social power remained in the hands of the old order, there was no hope of peaceful evolution; for the privileged classes resisted any alteration of the constitution of 1871, which was their charter of privileges, for fear that the flood-waters of radicalism, bursting through the breach, would tear down the whole dam."[124]

The glue which held German society together, and which had to be applied ever more liberally, was nationalism. The German government shamelessly shifted the blame for all its shortcomings on foreign countries. This kind of propagandizing found a rich source of support in the anti-Enlightenment romanticism which increasingly gained ground in Germany in the 19th century. Here the government could tap deep wellsprings of support for its otherwise hopelessly ungrounded policies, for the German intelligentsia and the German workers' movement shared the ruling classes' antagonism to the common-law tradition, castigating it as a tool of English domination. Thus there existed a significant common basis for German society transcending its deep social and political divisions.

The German left developed one aspect of this antipathy to a pitch of perfection: the rebellion against "bourgeois" morality. Nietzsche's distinction between "Apollonian" and "Dionysian" morality did yeoman's work here. Apollonian morality is conventional, objective, rational, and hypocritical, forcing people into an unrealistic mold and hindering them from realizing their true selves. Dionysian morality, on the other hand, overturns conventional morality and encourages natural, primal upwell- <**128**> ings as true guides to fulfillment. Nietzsche put it thus:

> The word Dionysian means: an urge to unity, a reaching-out above the person, the everyday, society, reality, above the abyss of offenses, the passionate,

---

[124] Barraclough, *Factors in German History*, pp. 126–127.

painful swelling-out in dark, full, floating situations; an ecstatic affirmative to the collective character of life as alike in all change, equally powerful, equally sacred; that great pantheistic conviviality and compassion that approves and sanctifies even the most fearful and questionable characteristics of life; the eternal will to procreation, fertility, return; the feeling of unity of the necessity of creation and destruction. The word Apollonian means: the urge to complete existence for oneself, to the characteristically individual, to everything which simplifies, distinguishes, makes strong, clear, unambiguous, characteristic, to freedom under law.[125]

The contrast could not be sharper. The revolt against the citizen ideal led directly to pagan organicism.

What bound left and right – otherwise poles apart – was a common allegiance to absolute government as the means to realize the destiny of the German nation. From the late 19th century onward, the cultural lead in Western Europe was taken by the new, transformed Germany. Unification and modernization spawned the most powerful economic and military power in the world. The theory of economic nationalism and the welfare state rose to challenge classical liberalism for primacy in economic theory and practice; the idea of liberation from the ethic of the middle class, the ethic of the citizen ideal, rose to challenge that ideal as the leading concept of culture. Germany exported these ideas to the world in a form against which no nation proved immune. The common denomi- <129> nator behind these ideas was a reliance on the absolute state, absolute sovereignty, to make them reality. The Enlightenment project to free the citizen ideal from its theocratic moorings led directly to the rejection of that ideal in favor of a return to the organic total community.

---

It would be difficult to add to this conclusion. It nicely encapsulates where we are at today, 100-plus years later.

---

[125] *Wille zur Macht* [Will to Power] (Krönersche Ausgabe, p. 683), quoted in Herbert Werner Rüssel, *Antike Welt und Christentum* [Classical Antiquity and Christianity], p. 40.

# Chapter 13

# Tragedy and Hope

GERMANY CONSTITUTED the further development, even fulfillment, of the civil-law tradition, which explains the attraction German thought and institutions has exerted on statist-minded intellectuals. One thing stood between it and the final victory: the continuing existence of the common-law Anglo-American tradition. Britain with its empire, and America looming in the background, were what kept Germany from realizing its destiny as newfound champion of the civil-law tradition. Britain represented the continued existence of a universal civilization embracing and conditioning all nations under law. Germany had undergone a transformation in opposition to that kind of universal order. Germany championed nationhood over against civilization.

This is not to say that everything Germany did was bad and everything Britain did was good. The ledger is full of credits and debits here. In particular, the role of the gold standard needs to be brought into the picture (see *Follow the Money*). But the underlying trend lay in the direction here described. The common-law tradition represented nationhood conditioned by limited government, while the civil-law tradition represented nationhood stamped by absolutism. And again, it must be emphasized that the lopsidedness inflicted on the common-law tradition by the loss of the theocratic framework created the vacuum filled by the civil-law tradition.

This conviction was the underlying impetus behind the first conflagration of this century, the Great War of 1914–1918. German *Kultur* was pitted against British *Zivilisation*. *Zivilisation* was a term of derision, applying to the universalist, cosmopolitan, rationalist culture of the Enlightenment, the commercialism and utilitarianism of classical liberalism; *Kultur*, by contrast, was the expression of the German national spirit, "concerned with 'inner freedom,' with authenticity, with truth rather than sham, with essence as opposed to appearance, with totality rather than the norm.... a matter of 'overcoming,' a matter of reconciling the 'two souls' that resided in Faust's breast."[126] Nietzsche's contrast between Apollonian and Dionysian culture was elevated to the stature of national myth. Germany had a mission: to overcome the imperial domination of Britain, to bring to the world the true freedom of spiritual expression beyond the restraints of bourgeois morality.

This mission was shared by German "conservatives" as well as "liberals." All of Germany experienced the citizen ideal as expressed in <131> Enlightenment classical liberalism as a betrayal of Germany's inheritance, an imposed restraint on Germany's destiny in favor of the *pax Britannica*. As Modris Eksteins in his book *Rites of Spring* brilliantly describes, Germany's conflict nevertheless was domestic first and foremost, a classic class struggle between power haves and power have-nots, which was resolved only by projecting the conflict onto the external world and summoning up a unified will to combat that world. This was the origin of World War I. Germans experienced the Kaiser's declaration of war on August 1 as an ecstatic release, as the realization of all their hopes on earth, as the end of dividedness and the dawn of a new age in which alienation would no longer exist.[127]

As the war dragged on, the enthusiasm and hopefulness was replaced by disillusionment and apathy in the face of the remorseless Moloch which the Western front had become. Germany's problems did not go away, rather they worsened, and not only because they lost the war. Germans had believed in war as itself an instrument of redemption and purpose, but war proved the biggest hoax of all.

Though Germany did not gain through the war, neither did the Allies. Germany's Dionysian affirmation in the face of lost certitude and meaning increasingly stamped Britain, France, and even America. Materialism, technicism, scientism, combined with unrelenting doubt about the very legitimacy of "bourgeois" civilization and an all-pervading relativism increasingly replaced the old Victorian value system which once made the middle class the vanguard of history.[128]

---

[126] Modris Eksteins, *Rites of Spring: The Great War and the Birth of the Modern Age*, p. 77.

[127] Eksteins, *Rites of Spring*, pp. 55–64.

[128] The classic description of this process from a Christian perspective was provided Francis Schaeffer in his trilogy *Escape from Reason, the God Who Is There,* and *He Is*

The promise of materialism and the backlash of the Great Depression left the Western world in a state of disorientation. The ideal of a universal civilization lost further ground as countries raised tariff walls and resorted <**132**> to programs of economic collectivism. Fascism moved in to fill the void, co-opting the same Dionysian tradition used so effectively by the left, but then crushing all opposition on the way to total power.

The Nazis under Adolf Hitler rejuvenated the *Deutschland über alles* vision which had lain dormant since the war. They took over the German *Kultur* motif and turned it into cheap imitation kitsch, suitable for mass consumption. The German nation was easy prey. Hitler hit all the right buttons.

Then came another world war, with virtually the same constellation of powers facing each other, with another nationalist power, Japan, thrown in for good measure. Once again, it was *Kultur* versus *Zivilisation*, and once again the good guys won. But once again as well, war led to the victors' adopting wholesale the mind-set and methods of the losers.

It purports to be common knowledge that the post-World War II era has been the American age. American culture is supposed to have been triumphant, to have spread throughout the world, as witness the presence of Coca-Cola even in darkest Africa. Especially since the end of the cold war, we are said to be living under a *pax Americana*, with America the only remaining superpower, the only country able to bring peace to the trouble spots of the world. Institutions ranging from the World Bank to the International Monetary Fund to the General Agreement on Tariffs and Trade (now the World Trade Organization) to the United Nations are products of American efforts to create a stable world order of peace and prosperity in the aftermath of the devastation of two world wars.

The question is, to what degree does this represent the advancement of the common-law tradition as opposed to the civil-law tradition? To what degree did the citizen ideal triumph over dependency and subjection? To what degree did limited government triumph over centralizing absolutism? Above all, to what degree did the Church and the absolutes she proclaims inform public policy?

---

*There and He Is Not Silent*, the first two published in 1968 by Hodder & Stoughton/ Inter-Varsity Press, the last in 1972 by Tyndale House.

On this score, it would be difficult to say that the "American Age" has <133> meant the triumph of the common-law tradition. Citizenship has certainly become more universal, but it has likewise become watered down. The citizen ideal itself informs actual citizenship but little. As far as government is concerned, though the worst abuses of communism are things of the past, government itself has come to occupy a greater role in the lives of citizens than ever before. And the Church – who would not say that the Church, rather than regaining her voice, has rather lost what little influence she had before the Second World War?

The clearest indication of the demise of true citizenship is the adoption of human rights formulas as supposed expressions of citizenship. The main codification of such human rights is the UN's 1948 "Universal Declaration of Human Rights." According to this version, human rights include "the right to social security" and "the right to a standard of living adequate for the health and well-being of oneself and of one's family, and the right to security in the event of unemployment, sickness, disability, widowhood, old age or other lack of livelihood in circumstances beyond one's control." What this means is that human beings have the right to the fruit of other human beings' labor regardless of their own contribution, a violation of the principle of reciprocity, the keystone of civil social order (see above, p. 24 [original pagination]). Such economic security can only be bought at the price of abandoning the civil contract to keep the public square free of the lordship/dependency relation, precipitating a return to the extended-household model of society, with the loss of freedom and permanent minority status that entails.

Further exploration of this theme is included in "Rights, Revolutions, and World Order" below.

This is precisely the reason Western civilization since the Second World War has continued to see the state expand its role in society to the point of virtually running citizens' lives. Such human rights doctrines require the establishment of a confiscating, redistributing authority to make them a reality. They are therefore incompatible with true citizenship. This is how citizenship itself has increasingly become a hollow concept. Awareness of the obligations, restraint, and self-reliance required <134> of true citizenship have virtually vanished, in favor of interest groups pushing their particular agendas, involving the use of political power to advantage themselves vis-à-vis other groups in the society. Once upon a time, society could assimilate and mediate the relations between different groups because the civil contract established rules by which no particular group could use political power for its own purposes; rather, political power was an instrument to preserve neutrality between different groups. Now, groups increasingly are urged to enter the political process for private gain, molding as much of the legal framework as possible in their favor as against other groups, pushing for as much government largesse as possible for themselves at the expense of other groups. This is how civil society has degenerated. This process is the harbinger of the disintegration of Western civilization and a return to pagan, organicist particularism.

This process promotes absolute state sovereignty in two ways. First, the state of necessity grows in power the more citizens turn to it to fulfill their demands for substantive results, whether legal privileges or economic booty. But as this process foments divisions and resentment within society, the state must grow to pacify the various antagonists and maintain the peace.

---

This passage presages the rise of the identity politics which plagues the contemporary polity.

---

Power as solution is, of course, the formula developed by Germany on its path toward unification and expansion. The parallels are uncanny between German unification in the 19<sup>th</sup> century and the most visible contemporary expression of the civil-law tradition, European unification. Then as now, political unification was preceded by economic union in the form of a customs union. The customs union created economic interdependency which was then used as a club with which to beat recalcitrant states into submission to the hegemon. Nationalist fervor was played up to the hilt to paper over deep divisions. Today, it once again is economic dependence fostered by customs union which is used as the rationale for going along with far-reaching political and monetary union. The question now is which role the United Kingdom is going to play: that of <**135**> a southern German state like Bavaria, eventually cajoled into submission, or rather something like Austria, entirely shut out of the new union. In fact, the arguments surrounding Britain's current relation with the European Union sound eerily like the *Grossdeutschland-Kleindeutschland* debate of the last century: would Prussia agree to allow Austria to join a unified Germany (the *Grossdeutschland* option) or would it keep Austria out (the *Kleindeutschland* option)? Today, the question is whether Germany and France are going to accommodate Britain in a loose union built upon national sovereignties (the *Grosseuropa* solution) or whether they are going to exclude Britain in advancing a unified single sovereign state of Europe (the *Kleineuropa* solution).

Indeed, it is a form of nationalism that drives European Union, likewise explaining the scorn and derision visited upon recalcitrants like the UK. The motto "Make Europe Great Again" is certainly applicable.

The question is anything but academic. On it hinges the future development of Western and world civilization. For the driving force behind the two world wars already experienced in this century – the clash between the common-law and civil-law traditions – is the same force behind the conflict in the EU between Germany and France on the one hand and Britain on the other. If the civil-law tradition wins out in Europe, then future conflict is inevitable between Europe and the only remaining common-law power in the world, the United States. *Germany is the key here.* As should be somewhat evident from the discussion this book has presented, Germany has been the central nation in European history. When Germany championed liberty, Europe enjoyed relative peace. When Germany championed power, Europe went to war. Since its defeat in World War II, Germans have been divided as to which tradition to follow, the civil-law variant or the common-law one. It is time for truly patriotic Germans to recognize in their history a great struggle between these two and to return to the inheritance they so carelessly cast aside.

With the benefit of hindsight, it is easy to see that these hopes have been dashed. Germany is pursuing the civil-law agenda with abandon. The current crisis surrounding "Brexit" is only the latest example of this. The civil-law tradition runs deep, and it is dividing the British nation in two, even as this is written.

But is the common-law tradition still viable, even in the United States? The ongoing culture war would appear to indicate otherwise. There is no consensus as to what America is all about; the citizen ideal itself has been rejected in its natural-rights form, the form upon which the <136> country's legitimation was grounded, and has been replaced by the mentality which views the political process as a means to satisfy substantive ends – entitlements – and as a vehicle to self-actualization and social engineering.

Francis Fukuyama's *The End of History and the Last Man*[129] argues that what is needed to supplement liberal democracy is an understanding of and respect for the need for recognition by citizens. But the drive for recognition, far from being a source of reinforcement, is actually one of the cancers eating away the heart of Western civilization. We certainly need to recover this category in our political philosophy, because only by doing so can we guarantee the foundations of civilization. So much is certain. But this idea of recognition is central not to citizenship but to the institutions and framework which precede citizenship. *Recognition is a theocratic category*. Recognition is how the social order establishes extra-societal foundations.

Recognition has to do with honor. What we recognize, we honor. The Bible admonishes us to honor God (e.g., I Samuel 2:30; Malachi 1:6), our parents (Exodus 20:12), the elderly (Leviticus 19:32), all to whom it is due (Romans 13:7). Our cultural elites now encourage us to despise traditional morality and authority and honor those who overthrow the moral foundations of civilization, as for example in countenancing homosexual marriage. To recognize the legitimacy of homosexuality is to institutionalize the sexual revolution and the overthrow of the nuclear family. Sexuality is a destructive as well as a creative force, it must be restrained and subordinated in terms of its original purpose, to bind husband and wife together as "one flesh," so establishing the nucleus for a nurturing home in which to raise the children that are the fruit of sexuality. Apart from this context, sexuality is a force for dissolution. Homosexuality is promiscuity taken to its extreme and the death warrant of a civilization. <**137**> It severs the link between sexuality and child-rearing. In dissolving in this way the bond of the home, it puts the individual on his own in the face of a faceless society. If society is to countenance homosexuality it must likewise recognize that it has rejected homes. And no amount of wishing can make it otherwise.

---

The problem is, we are recognizing all the wrong things. Recognition of the effluence of the sexual revolution is dismissal and negation of the tradition-

---

[129] See appendix.

al family, the church, the Bible. The question is not whether the state will recognize a set of values or not, it is which values will it recognize?

Recognition is also what drives the human-rights doctrine: persons need to be recognized as persons by guaranteeing them entitlements. But such recognition only subverts the civil social order. The human rights/entitlement doctrine stands as a massive roadblock in the road to Mr. Fukuyama's end of history. This doctrine legitimizes modern-day slavery in the name of freedom and destroys the true concept of citizenship in the name of rights. Those who earn, save, and are thrifty are forced to share with those who do not, as if everyone were the member of one big happy family with an equal right to support within that family. Until citizens recover the true concept of citizenship *as a bond which supersedes the family, not one which extends it,* modern society will continue to suffer contortion and confusion.

And certainly not as a bond which substitutes for it. Feminism, the gay rights agenda, transgenderism, all are destructive of the family. This leaves an inevitable void, which they seek to fill with the government as ersatz householder, provider, protector. Here again, it is not a question of recognition per se, but which recognition: which family will be recognized?

The reason for liberal democracy's relative success lies not in its superiority in "delivering the goods," satisfying material demand. Fukuyama goes further: he sees the key to that success in liberal democracy's attribution of equal recognition to all its citizens. But neither of these in actual fact explain liberal democracy's success. The true reason is liberal democracy's adherence to a fundamental form of justice, what Aristotle called commutative, embodied in the principle of reciprocity, which establishes a precise relation between what one contributes and what he gains – one reaps precisely what he sows. Where this principle is established, citizens gain the respect derived from knowing that they are no man's slave and no man's master; they are equal partners in the great project of liberty under law.

This great project cannot stand on its own: that was the error of the natural rights theorists, who considered the institutions of civil society to <138> be self-evident and acceptable apart from a prior faith commitment to anything outside civil society. Subsequent history proved them to have been hopelessly misguided in this respect. Fukuyama's call for recognition is muted testimony to the need for a transcendent ratification of the institutions of civil society. That ratification can only come through the institution which did the most to establish civil society in the first place, the Church. The Church is the Ark of the Covenant, the repository of the tablets enshrining the principles without which civil society cannot survive. The Church's ministry of Word and Sacrament remove ultimacy from the social order, providing the liberty for individual choice and action consonant with man's being made in the image of God and necessary to fulfill the calling of each to work out his own destiny in fear and trembling (cf. Philippians 2:12). Its ministry of the diaconate is the true ministry of health, education, and welfare; the modern state shoddily imitates this ministry, and it does so only to make its domination of civil society the more effective.[130]

Thus Western civilization today is at a crossroads. On the one hand, the institutions of the common-law tradition seem to be making headway as never before; on the other, the mind-set and belief-system underlying the civil-law tradition seem to be following right along in its wake. The more markets conquer, the more nihilism and the urge to collectivism seem to spring up from the rubble. This double-mindedness cannot be papered over, nor can it go on forever. The final showdown between the two great forces of world history still has yet to take place.

The conflict is really one between the head and the heart. With his head, modern man realizes that markets and true citizenship are the way forward – they work better, they are superior in providing for people's needs – but with his heart he still holds on to the civil-law vision of security through absorption in the collective womb. Modern man is a capitalist <**139**> in his head and a socialist in his heart. By way of justification he attributes the baser motives of private gain to capitalism, the higher motives of community spirit and generosity to socialism. The result is the unsatisfactory compromise of the welfare state, where people convince themselves that they are only being smart, i.e., pragmatic, by participating in the market economy, but purchase atonement for their guilt by voting for redistribution and restriction and other forms of self-flagellation. Modern man has to come clean with himself, and realize that it is precisely because capitalism, markets, the citizen ideal answer to fundamental principles of justice that it has proven successful. And

---

[130] On this point see Oakeshott, *On Human Conduct*, pp. 280ff.

those conservatives who embrace the citizen ideal must realize that all this is not an end in itself but only a necessary to stage to a higher goal. Its purpose is to prepare the way for the true end of history, when each will have to give account of his deeds before God – beyond the earthly city.

# Appendix: Fukuyama's End of History

WHAT is the meaning of history? Lately, and happily, this question is being reasserted with renewed vigor. People instinctively realize that with the end of the Cold War and the approach of the third millennium, history has reached a crossroads. They see in the collapse of the Iron Curtain and the world-wide triumph of liberal democracy events of prime historical importance. Sadly, however, though few doubt this, even fewer seem to grasp the full significance of these events. After a century including two world wars and the advent of the prospect of nuclear annihilation, they offer an opportunity for fundamental improvement that must be seized. But if this is to happen, some perspective must be gained on the present situation, a perspective which can only be provided from the viewpoint of broader history; and it is precisely such historical awareness that is so painfully lacking in our day. How can we see in which direction we have to go if we have no idea how we arrived where we are in the first place?

The urgency of this task provided the motivation for the present book. This is not to say that others have not gone on ahead. The most celebrated effort thus far is certainly Francis Fukuyama's *The End of History and the Last Man*, published in 1992 as a follow-up to his article "The End of History?", the announcement of the end of communism which prophetically appeared in the quarterly *The National Interest* in the summer of 1989, just prior to the total collapse of Communism in Eastern Europe. Fukuyama's thesis in both the article and the book is that liberal democracy triumphed over its main rivals, fascism and Communism, and that this triumph constituted no less an end to history than would have been the case had nuclear war between the superpowers actually taken place.

The strength of Fukuyama's argument is his presentation of the victory of <141> liberal democracy as an accomplished fact. Since the start of the 1980s and the twin triumphs of Ronald Reagan in the United States and Margaret Thatcher in Great Britain, liberal democracy has gone from strength to strength, winning the struggle with Communism in something of an anticlimax, as the former Iron Curtain countries one by one collapsed like out-of-shape joggers. In Asia capitalism showed an unimagined capacity to transform; in Latin America the mantras of development economics finally gave way to monetary and fiscal realism, while dictatorships fell before the inexorable wave of democratization.

None can argue that the world is a changed place, a relatively homogeneous, "Westernized" place. Liberal democracy is the form of social order to which all peoples either aspire or have already attained. This is the presupposition of Fukuyama's argument and to this author it seems unassailable. What Fukuyama then attempts, however, is to explain this phenomenon. What is it about liberal democracy that *explains* its universal triumph, and what does that mean for the further course of history?

In the first place Fukuyama is sure that the traditional Anglo-American, what historians call Whig, justification is insufficient. In Fukuyama's view this tradition, spawned by Thomas Hobbes and John Locke and carried forward by Adam Smith and the Founding Fathers of the United States, celebrated a *novus ordo seclorum* centered in freedom of acquisition based in a renewed appreciation for the positive role of the appetites. Classical political philosophy had argued against such a viewpoint, opposing virtues to appetites, arguing that the virtues needed to gain ascendancy over the appetites if ever a just social order were to be established. In the Lockean tradition, argues Fukuyama, these very appetites were rehabilitated and harnessed to a framework in which they could work for the common good. Adam Smith called this "enlightened self-interest." Each by seeking his own good within the framework of property rights and markets would simultaneously promote the common <142> good.

Fukuyama believes he has found a better explanation for liberal democracy's success in the work of the 19th century German philosopher G.W.F. Hegel and Hegel's 20th century interpreter, Alexander Kojeve. At the core of this explanation is not the pursuit of appetite but the pursuit of recognition. Fukuyama, following his guides Hegel and Kojeve, draws on Plato's discussion in *The Republic*, which postulated the existence of a third faculty besides reason and appetite, called *thymos*, the seat of emotions like honor and shame. Fukuyama attributes to this faculty the desire for justice above and beyond self-interest. "*Thymos* is something like an innate human sense of justice: people believe that they have a certain worth, and when other people act as though they are worth less – when they do not *recognize* their worth at its correct value – then they become angry."[131] The success of liberal democracy, beyond its ability to generate economic wealth – an insufficient basis in Fukuyama's view – lies in the fact that it answers to every individual's innate "thymotic" demand for recognition, by attributing equal civil and political rights to all rather than reserving them to a privileged few. This development has removed the fundamental feeding ground of social conflict and eliminated the internal contradictions which kept history from attaining a final resolution.

After explaining the reason for liberal democracy's success, Fukuyama goes on to address possible flies in the liberal ointment. Are there really no more challengers to the throne, no viable options to this form of social order? Is it really true that liberal democracy harbors no internal contradictions? Fascism and socialism have been weighed in the balance and found wanting, as has nationalism. Only two main challengers remain, one from the left of the political/intellectual spectrum, one from the right. <**143**>

From the left comes the charge that, despite its undeniable advances, liberal democracy has insufficiently provided for equality. Instead of satisfying the demand for equality, liberal democracy in fact has made the demand more urgent. When inequality was understood as something ingrained in the way things are, it was also more easy to accept. But when liberal democracy came along and obliterated the conventional barriers, remaining obstructions to equality became even more problematic. "Tocqueville explained that when the differences between social classes or groups are great and supported by long-standing tradition, people become resigned or accepting of them. But when society is mobile and groups pull closer to one another, people become more acutely aware and resentful of the remaining differences."[132] It is the resulting resentment that provided the motive power behind Marxism and socialism. Liberal democracy's recent triumph put an end to the hardcore Marxist doctrine of class struggle, but other forms of egalitarianism are surging forward to fill the gap, in the form of feminist, homosexual, and environmentalist agendas. Answers to these pressing threats will have to be

---

[131] Francis Fukuyama, *The End of History and the Last Man*, p. 165.

[132] Fukuyama, *The End of History and the Last Man*, p. 295.

found if the history is to remain at an end, for these agendas spell the overthrow of liberal democratic institutions.[133]

Fukuyama sees an even greater threat to liberal democracy stemming
from the right. On this end, the problem with liberal democracy is not that
it has not gone far enough in extending equality, but that it has gone too far
in doing so. This was Nietzsche's critique, that liberal democracy established
the triumph of the slave mentality, not the supersession of that mentality.
Nietzsche felt that the driving force behind great achievement was the desire
to be seen not as the equal of others but as their superior. Liberal democracy
stifles natural aristocracy/inequality and in doing so cuts off the sources of
excellence, innovation, and improvement. Ambitious men and women will
subvert the liberal democratic order <144> rather than allow themselves to
be submerged in the mass, essentially by seizing the reins of politics and government, steering things in an authoritarian direction.[134]

In this manner Fukuyama "covers the bases," anticipating and answering
the most powerful arguments he can come up with against his thesis. But the
existence of these threats from left and right seem to me to undermine the
conclusion Fukuyama has tried so hard to draw: for by his own account, as it
were, liberal democracy harbors the very seeds of its own destruction that the
"End of History" thesis demands to have been eliminated. The threats Fukuyama sketches are quite real, but they must be understood at a more fundamental level than Fukuyama has achieved to grasp the magnitude of the peril
they entail.

Contrary to Fukuyama's claim, I believe that the threat to liberal democracy is less to be feared from the right than from the left. In fact, liberal democracy quite successfully wards off the danger from the right – that dis-
gruntled achievers will be tempted to subvert the liberal order so as to establish their personal authority – in the very manner that Fukuyama describes,
by securing fields of endeavor in which only superior performance provides
advancement, not political favoritism – as in business entrepreneurship. The
threat from the right as Fukuyama describes it really could only get off the
ground if the threat from the left – the use of human rights doctrines to establish the egalitarian "equality of outcome" agenda – first gains the upper

---

[133] Fukuyama, *The End of History and the Last Man,* ch. 27.

[134] Fukuyama, *The End of History and the Last Man,* chs. 28–29.

hand. When the equal-opportunity society becomes the equal outcome society, the true achievers will turn to political power as the only means to realize
their ambitions and restore their presumed sense of superiority.

Fukuyama's failure to convince on this score stems from his confused
concept of liberal democracy. At one point he equates it with classical liberalism, what Americans call conservatism, the social order espoused <**145**> by
the likes of John Locke and Thomas Jefferson. Along these lines Fukuyama
falls back on James Bryce's definition in *Modern Democracies* and the U.S.
Bill of Rights.[135] The problem is, not even the U.S., let alone the Western
European democracies, can be understood as classical liberal democracies. If
Fukuyama speaks of socialists' penchant to expand the list of rights to include "second and third-generation economic rights" to cover employment,
housing, and health care – and so excludes them from his definition of liberal
democracy,[136] he has forgotten that it is not only socialists but mainstream
democrats the world over who understand rights in these terms, beginning
with the signatories to the United Nations' Declaration of Human Rights, a
prime example of entitlements masquerading as rights (this thought will be
picked up again in the conclusion). The confusion is made complete when
Fukuyama speaks of European "Christian democracy" and even Scandina-
vian social democracy as legitimate versions of liberal democracy, like any
other.[137] By way of exoneration, he argues that European social democrats
have given up on the old-fashioned Marxist class struggle and accepted the
legitimacy of capitalism. But this begs the question. The principle underlying
the class struggle – the illegitimacy of any private gain that leads to inequality
– has not been denied but only converted into an argument for massive redistribution. The only factor staving off a return to full-fledged class struggle
is economic growth sufficient to provide both rising real incomes and undi-
minished welfare benefits.

Fukuyama's exposition certainly goes far in explaining the success of liberal democracy and its prospects for maintaining that success. But he does
not go far enough in explaining the phenomenon itself. This shortcoming is
grounded in his choice of sources: essentially Locke on the one hand and

---

[135] Fukuyama, *The End of History and the Last Man*, pp. 42–43.

[136] Fukuyama, *The End of History and the Last Man*, p. 43.

[137] Fukuyama, *The End of History and the Last Man*, pp. 293–294.

Hegel on the other. But one must do better than that if one <**146**> is to grasp the significance of this historical movement. What is required is a thorough reexamination of the origins and development of Western civilization itself. For liberal democracy is nothing other than the latest stage in the development of that civilization.

Such a reexamination demands a bit of intellectual effort, for it entails rejecting one of modernism's besetting sins: complacency with respect to the past. Since the Enlightenment, our ancestors and we with them have become increasingly condescending about the achievements of our forefathers. Current intellectual fads like multiculturalism are only the latest forms of this condescension, and border on outright rejection of our civilization's patrimony. Such an attitude is blind, to say the least; if we allow ourselves to be led by its adherents, we will all end up in the proverbial ditch. Rather than rejecting our past, we must recover it. And to truly recover it, we must go back and retrace our steps, through the entire course of our civilization's history. This book was written for those willing to take that journey.

# Since 2001

The year 2001 forms a watershed in contemporary history. Two events took place which transformed the global landscape. First, the terrorist attacks on the US mainland, most glaringly the Twin Towers in New York City. Second, the introduction of the euro as the centerpiece of European Monetary Union. These two events stamped the further development which followed, feeding not only a European "nationalism" as manifested in divergence from shared interests with the US, but also a transnational "nationalism" putting the very concept of the nation-state at risk. These articles pick up where *A Common Law* left off, and show the effect of those changed circumstances.

With regard to the Iraq War, certain distinctions need to be made. The major one is that the war was not illegitimate in terms of international law per se, but only by decree of international institutions who took it upon themselves to be the arbiters of relations between sovereign nations, thus asserting an incipient claim to universal jurisdiction which in turn was disregarded by the "unilateral" action of the US. If the Iraq War conducted by George W. Bush was illegal, then so was the one conducted by his father – but no one is claiming that. No, the one implies the other, because it finished the business of the other. The more salient question is whether it was a wise or prudent thing to do. That is significantly more difficult to decide. What is clear is that the decision by the Obama administration to withdraw from Iraq in 2010 precipitated a drastic deterioration in conditions in the region. These articles were written with this perspective in mind.

# Rights, Revolutions, and World Order (2003)

*"Que la révolution a commencé par la déclaration des droits de l'homme, et qu'elle ne finira que par la déclaration des droits de Dieu."*[138]

MUCH INK has been spilled explaining the rationale of opposition to the US and its "coalition of the willing" in the war against Iraq. Much of that effort has been wasted. That China and Russia would oppose the war was to be expected; for them, such affairs are mere bargaining chips in ongoing efforts to neutralize the influence of the US on the world stage. Furthermore, in Russia's case significant economic interests were at stake. The same of course holds true for France. And Germany is riding on a wave of anti-war sentiment that would not brook any breach of the peace no matter how inherently justifiable.

What the pundits have missed is that the issue goes far deeper. The Iraq war is merely the latest in a series of events bringing to light an agenda on the part of France and Germany, an agenda which those of us who over the years have followed the development of the European Union (EU) have seen wax in strength and coherence; but to which the world at large has been oblivious. Yes, the Franco-German axis wishes to establish itself as an alternative power to the US, but more than this: it wants to establish itself as the *supreme* power in the world. And why does it want to do this? Because it is possessed of a *moral vision* by which it believes the world should be ruled – and it sees the US standing squarely in the way of the realization of this vision.

The moral vision of the Franco-German axis can be summed up in two words: *universal jurisdiction.* Universal jurisdiction – legal sway extending across and into every nation, usurping and supervening national sovereignty – is the solution to the crises, the conflicts, the insuperable problems seen the world over. All these problems are global in scale, they believe, and therefore require a global solution, imposed on a global scale.

This is why France and Germany in particular are so staunchly opposed to US-led efforts to keep the peace in the world. France and Germany harbor

---

[138] M. de Bonald, *Œuvres Complètes,* vol. 1, column 1133.

an alternative vision of world peace – attained not through the concerted efforts of nation-states, but through *world government*. The United States, the supreme sovereign nation in the world today, would rather maintain a world-order of nation-states, and it is willing to maintain that order through its own efforts. That is the conflict, and it is being waged across the board.

The focus of these efforts is the United Nations. A doctrine is now abroad, and has gained astonishing currency – that the UN is the supreme arbiter of the affairs of nations, that it must decide on all matters of war and peace, and that its decisions are final. The UN has gained a moral status among the nations of the world that cannot be gainsaid. It is the withholding of UN approval for the war of Iraq that has sparked such a high degree of opposition worldwide to the US-led coalition.

These developments are behind the yawning divide separating America from Europe, also visible in initiatives ranging from the Kyoto Protocol to the newly-established International Criminal Court (ICC). Seventy-odd nations have signed on to the ICC, the most pointed example of universal jurisdiction yet to make its appearance. Its first judges have already been elected. The nations of the EU not only have signed on but are actually making participation a *sine qua non* of respectability and belonging. Behind this cover, the Franco-German axis is pursuing the identical strategy of arm-twisting and incessant needling they used to such effect to form the EU in the first place. At the level of the EU, it was Great Britain that was the focus of odd-man-out tactics; at the level of the UN and of world government, it is the US. Any tactics to discredit and isolate can and will be used to achieve the goal.

So it should be no cause of wonder that the Franco-German axis, the leading force within the EU, opposes US foreign policy at every turn. For it sees the US as the biggest obstacle standing in the way of making world government a reality. They are shocked – shocked! – that anyone, even the world's only superpower, could conceive of opposing their plans to establish their vision – ostensibly, justice rather than power – at the heart of the world order.

Aye, there's the rub. For in the eyes of many, the European effort to make the world safe by ridding it of sovereign states is the expression of the ideal of replacing power with justice as the decisive principle of international affairs. A recent article by Robert Kagan[139] makes the case that this effort to replace

---

[139] "Power and Weakness," *Policy Review* (Number 113; June/July 2002), pp. 3 ff.

power with justice is simply a strategy dictated by weakness: like lesser powers throughout history, Europe is now relying on appeals to international law and human rights as a substitute for the exertion of brute force in international affairs. But this analysis remains unconvincing, for Europe, although lacking in military strength, has plenty of economic and diplomatic clout to throw around. Europe is not eschewing power in this instance; in fact, it will require a great deal of power to establish of the kind of international judicial regime it and its allies seek. The replacement of national sovereignty with global hegemony cannot help but be realized through the use of force, though it be non-physical.

Is the issue really justice versus power? Is it a question of superpowers like America acting in disregard of principles of right simply because they have the power to do so? In this way of thinking, the problem at bottom is simply sovereignty itself. National sovereignty stands in the way of a universal order of justice. Countries with power will act with impunity, like it or not – and those without power, which harp on the need for justice in international relations, would act the same way if they had power. This view is widespread, but it is fundamentally flawed. For it entirely overlooks the history of the development of international law out of the original law of nations, which first provided flesh and bones to the fledgling international order of early modern times.

The history of this development is crucial to understanding the current divide between Europe and America. It is also crucial to understanding the greater conflict beyond passing policy issues. For this issue will not go away. In fact, it is this conflict that in the long run will be more determinative of world peace and world order than even the threat of terrorism.

The story revolves around the twin poles of human rights and the definition of sovereignty. Tracing it out pays handsome dividends, for it explains the motive forces driving current events.

Kagan puts forward the either/or of a Kantian or a Hobbesian world order: the Kantian order, standing for universal peace, provided by the establishment of a world government; and the Hobbesian order, a war of all against all, the current situation of independent sovereignties. What he did not mention was that the vision of a world order governed by universal law but policed by national sovereignties was not the vision of

Thomas Hobbes but of the true father of international law, the Dominican priest Francisco de Vitoria, in whose lectures on the Indies this order of law and sovereignties first took definite shape.[140] Vitoria refuted the claims to universal jurisdiction propounded by champions of the Holy Roman Emperor on the one hand and the papacy on the other, instead arguing that the nations of the world, rather than being subject to any a priori universal jurisdiction, were sovereign in their own right and under no obligation to submit to foreign rule. What binds the nations is not overarching sovereignty but an overarching set of principles enshrined in the *jus gentium,* the law of nations.

These principles Vitoria summarized as rights of communication. They include freedom of trade; freedom of movement – open borders, freedom of the seas, freedom of domicile; freedom to spread the Gospel. These are the basic rules which, he argued, bind nations to each other and which they cannot get out from under, which establish peaceful communication, the indispensable condition for civil society lived for the sake of citizens rather than rulers.

The Vitorian law of nations is therefore more than simply a law governing international (read: inter-state) relations. It is much rather a law over nations, a law binding them, setting forth relations both between the nations and within the nations themselves. Peter Stanlis correctly underscores this point when he writes of the *international* and *constitutional* law of nations as two sides of the same coin.[141] The Vitorian *jus gentium* spawned two major developments: the doctrine of the freedom of the seas, and that of limited, popular sovereignty; the former best exemplified in Hugo Grotius' *Of the Freedom of the Seas*, the latter in Johannes Althusius' *Politics*.[142]

These doctrinal positions were not advanced in a vacuum; they did battle against formidable opponents, themselves taking their stand ultimately in the grounds of absolute sovereignty centered in "the king that could do no wrong." For these thinkers, sovereignty was an all-encompassing power, the source of all law. There was no law binding the sovereign, all such higher law partook of morality, not legality proper. The premier exponent of this

---

[140] Vitoria's major works are available in translation in Anthony Pagden and Jeremy Lawrance (eds.), *Vitoria: Political Writings.*

[141] Peter J. Stanlis, *Edmund Burke and the Natural Law*, p. 85.

[142] A fine edition of which is now available from the Liberty Fund.

viewpoint was the French polymath Jean Bodin, whose *Six Books of the Republic* is considered the founding document of the modern concept of sovereignty.

It is no coincidence that this conflict between constitutionalism and absolutism, between freedom and hegemony, progressed in tandem with the major conflict of the period, the war of religions sparked by the Protestant Reformation. It was the wars of religion in France and the resultant upheavals they caused that had led Bodin to develop his path-breaking treatise. It was at this time as well that the crucial step was taken, not only beyond Europe's wars of religions, but to modern human-rights-based international law, the legal order to be effectuated by universal jurisdiction. The conflict between Vitoria and Althusius on the one hand and Bodin on the other led to the emergence of a third way, personified in Grotius himself.

Grotius provided a new outlook on the origin and legitimacy of sovereignty. Such was required in the wake of devastating religious warfare: the consensus was that an alternative foundation to sovereignty had to be established in the place of religion, of "divine right." The theocratic root of legitimacy was insufficient because it could not command universal consent. Rather than the continuation of religious warfare, what was needed, it was thought, was to supersede religion in public life altogether. This alternative foundation was discovered in the doctrine of natural rights. It was a doctrine that promised release from the need to agree on absolutes; but in doing so it opened the door to a radically different form of confrontation.

History has assigned the status of "Father of International Law" to Grotius, and not entirely without reason. Although he was not the father of the notion that it is the nations, not the Roman empire, that are sovereign – that honor goes to Vitoria – he was the first to wed this notion of national sovereignty to the idea of natural rights. In fact, he pioneered the very notion that natural rights function as the source of sovereignty. And in so doing he provided the alternative to divine right that the age seemed to be demanding.

The nuts and bolts of Grotius' theory will be developed further along in this discussion; for now it is enough to note that in making this move Grotius spawned a plethora of followers who continued the development of this core idea until it gained ascendancy in the Enlightenment. Some went in the direction of Thomas Hobbes, justifying absolute sovereignty on the basis of an unconditional surrender of original rights; but most ended up in convoy with John Locke, establishing sovereignty as a grant from its original holders, the citizens, which they might revoke at any time it might suit them.

So governments existed at the pleasure of their citizens, and might be disbanded at their whim, should their original rights, the rights they possessed in the state of nature, be infringed by this artificial institution. And what if the government refused to disband? Why, in that case there was Locke's "appeal to heaven" – a call to arms – to force the issue. Bad governments had now had notice served.

Theory became practice in France, where the received institutions of the Ancién Regime fell afoul of the natural rights ideology, tried and convicted on the charge that the French social order bore little resemblance to the state of nature. As such, it deserved abolition, and the sentence was carried out with verve. The monarchy, the aristocracy, the church, all were put to the sword and the torch, to make way for The Rights of Man and Citizen, which now surely would come to bloom with the removal of these offending institutions.

But this did not take place. Rather than citizens blossoming into their roles as preached in the theory of natural rights, French society descended into chaos, and was only saved by the emergence of a full-fledged dictator who not only established absolute government but took a step that no previous monarch had ever done – impose a nationwide law code, outside of which there was no law.

Thus did the doctrine of natural rights begin to bear its unintended fruit. There were those, such as Edmund Burke, who laid the blame for these fruits at the door of the doctrine itself. But there were others who took a different tack. The problem, to their minds, was not natural rights per se; it was the definition of those rights.

In the original formulation of natural rights, private property stood central. Locke's triad of life, liberty, and property rang true with every one of its proponents. Grotius, the original developer of this framework, characterized it as the expression of strict justice, the kind of justice which could be enacted in law and enforced by the state, as opposed to a broader category of justice which partook of a moral rather than a legal character. Rights of liberty, authority over one's household, property and credit, and self-defense, were natural and formed the basis of what it was the state was there to protect. Grotius accurately characterized these rights as expressions of commutative justice, following the Aristotelian and Thomistic tradition; the broad category of justice he termed distributive justice, which he thus removed from the state's purview. As he explained it, "For a long time many have considered this [distributive justice – RCA] to be part of law in the actual and strict sense, even though the latter actual law is of an entirely different character, resting as it does on the notion that what is another's is left to him or transferred to him."[143]

With this decisive move, the novelty of which Grotius was fully aware,[144] a great swath was cut through the received legal and political tradition. The distinctive medieval constitution, overseen in its development by the cooperative effort of kings and the church, incorporated substantial elements of distributive as well as commutative justice: in fact, the two formed part of the same coin. Aquinas gave definitive shape to this dual form of justice when he introduced Aristotle's ethical teaching to the church, and so to society at large. But this formulation depended upon shared values, an agreement as to ultimate reality; and when this was lost, the system of justice upon which it was based began crumbling. Grotius, in his zeal to provide a common ground for law agreeable to all, sheared the distributive element out of the legal system, thus leaving the commutative element freely standing. This was possible because commutative justice "presupposed a minimum of criteria, all of which on the horizontal, secular plane, regarding human nature as such, not theology, not dogma."[145]

Grotius thus distilled natural rights in their classic form, but only at the cost of going massively in hock to the future. For distributive justice would not remain in abeyance forever. Like a ghost from the dead, it would return, only in a form wholly other than in its original, Christian-classical shape.

Property could not remain the cornerstone of the enlightened blueprint for long, for property yielded inequality. And, when push came to shove, inequality could not be tolerated; not even liberty was worth this price. In this manner, liberty yielded pride of place to equality in the pantheon of enlightened values, and natural rights were reforged on the anvil of political will. For

---

[143] Grotius, *The Law of War and Peace,* Prologue, section 10.

[144] *A Common Law,* p. 94 [original pagination].

[145] *A Common Law,* p. 92 [original pagination].

a new set of priorities were arising in the wake of revolution political, social, and industrial.

Natural rights in their revised form no longer emphasized liberty and property, but rather solidarity and "stakeholding." No longer was it enough to affirm a right to pursue happiness and reap the rewards; what now became primary was the notion that man qua man, created in the image of God (this helped greatly to convince those recalcitrants who still held to religious faith), was entitled to a certain level of existence, a certain standard of living, simply by virtue of his existence.

The idea took much longer to put into practice than to take the high ground theoretically; Bismarck got the ball rolling with his universal pension scheme, which also demonstrated the vote-buying power of welfare politics. His lead was followed throughout Europe, welfare politics forming a solid buttress for the neo-mercantilist, protectionist policies already being pursued.

Rights now had come to signify entitlements to largesse: distributive justice had made its triumphant reappearance on the political stage. Conflict was the result, in that the two forms of rights, the original commutative form and the resurgent distributive form, were incompatible: the one negated the other. One cannot argue both for a right to property and a right to redistribute property without entangling oneself in interminable inconsistencies. What happened then is that rights theory became subtly remodeled: rights became interests.[146] Where rights are absolute claims that cannot be gainsaid, interests are relative, can be balanced, can be weighed against each other. But what this means is that a higher authority is needed to make the decisions as to which interest is to prevail. It means that private law has to give way to administrative law. It means that commutative justice gets swallowed up by distributive justice. Once again, the holistic order of justice was mutilated to accommodate a political predilection: with the earlier natural rights theory it was commutative justice that subordinated distributive, now it was distributive justice that trumped commutative.

Consider what this means. The original natural-rights agenda promised to establish a social order in which individuals could act freely as

---

[146] The pioneer here was the great 19th century German jurist Rudolph von Jhering, who defined rights as legally-protected interests.

independent agents without subordinating their lives and estates to an absolute authority, returning to the extended family-order of the medieval manor. But what happened is that this natural-rights theory, in eliminating the Christian-classical distributive background against which commutative justice had developed, simply prepared the way for a new form of social subjection in which all property, all estates, were subordinated to a common distributing authority ruling not on the basis of rights but interests. The circle was complete.

The welfare state is built on the legitimating framework provided by these rights theories. And now we have looming ahead of us the prospect of a global welfare/police state dispensing total justice, against which there can be no appeal, for national sovereignty will have been sacrificed on this altar as well.

*Human rights ideology is the driving force behind the notion of universal jurisdiction.*

Is there an alternative to this ideology? The answer is yes; but that alternative is unpalatable, in view of the underlying prejudice in favor of human rights – which is the reason why this ideology remains so popular in the face of its manifest unworkability.[147] But this alternative needs to be explored, and once the true underlying issues are examined, perhaps it will come in for a reappraisal.

Such a reappraisal must needs begin with Edmund Burke, the founder of the modern conservative movement, the launcher of the first effective attack on the natural rights school of thought. It was his counterattack against the French Revolution that caused the scales to fall from the eyes of so many of the latter's sympathizers, for the first time generating substantial argument against what hitherto had become virtually received wisdom.

Burke argued that natural rights were unsuitable to found civil society because their abstractness could not be translated into workable practice. "These metaphysic rights entering into common life, like rays of light which

---

[147] Nicely encapsulated by F.A. Hayek, *Law, Legislation, and Liberty: Volume 2: The Mirage of Social Justice*, "Appendix to Chapter Nine: Justice and Individual Rights," pp. 101–106.

pierce into a dense medium, are by the laws of nature refracted from their straight line. Indeed, in the gross and complicated mass of human passions and concerns, the primitive rights of men undergo such a variety of refractions and reflections, that it becomes absurd to talk of them as if they continued in the simplicity of their original direction. The nature of man is intricate; the objects of society are of the greatest possible complexity; and, therefore, no simple disposition or direction of power can be suitable either to man's nature or to the quality of his affairs."[148]

Natural rights could not be used to call received historical institutions into question. There was too much of a disparity between abstract ideas of what rights pertain to man in a so-called state of nature and what rights he might enjoy in a concrete, historically conditioned society. Rights are the product of historical growth in terms of the advancement of culture. It is useless to talk of which rights ought to pertain to a hypothetical individual; we can only speak of what rights pertain to citizens and subjects of actual regimes, what institutions exist which uphold and support those rights, what constitution and legal order has developed in which these rights are framed. The correct approach to such issues is not abstract philosophizing or "metaphysics," as Burke put it, but a basic acceptance of received institutions, especially in the context of Western civilization, in which the common law and institutions of Europe have grown on the basis of Christianity. The principle to be applied is that of prescription.

Prescription is a concept originally derived from Roman law, being one of the modes of acquiring landed property (the comparable form of acquiring movables is called *usucapio*). What it concerns is how title is acquired to property absent the transfer of a title deed. What is required in that case is possession for a statutory period of time, usually 30 years.

The significance of this is the allowance of the acquisition of a right without having to point to a definitive act whereby that right was acquired – under certain conditions, time alone is enough to establish rights.

This principle came to be applied in the English common law in the criterion of "time out of mind" to justify the possession of rights – thus,

---

[148] Burke, *Reflections on the Revolution in France,* p. 70.

immemorial usage, custom extending back into the mists beyond memory.[149] The significance of this for Burke is that prescription provides a historical origin to rights as opposed to a natural origin. Burke took his stand on the English constitution to cut off the natural rights ideology at its root. Christopher Brooke, a leading member of the House of Commons 150 years before Burke, put it this way: "We hold our privileges by prescription and prescription is inheritance."[150]

But Burke did not restrict this conception to England. He viewed this prescriptive constitution as a part of what he called the common law of Europe. This is how he could argue against natural rights in the context of the French Revolution, maintaining that the French could have returned to their indigenous, historically conditioned constitution and revitalize it rather than throwing it overboard. The argument from prescription held for all the countries in Europe which had grown out of the common root of Latin Christianity.

In the argument from prescription, therefore, we have not simply a principle from the English common law; we have a principle which forms the heart of what was the common law of Europe. And it is this principle which may guide us to an alternative approach to the source of law that can solve the conflicts inherent to the human-rights paradigm.

If we go back to the beginning, if we go back to the sources on which Grotius relied to develop his natural rights theory, we plunge into the classical and scholastic legal tradition of early modern Europe, the world of this common law of Europe, the *ius commune*: a corpus of Roman law, canon law, feudal law, law merchant, covering both private law and public law, the cradle of which was Italy but which spread throughout the Latin West to the point of being officially "received" in the Holy Roman Empire of the German Nation. Every legal system in the West, even England's, was decisively influenced by this overarching body of legal doctrine.

The theories of rights which have so come to dominate Western political thought were originated in this matrix. Blow-by-blow accounts of that

---

[149] Corinne C. Weston, "England: Ancient Constitution and Common Law," in *The Cambridge History of Political Thought: 1450–1700*, edited by J. H. Burns, p. 376.

[150] Quoted in Weston, "England: Ancient Constitution," p. 377.

development can be found in such works as Richard Tuck's *Natural Rights Theories* and Brian Tierney's *The Idea of Natural Rights*.[151] The upshot is that the notion of rights accruing to people as expressions of universal human nature was then developed.

Rights are more than mere external imputations – they are expressions of a power inherent in human beings. Witness their description by one of the ablest theorists of these rights, the 19th century German statesman and philosopher Friedrich Julius Stahl:

> By virtue of the personality of men... the sphere which is allotted to him through the ethical power of law is of necessity *his own ethical power inhering in himself over against others*, who then are ethically bound *to him* – not merely to God or their conscience or the legal order with respect to him – he is not merely an *object* of their duty but the *cause* of it. This is law *in the subjective sense* or *rights*..... Accordingly, law in the subjective sense is the *ethical power* which a man has over against others in the sphere allotted to him by the legal order, by virtue of that order.... Law in the subjective sense, e.g., the right of men due him in all his life positions, constructs, in that it is his own power inhering in him, a true center about which the entire external world (things, actions of others, etc.) is related as controlled object, and in accordance with which the content of legal norms is often determined.[152]

It took some time for this doctrine to gestate; it was not until Fernando Vasquez de Menchaca, the great Spanish jurist of the 16th century, took the crucial step of equating *iura* with *dominia*, rights with property, that it was completed.

The equation of rights with property was crucial because it made the possessor of rights, the person, a *dominus*, a lord, empowered to deal with the world about him. *Dominium* in the tradition of the *ius commune* is an absolute power to deal with an object, a *ius utendi et abutendi*, a right to use or

---

[151] Richard Tuck, *Natural Rights Theories: Their Origin and Development*; Brian Tierney, *The Idea of Natural Rights: Studies on Natural Rights, Natural Law and Church Law 1150–1625*.

[152] Friedrich Julius Stahl, *Principles of Law* (Aalten: WordBridge Publishing, 2007), pp. 97–98.

abuse, however the owner, the *dominus,* thinks fit. Vasquez's object in extending *dominium* to rights in general was to secure for all rights the same kind of protection from state power that strict *dominium* enjoyed. "Considering that, in accordance with the dominant view of jurists of that time, state power could not interfere with the *dominium* of individuals without cause, this extension of the definition of *dominium* was urgently needed if one desired to preserve other rights from state interference as well."[153] *But it also extended to rights the concept of dominium* as a relation of expansive lordship of men over their world. Vasquez's innovative definition of subjective rights thus accomplished two complementary goals: it made rights-bearers into power-holders, and it restricted the power of the state over those rights and their bearers.[154]

The equation of rights with property paved the way for Hugo Grotius' new approach to law and government, enshrined in the original natural-rights doctrine. For property is preeminently the subject matter of commutative justice; by restricting justice to the maintenance of each in their rights, Grotius established the basis for the de-theocratized social order his times were demanding. And in fact Grotius was heavily dependent on Vasquez for his own innovation.

Vasquez himself took an entirely different tack when it came to presenting a vision of the social order in terms of this new doctrine of rights. For he did not speak of a state of nature in which individuals came together to erect a government in order to preserve them in their rights, as did Grotius and his followers. Instead, Vasquez followed the classical, Stoic doctrine of a "golden age" in which all were free and all was held in common, followed by a sort of "fall" (though Vasquez, unlike others, did not directly mention the biblical teaching of the fall of Adam in this regard) when the nations introduced *dominium,* dominion, expressed in the institutions of property and slavery. Thus rights as legal positions held by persons over against others and over against the state made their entry later on in history – and were not there in the beginning.

---

[153] Kurt Seelmann, *Die Lehre des Fernando Vazquez de Menchaca vom Dominium* [Fernando Vasquez de Menchaca's Doctrine of *Dominium*], p. 153.

[154] Seelmann, *Die Lehre,* p. 153–4.

So how did rights arise? Vasquez devotes the entire second volume of his magnum opus, the *Notable and Frequent Controversies,* to his answer: prescription, the importance of which cannot be overstated, he says, because "if one examines with care the frequent practice of the courts one will find nothing more in use than the matter of prescription, considering that it is virtually the only hope and proof and the treasury both of all property and all rights of the human race; or if one investigates as well the rights and state even of kings, princes and emperors, one encounters them safeguarded in mere prescription and the extended passage of time, as if in some most bounteous and secure treasury."[155] Prescription is the source of property and of rights; without it, nothing would be secure, no legal order would be possible. "[Vasquez] supplemented the doctrine of inalienable individual rights with acquired rights; both spring from the same root, the doctrine of prescription, and in the final analysis refer to natural-law criteria. These individual rights could only develop and maintain their existence on the basis of the general doctrine of natural law and in the climate of the constitutional state."[156]

Realizing the significance of this appeal to prescription as the basis of rights, Vasquez stipulated that prescription operated only on the level of national law, not at the level of international law. Rights were thus the creature of sovereignty, and by no means could be made to be the source of sovereignty. The rule of law, the constitutional state, preceded rights and provided the background against which they could arise.

Vasquez's ground-breaking doctrine of rights made them to be the product of prescription, thus originating in the lapse of time; the product of sovereignty, because prescription only operates at the level of national law; yet nevertheless enjoying the protection against state interference or abolition

---

[155] Fernando Vasquez de Menchaca, *Controversiarum Illustrium aliarumque usu frequentium libri tres* [Illustrious Controversies and Others of More Frequent Usage in Three Volumes] (Venice: Franciscum Rampazetum, 1564), vol. II, Question 51 section 1. I am using the edition prepared and translated by Don Fidel Rodriguez Alcalde (Valladolid: Cuesta, 1933).

[156] Ernst Reibstein, *Die Anfänge des Neueren Natur- und Völkerrechts: Studien zu den "Controversiae Illustres" des Fernandus Vasquius (1559)* [The Beginning of the Modern Law of Nature and Nations: The "Illustrious Controversies" of Fernando Vasquez], p. 137.

that property rights in the strict sense enjoy. It is thus historically conditioned, gradually developed rights of which Vasquez speaks, prescriptive rights, rights as inheritance rather than natural endowment. And it is against the background of Vasquez's doctrine that Grotius developed his own theory, which he took, as has been shown, in an entirely different direction.

The doctrine of the prescriptive constitution was a viable force on the early-modern political scene, in that it was the outgrowth and expression of the medieval constitution with its reciprocal rights and duties, its plethora of associations, its many concurrent jurisdictions. The medieval constitution demonstrated a fantastic capacity to generate rights; but this was because at its foundation was a clear conception of justice and law, rooted in nature and nature's God. The medieval constitution adhered to Stahl's conception of rights, that they form "a *secondary principle of the legal order* alongside the primary and absolute principle: the *purpose* (τέλος) of *life relations*. As secondary principle, however, it is always based upon this latter. Its own content and range is originally and essentially derived from, and the coherence of all the rights of all men lies in, this objective higher principle."[157] Thus rights did not exist prior to the law nor to the state; their existence in fact depended on the prior existence of law and the state. This is the world-historical significance of feudalism: that it provided this framework and platform upon which a constitution of reciprocal rights and duties between sovereign and subject might arise.

The emergence and ascendancy of natural-rights doctrines unsettled this received constitutionalism. Again, Grotius was the pioneer here. His treatment of rights required him to explain deviations from the original condition of life, liberty, and property in the state of nature; and he did so by resorting to the notion of the tacit contract, arguing that where subjection existed, it was because in the mists of time agreements had been made to surrender those rights and enter into these arrangements of subjection.[158] The principle of inalienability introduced by Locke placed a keg of dynamite under this theory by de-legitimizing such transactions. Assuming Locke's theory, where conditions of subjection existed they were in principle unjust and thus intolerable. Rousseau drew the obvious conclusion: "Grotius denies that all

---

[157] Stahl, *Principles of Law,* pp. 98–99.
[158] Reibstein, *Die Anfänge,* p. 141.

human power is established for the benefit of the governed, citing slavery as an example. His usual method of reasoning is always to present fact as a proof of right. A more logical method could be used, but not one more favorable to tyrants."[159] Thusly did first Grotius, then Locke, and finally Rousseau pave the way for the full-scale condemnation of the received historical constitution and the ascendancy to the moral high ground of the human rights ideology.

Natural rights likewise provided the legitimation of the *novus ordo seclorum* known as the United States of America, but in an entirely different manner than with the French Revolution. For the American revolutionaries were not interested in overthrowing the received order; they were interested, rather, in maintaining their received institutions, customs, and laws in the face of an overweening British monarchy and parliament. The American revolutionaries were trying to secure their historic, prescriptive rights as Englishmen; and no less a proponent of prescription than Edmund Burke regarded them as such.

But undeniably there was more to the American revolutionary movement than prescriptive rights. The natural rights based theory originating in Grotius had here borne significant fruit: "Many of the Revolutionary patriots believed with Thomas Dickinson that liberties do not result from charters; charters rather are in the nature of declarations of pre-existing rights."[160] Historical rights were therefore confirmations of pre-existing natural rights rather than being acquired and therefore precious heirlooms. Grotius had triumphed over Vasquez.

It is instructive in this regard to compare the first of the American revolutionary documents, the *Resolutions of the Stamp Act Congress* of 1765, with the *Declaration of Independence*. The former declares "That his majesty's subjects in these colonies, owe the same allegiance to the crown of Great Britain, that is owing from his subjects born within the realm, and all due subordination to that august body, the parliament of Great Britain," and, concurrently, "That his majesty's liege subjects in these colonies are entitled to all the

---

[159] Jean-Jacques Rousseau, *The Social Contract Or Principles Of Political Right* (1762), book I, ch. 2, in *The Basic Political Writings*.

[160] Charles Grove Haines, *The Revival of Natural Law Concepts*, ch. II, sec. 2.

inherent rights and privileges of his natural born subjects within the kingdom of Great Britain." Here there is no trace of a claim derived from natural rights; all rests on historical rights, acquired rights. But the matter is entirely different once we reach the Declaration itself. "The actions of that monarch were [there] declared to be in violation of the inalienable rights of man; they had as their object the establishment of an absolute tyranny over the states. No mention was made... of the rights of Englishmen."[161]

Yet, although both the American and the French Revolution partook of the elixir of inalienable natural rights, the underlying constitutions which they established are of a fundamentally different sort. Post-revolutionary France had put paid to its feudal past; America, on the other hand, had carried out "a conservative counter-revolution."[162]

The French legacy can be summed up as the paving-over of the Old Regime and the establishment of a system emanating wholly from the center; although the latter might well be viewed as an inheritance, for this was precisely what the French monarchy had expended so much effort to attain.[163] And while the new French Civil Code included substantial elements of received legal tradition, both Roman and customary, it firmly established the principle of law being a creation of the sovereign and having no existence outside the promulgated code. The revolutionary principle is thus that of absolute sovereignty, vested in autonomous man; it is what I have elsewhere characterized as the civil-law approach to law and government.[164]

The American legacy, on the other hand, truer to the original Grotian than the later Rousseauian form of natural rights, maintained continuity with the past and in fact revered that past, while marrying it to a theory that put paid to certain elements of that past – the theocratic inheritance, the public role of the church, the divine right of kings. Thus the American system maintains the common-law tradition, albeit in an inherently unstable compound that ever threatens to fall apart, as witness the contemporary phenomena of political correctness and culture war.

---

[161] Richard L. Perry (ed.), *Sources of Our Liberties*, p. 318.

[162] Rousas John Rushdoony, *This Independent Republic: Studies in the Nature and Meaning of American History*, p. 21.

[163] Alexis de Tocqueville, *The Old Regime and the French Revolution*.

[164] *A Common Law.*

For the theory of natural rights constitutes nothing other than a Trojan Horse in the body politic. Without a standard of reference outside of natural rights, the law, the judiciary, political action become nothing other than competing visions of what those natural rights should be. Every expansion of government intervention into previously sacrosanct areas of private action – the realm of private law – has been sanctioned by an appeal to someone's or some group's rights. I repeat: the regime of rights then becomes not a regime of rights at all, but of interests, and private law becomes subverted by administrative law.

We now are witness to the audacious attempt by proponents of the human-rights vision to establish a world government to impose by force a certain vision of rights, informed most emphatically by the civil-law tradition, which will convert the entire world into an administrative department. Thus what is now taking shape is a conflict between that tradition and its mortal enemy, the common-law tradition. But the contemporary champions of the common-law tradition are hampered from the beginning by the common root they share with the civil-law tradition, which is the basis in natural rights, human nature, a horizontal, a secular measure, excluding appeal to that which is truly transcendent.

It was Plato who laid the finger on this fatal flaw, when in *The Laws* he contrasted Protagoras' dictum man is the measure of all things with his own: God is the measure of all things.[165] It was the glory of the Christian moral-theological tradition that it was able to integrate the two forms of justice that both Plato and Aristotle identified, distributive and commutative, in a fruitful synthesis that produced not only constitutional government and liberty under law but also free-market economics, laying the foundations for both Adam Smith and the Austrian school. This was a tradition carried forward by both Catholic and Protestant scholars[166] but which ran aground on the

---

[165] Plato, *The Laws*, 716C.

[166] Ernst Reibstein, *Johannes Althusius als Fortsetzer der Schule von Salamanca*; Joseph Schumpeter, *History of Economic Analysis*; Marjorie Grice-Hutchinson, *Early Economic Thought in Spain, 1177–1740*; Alejandro A. Chafuen, *Christians for Freedom: Late-Scholastic Economics*; Julius Kirshner (ed.), *Business, Banking, and Economic Thought in Late Medieval and Early Modern Europe: Selected Studies of*

shoals of unbelief. It was the tradition that sustained the idea of justice that underlay and provided sustenance to the medieval growth of rights and reciprocal government.[167]

Stahl most clearly identified the rights-generated conflict, emphasizing, while recognizing the legitimate claims of those "rights of man," the need to maintain the fear of God as one of the two principles of the social order.

> This is therefore the shadowy side of recent times along with its higher worth: that it only seeks man while being detached from what stands above man. Of the two parts through which the law is fulfilled – you shall love the Lord your God above all things, and your neighbor as yourself – it has arbitrarily picked out the second while ignoring the first, it has demolished the first of the two tables of the law while proposing to establish only the second. This is however contrary to the eternal ordinance. No building can stand when one removes the foundation, no tree can live when one lays the ax to the roots. The task of the times is therefore not the ongoing one-sided advance of humanity and the rights of man, but the restoration of the fear of God as the energetic principle in both hearts and public institutions, while in it and through it preserving humanity and the rights of man. This is the union of the truth of former times with contemporary times. It gives the testimonies of the one and the other principle their pure shape and their complete meaning and worth.[168]

If we recognize this, we recognize that there is built into the creation an order which cannot be trifled with, which ordains among other things that it is nations, not individuals and certainly not imperial impositions, that are sovereign, and that this sovereignty is to be used to enforce the law rather than to create it, and that the nations have the right and duty to assert and defend their sovereignty precisely because of this divine command to enforce the law. If this system of multiple sovereignties is eliminated, then the law

---

Raymond de Roover; Murray Rothbard, *Economic Thought Before Adam Smith,* 2 volumes; Harold Berman, *Law and Revolution.*

[167] Gerd Tellenbach, *Church, State, and Christian Society at the Time of the Investiture Crisis;* Berman, *Law and Revolution.*

[168] Stahl, *Private Law,* pp. 40–41.

will become the monopoly of a single sovereign voice, outside of whose juris-diction there is no appeal. In this regard, the biblical story of the Tower of Babel (Genesis ch. 11) stands as a warning to the ages.

This is what it means to recognize the category of distributive justice as a fundamental building block of the legal order along with and complemen-tary to commutative justice. Distributive justice entails making and enforc-ing value judgments. It entails recognizing certain institutions as expressions of the creation order, with their own particular, created structures that can-not be remade to suit taste or desire. The family is the prime example of this: try as one might, one cannot efface the reality that families are first and fore-most husband-wife-children. It is a fact rooted in biological reality, although even such plain truths cannot stand in the way of determined human-rights judiciaries to remake reality as it suits them.[169] Ultimately, distributive jus-tice rests on a confession of faith, on a vision of reality, the world, nature, grace. It was precisely for this reason that the grand attempt was made to do without it, to soldier forth solely on the basis of commutative justice; but man does not live by liberty and property alone, and the vacuum was filled by redistributive "social" justice and human-rights ideologies that make a mockery of the rule of law.

What must be recognized is that the Founding Fathers of the United States, in throwing in their lot with the natural-rights theories that reigned in the 18th century, opened the door to the conundrum we now face in stav-ing off a human-rights global hegemony. Appeals to natural rights have been made in judicial decisions throughout the history of the Republic, thus mak-ing an appeal to such rights a part of the warp and woof of its legal

---

[169] A clear-cut illustration of this is seen in a recent decision by the European Court of Human Rights, *Christine Goodwin v. the United Kingdom* (link: http://hu-doc.echr.coe.int/eng?i=001-60596), in which the human rights of a transsexual were ruled to have been violated in the refusal to recognize her marriage. The rationale? "While it was true that Article 12 [of the European Convention on Human Rights] referred in express terms to the right of a man and woman to marry, the Court was not persuaded that at the date of this case these terms restricted the determination of gender to purely biological criteria." Purely biological criteria? What else defines a man, or a woman, or a cow for that matter?

tradition.[170] The genie has been let out of the bottle; the inexorable logic of human-rights theories has now produced a most virulent strain, and every fiber of the national will be required to divert it from its totalitarian course. In the end, though, there can be no relief from this particular malady until a fundamental change takes place in that most sensitive of all areas of public debate: the way we view religion in public life. For this situation is part and parcel of the naked public square.[171] As de Bonald put it: "The Revolution began with the declaration of the rights of man; it will not end until the declaration of the rights of God."

---

[170] Haines, *Revival of Natural Law Concepts,* "Part II: The Acceptance of Natural Law or Superior Law Concepts in the Public Law of the United States"; "Part III: The Fourteenth Amendment and Natural Law Theories."

[171] Richard John Neuhaus, *The Naked Public Square: Religion and Democracy in America,* 1984).

# What We Are Up Against (2006)

## The Current Situation in the Light of an Historical Example

---

This article fixes the precise moment in history in which absolutism became emancipated from the strictures of the received constitutional tradition, thus paving the way for an autonomous civil-law orientation. Through the War of the Spanish Succession and the subsequent Treaty of Utrecht, the French monarchy cemented a post-Christian basis for absolutism which the French Revolution finalized. As such, this article supplements the discussion in ch. 11, "The Apotheosis of Liberty."

---

*What a spectacle was presented to us from the crown of the hill! The great space was covered by the most magnificent tents. The frightful thunder from out of the mouths of the enemies' guns and the answering fire from the walls of the town filled the air. Smoke and flames enveloped the city so much that only the tops of the towers were visible. All around the city, 200,000 Ottomans were spread in battle formation from the Danube to the hills, and further to the left of the Turks immense hordes of Tartars approached the heights and forests.*[172]

SUCH was the prospect from the Kahlenberg overlooking Vienna on the morning of September 12th, 1683. The city was now into its 62nd day of siege and cannonade by the Turks. The defense was in imminent danger of collapsing. But relief was on the way, in the form of an army of Poles, Bavarians, Swabians, Franconians, Saxons, along with troops from other parts of the Empire, albeit fewer than 70,000 in all. What was such a number against 200,000?

Nevertheless, the Christians had one thing working in their favor: the hubris of Kara Mustapha, the Grand Vizier in charge of the siege. Mustapha refused to lend credence to reports of an approaching relieving army, thus

---

[172] Quoted from a French engineer in the service of King John Sobieski: Alfons von Czibulska, *Prinz Eugen: Retter des Abendlandes* [Prince Eugene, Savior of the West], pp. 35–36.

neglecting to occupy the surrounding hills and so halt the relief effort in its tracks. When the Christians stormed down the hill on that fateful morning, the Turks, suddenly fighting on two fronts, proved unable to withstand the assault. The Polish cavalry overwhelmed the center of the Turkish resistance, where stood the symbolic red tent and the flag of the Prophet "brought every year with great piety from Mecca,"[173] where the command to the Turkish soldiers was to stand, either to triumph or to die. They met with the latter fate, the tent and flag falling to the Polish onslaught, while elsewhere the soldiers of the Cross drove all before them, partly from "the cowardice of our enemies, whom we drove like herds before us from post to post, and from morning well into the night."[174]

There were also members of the French chivalry among the combatants, princely knights, volunteers in the Imperial army, come to defend Christendom from the Saracen scourge – one of whom will loom large further on in this story. For the siege of Vienna had captured the imagination, and the sympathy, of all of Europe. All, that is, except the King of France, the *Rex Christianissimus*, "Most Christian" Louis XIV, who in fact had discovered the uses of such a Turkish invasion against his arch-enemy. This would be Leopold I, the head of the Holy Roman Empire, whose throne was located in Vienna albeit relocated to Passau during the siege. For while Leopold's attentions were occupied in the east, he could do nothing to avert the ongoing aggrandizement of territory being conducted by Louis on the Empire's western border, the Rhine.

Ever since assuming the reins of power in France, that is, after the death of the great Cardinal Mazarin, who hitherto had guided the affairs of state, Louis had pursued a plan of land-grabbing beginning with the Belgian province of Brabant, then Lorraine, and then, in 1672, the all-out invasion of the Netherlands, precipitating the accession of a young William III of Orange to the stadhoudership (captain-generalcy) of that country. The obstinate and valiant defense led by William put a temporary halt to Louis' gains; but despite the conclusion of the Peace of Rijswijk (1678), Louis continued his rapacious ways, this time going straight for members of the Holy Roman Empire such as the Palatinate, which he subjected to the most outrageous and

---

[173] Paul Frischauer, *Prince Eugène: A Man and a Hundred Years of History*, p. 124.
[174] Count Taafe, quoted in Frischauer, p. 125.

destructive treatment, and Strasbourg, about which Charles V had once said that if both Vienna and Strasbourg were threatened, he would rush to the aid of Strasbourg. Leopold's preoccupation with the Turkish threat in the east forced his hand into acceding to this treatment.

Louis' game was simple: he hoped that Austria would fall; for then his would be the only power standing in the way of an Ottoman primacy over the Western Christian Empire, the only power able to stave off a fate similar to that of the Eastern Christian Empire, Byzantium, where the Ottomans conquered Constantinople in the 15<sup>th</sup> century. Then Louis' dreams would be realized, in which he himself would rescue the West and become Holy Roman Emperor, the universal monarch in the likeness of Charlemagne. Who could stand up to him then? And his duplicitous game would have paid off, for he himself had encouraged the Turks into pursuing their plan of invasion in the first place.

Indeed, Louis' France posed as great, if not greater, a threat to Christendom than the Ottomans. The threat was most obvious militarily, in the attempt to subjugate neighboring states. But there was more, much more. The great polymath Gottfried Wilhelm Freiherr von Leibniz summed them up in a polemic written in the context of a later Louis-inspired crisis, the War of the Spanish Succession (1701–1713). Despite its relative obscurity, this war constituted one of the great turning points in European history, as we shall see.

The conflict here was between two aspirants to the vacant throne of Spain: Philip, grandson of Louis XIV, and Charles, son of Leopold I. Leibniz argued that the prospect of France uniting with Spain in the form of Philip's accession to the throne would spell doom not only for Spain but for Christendom as well. French manners would corrupt the Spaniards. "The manners of the French are absolutely alien to the manners or customs of Spain. There is in France a great freedom, particularly in respect to sex, and it is to be feared that they will bring this with them to the prejudice of good morals." Spanish mores were quite the opposite: "everyone is grave, serious and steady; everyone is for the exact observation of laws and customs; everyone is content to conform himself to them, and wants others to conform themselves; for those matters which the law has not regulated, the wisdom of the nation has provided, and has introduced customs which take the place of laws. In conversation and in social intercourse, just as no one wants to inconvenience others, no one wants to be inconvenienced by them, and even the youth partake of the gravity of the nation." What effect would French mores have on this austerity? "On the French side, it is quite the contrary. Everyone allows himself no repose, and leaves none to others; the grave and the serious pass for ridiculous, and measure or reason for pedantic; caprice, for something gallant, and inconstancy in one's interactions with other people, for cleverness: everyone meddles [with others' affairs] in [private] houses, and pursues people to their very homes, and picks shameful fights. Youth above all glories in its folly and in its disorders, which go quite far today, as if this were a sign of wit; it respects neither sex, nor age, nor merit."[175]

The effect of such manners is to corrupt domestic relations, which is even worse than corruption in public office; for "it is incomparably harder to be troubled, laughed at, affronted and mistreated in one's domestic life, in one's person, in what is one's own, and to drag through a life full of sorrow caused by the contempt and the insolence of those with whom one must live, and whom one is obliged to put up with despite himself and despite even fear, than to be put under the yoke of a conqueror, or to be oppressed by a tyrant who affects one only in general or in the purse."[176] Such is the effect of the total revolution French manners would bring about in the Spanish, and by extension European, social fabric.

The effect of the French way on religion would be as deleterious. The upstanding members of the Catholic church there are mistreated and abused. The Pope is only obeyed to be flattered, the better to gain his subjection. The French were responsible for "a thousand affronts" to Pope Innocent XI, "a saintly pontiff, because he was devoted to justice and did not approve the ambitious schemes of France." French policy was to undermine the authority of the Holy See in order to bolster the primacy of the throne in ecclesiastical affairs; the defenders of the church are "persecuted as heretics." The liberties of the church were being subjugated by dubious regal rights; "exemplary bishops, who were not the slaves of the court, to the prejudice of their conscience, were treated with the last degree of inhumanity."[177]

---

[175] "Manifesto for the Defense of the Rights of Charles III," in *Leibniz: Political Writings*, p. 157.

[176] *Ibid.*

[177] *Ibid.*, p. 158.

France's perfidy was especially visible in their support of the Ottoman offensive against Austria and thus Christendom. "The ambition of France has
also kept the Mohammedans in Europe, of whom the Emperor was on the
verge of chasing out." The French argued that this was done to restrict the
aggrandizements of the Emperor, but in fact if France would participate in
the war against the Ottomans it would also gain territories for itself: "Greece
together with Thrace (to say nothing of Asia) awaited her and were assured
to her." But Louis XIV instead saved his forces for the invasion of Spain. "It
is this crown which, by its greediness, has caused a horrible letting of Christian blood for nearly thirty years, by constantly attacking others; and almost
all the evils that Europe has suffered during that time ought to be imputed
to her."[178]

These things were bad – "But the worst thing of all is that atheism walks
today in France with its head up, that pretended great wits are in fashion
there, and that piety is turned to ridicule." France's ultimate gift to Christendom was an acidic skepticism that undermined the very foundations of
Western civilization. "To submit to French domination is to open the door
to dissoluteness and to libertinage; one can be sure as well that piety cannot
reign where justice is trampled underfoot, as France has done to it so many
times, and with so much haughtiness; and if the insolent spirit of the French,
as soon as they are the masters, must oblige honourable people not to allow
them to get the upper hand in their country, their feelings and their impious
actions must frighten men of good will and good prelates, as much as all those
[members] of the clergy who are zealous for the house of God." Even if the
king were pious and just, these manners are enough to ruin a people and
make them unfit for liberty: "bad habit, once minds have got the taste of it,
is stronger than ordinances, and we see it now in France itself."[179]

The upshot is a system of government which everyone knew to be despotism, and which France in pre-eminent degree exhibited to the world. "Everyone knows that this form of government is established in France, that it is
exalted there by flatterers, and that a grandson of a king of France cannot fail
to be imbued with these maxims. There the liberties of the great and of the
people have been reduced; the good pleasure of the king takes the place of

---

[178] *Ibid.*

[179] *Ibid.*, p. 158–159.

everything else; even the princes of royal blood are without the slightest authority; the great are only title-holders and are ruining themselves more and more, while persons of little importance are elevated to serve as instruments for oppressing the others." The estates have been suppressed, the nobility made subservient and fawning. "In the *pays d'États* the Estates are assembled only for form's sake, and these assemblies serve only to execute the orders of the Court, without any regard for their grievances. The nobility is impoverished to the last degree, vexed by quarrelling and investigations, obliged to use itself up in service to the king and to sacrifice its welfare and its blood to the ambition of a conqueror, while it nourishes only hopes for chimerical riches and for advancements which are given only in very small numbers." The administration itself is based on self-aggrandizement and mutual extortion. "Those who occupy civil positions, particularly lucrative ones, having once enriched themselves at the expense of the community because they were given free rein, are now squeezed like sponges by re-examinations of their accounts and their affairs, by the venality of offices, by the creation of new burdens, and by great sums which are demanded of them without any reason, and which they are obliged to pay to save themselves from harassment." And the burden of taxation and regulation has taken on oppressive proportions. "The people are trampled upon without mercy and reduced to bread and water by tithes, taxes, imposts, head-taxes, [by being required to supply] winter-quarters and passage for war-makers, by monopolies, by changes in [the value of] money which take suddenly from everyone a good part of his goods, and by a thousand other inventions; and all of that is only to serve the insatiability of a court which cares not at all about the subjects which it already has, and which seeks only to augment the number of miserable people by extending its estates."[180]

Leibniz's view of France was not an isolated one. It was shared by many who had come to see in France not merely a military threat but a total cultural one. And not only Louis' agenda generated opposition; his methods as well created enemies he would have been better off not having, who shared Leibniz's opinions not by observation but from cruel experience.

---

[180] *Ibid.*, p. 159–160.

There was a volunteer in the Imperial army on that fateful day at the Kahlenberg, a scion of the ruling house of Savoy; his father had been a general in Louis' army, distinguished for bravery, rewarded with command of the crack Swiss Guard. His mother was a niece of Cardinal Mazarin, and Louis' favorite playmate in his youth. Olympia Mancini was one of the most influential ladies at court, and an intriguer of the first order. Even though she conducted numerous affairs, her faithful husband stood by her, that is, until he was killed in battle.

Eugene, the youngest of five sons (he also had two sisters), was also the runt of the family. Because of his physical shortcomings, he was intended for an ecclesiastical career. From the age of five his hair was cut in a tonsure and he was forced to wear the habit of a monk. Louis himself, it is said, was the one who dubbed him "the little Abbé," the little abbot. But Eugene had other ideas. Fascinated and enthralled by the military – France's army was by far the best-equipped and best-trained, and Eugene daily witnessed the pageantry thereof – Eugene set himself, in spite of opposition at home, to lead men in battle. His choice of occupation was hindered by his father's early death; it was not made any easier by his mother's being exiled to Brussels by Louis after having been accused of a plot to poison the King himself. It was rubbish, of course, and was only the upshot of court intrigues which this time got the better of Olympia. When the time came for Eugene to request a commission in the King's army, Louis simply refused him. The road here was closed. And because Eugene likewise refused his family's career choice for him, he was left virtually penniless.

But then came news from the east: Eugene's brother, Louis, had been killed in a rearguard action against the Turks, fighting for the Emperor and Christendom. Eugene immediately knew what he was to do: he himself would go and offer his services to the Emperor and pick up where his brother had left off. Having no means to do so, he convinced his cousin, Prince Conti, who had married into the King's immediate family, of the need to ride to the defense of Christendom. The two literally rode off in the night. When Louis heard of it, he immediately sent after Conti to retrieve him; he would have no prince of the blood fighting in the cause of his avowed enemy. Louis' messenger caught up with the two across the border, in Frankfurt. Conti must return; Eugene was left to make his own decision. With a small gift of a ring and money from his cousin, Eugene could now make his way unhindered.

It is said that when he heard of young Eugene's departure, Louis remarked sarcastically, "Do you think that I shall suffer a great loss if the Little Abbé does not return?" As if he had overheard them, Eugene meant to make him regret those words. Louis' treatment of his mother, his treatment of himself, the debauched lifestyle at court to which they all had been subjected and from which Eugene only with great difficulty managed to extricate himself, the subjection of the common good to the good of Louis and to France, all of these drove the Little Abbé into the arms of the major power standing in the way of the Sun King's universal dominion. As Frischauer observed, "Eugene's life, up to a certain stage at least, is one great reaction to the life and deeds of Louis XIV. It can be observed already in his earliest youth.... The habit, which was forced upon him in his parent's house of noting Louis's every movement, and of listening – at least indirectly – to his every word and taking account of it to himself, predestined him to become either a devoted adherent or an enemy."[181]

When Eugene charged down the Kahlenberg he knew that here was where he was meant to be, fighting for the existence of Christendom and not for the greater glory of Louis XIV. In this and subsequent actions against the Turks, driving them out of Hungary, where they had ruled for upwards of two centuries, Eugene rose meteorically through the ranks, by the age of 29 attaining the rank of imperial field marshal. Partly through his efforts, Austria was able to secure its eastern front against the Ottoman threat – thus freeing up the Emperor to meet the threat in the West. Louis' dismissal of Eugene would bear him bitter fruit.

While Belgrade was falling to the Imperial army in 1688, Louis was sending his troops across the border into the Palatinate, precipitating the Nine Years' War (1688–1697). This latest outrage led to the cementing of the so-called Grand Alliance led by William III, who, by invading England – on invitation – and acceding to the throne in the "Glorious Revolution," brought that country into the alliance as well.

---

[181] Frischauer, pp. 49–50. My main sources for the life of Eugene are this work (which, although accurate in terms of historically verifiable material, also includes much unsubstantiated gossip), along with Derek McKay, *Prince Eugene of Savoy*, and Max Braubach, *Prinz Eugen von Savoyen: Eine Biographie*, 5 volumes.

The Emperor, still smarting from Louis' previous annexations, was bound and determined to put a halt to encroachments on German land, and this time he had most of the German princes on his side, chiefly Max Emmanuel, Duke of Bavaria.

Eugene was sent to Savoy to battle at the side of his cousin Victor Amadeus, ruler of that country. After his first incursion on French soil, he is said to have remarked: "Didn't I say I would only return to France sword in hand? Louis exiled my mother... and I have just exiled thousands of his subjects by making them flee from their houses and country."[182] But the war here proved inconclusive; Victor Amadeus switched sides, leaving cousin Eugene in the lurch, while elsewhere the war ground down into a stalemate. With the Peace of Rijswijk (1697), Louis yielded the Palatinate but retained Strasbourg and his gains in Alsace.

Two years of peace were followed by the aforementioned War of the Spanish Succession. Leopold, noted for his indecisiveness, this time proved unmovable: he would not allow the House of Bourbon to accede to the throne which by right, he felt, belonged to the House of Habsburg. When the Bourbon prince Philip did ascend the throne by virtue of Charles II's will, Leopold decided upon war, even if he had to go it alone.

Eugene was given command of the Austrian forces, and the seemingly insurmountable task of facing France's superior forces in the field. The first stage of the war concentrated in Italy. Here the French forces had sealed the border and all the mountain passes into the country. Undaunted, Eugene had the army cross over the easternmost part of the border, hitherto considered impassable – a "remarkable feat," compared by contemporaries "with that of Hannibal; engravings of it were published almost at once."[183] Having caught the French by surprise, Eugene by virtue of superior generalship was able to inflict telling blows. But the general inferiority of his forces precluded his gaining a decisive victory; the most he could hope for was to pin the French down.

One of the major shortcomings of the Austrian forces was poor logistical and financial backing. This alone would keep them from giving the French more than a scare. But it was made up for by the entry of the English and the

---

[182] Quoted in McKay, *Prince Eugene of Savoy*, p. 36.

[183] *Ibid.*, p. 59.

Dutch into the war. As one of his last acts, William III renewed the Grand Alliance with Leopold. The Maritime Powers brought not only ground forces and naval superiority but also indispensable funding, which enabled the German forces to continue.

The entry of the Maritime Powers came not a moment too soon. Max Emmanuel, who had also fought at the Kahlenberg, by this time had been brought around to Louis' view of things, and threw Bavaria's lot in with France. This opened the door down the Danube directly into Austria and the gates of Vienna. Rebellion in Hungary, inevitable in the wake of the devastations of the Turkish wars and subsequent Austrian misrule, tied down Austrian forces. Eugene by now had been made President of the War Council and thus put in charge of the creaking Austrian war machine, furthermore hamstrung by the quietism of the overly pious Leopold, whose habit was to leave pressing matters "to God;" Eugene for his part "reminded Joseph [Leopold's son and heir] that 'The proverb says that God helps him who helps himself.'"[184] In January 1704 the Bavarians took Passau, where the Habsburg court had taken refuge during the siege of Vienna. Vienna was being pressed by the Bavarians from the one side and the Hungarian rebels on the other, and was close to panic.

In the summer of 1704 a combined Franco-Bavarian force occupied the Danube valley; it was only a matter of time before it would move on Vienna. Another substantial force stood on the Rhine at Strasbourg, waiting to join forces. Opposing it, Eugene had at his command a force smaller than either of those armies. But help was on the way, in the form of the Duke of Marlborough's allied force of English, Dutch, Danish, and German troops. In a remarkable feat of deception, not only with regard to the French but also the Dutch, who by no means would have agreed to the maneuver, Marlborough marched down the Rhine and through the Black Forest to join forces with Eugene. The French and Bavarian armies also combined; they met in August the battle of Blenheim, precipitating a crushing allied victory, the first Louis had ever suffered.

From this point on the tables were turned; it was France and Louis who were fighting for their lives. A series of splendid victories followed: Ramillies, Turin, Oudenaarde, even Malplaquet (although this latter was tarnished by

---

[184] *Ibid.*, p. 74.

the horrendous losses suffered especially by the Allied forces). France was brought to its knees, and a peace securing Christendom against domination by that country was in the offing.

But defeat, or at least an unsatisfactory conclusion, was snatched from the jaws of victory. What France failed to secure on the battlefield, it could gain through intrigue, by taking advantage of English party politics.

The English contribution to the war effort had been decisive, and it was made possible by what historians have termed "the Financial Revolution," involving the establishment of a central bank, the Bank of England, which issued bonds against the credit of the government. What made this so effective was that the government's credit was no longer based simply on royal promises, as was the case hitherto in most European polities, including France and Austria. It was rather based on the Parliament's power of the purse, thus the ability of popular representatives to allocate funds and earmark tax revenues. Such a system of taxation proved more effective: by involving the taxed more closely in decisions regarding taxation, it inspired greater cooperation and tended toward a more equitable tax base, hence less evasion.

With Parliament voting the tax revenues to cover the government's loans, the Bank of England found it much easier to find lenders. This led to the growth of a money market, the foundation of the modern investment regime; but that is another story. The important point here is that England by this method was able to raise revenues that the Emperor Leopold, for instance, could only dream of. England became the chief financier of the Allied war effort.

There was a fly in the ointment, however, and that was faction, which had already played such a mighty role in English politics. The financiers and the whole method of a "perpetual" national debt, which is how the new system came to be typified, had been institutionalized during the reign of William, whose support lay mainly with the Whig party. Whig politicians benefited from the new system, as did Whig financiers. This did not go down well with the Tories, the economic center of gravity of whom lay in landed rather than fiduciary property. The country squires viewed the newfangled system with complete distrust, while also harboring political jealousy because that system perpetuated a Whig pre-eminence in politics.

When William died in 1702, he was succeeded to the throne by Anne, the sister of William's wife Mary and the daughter of James II, the abdicator. Anne, while intent on preserving the Protestant succession, abhorred the Whigs and did everything she could to free herself from their influence in government. But William had already gotten England into the war, and John Churchill, the Duke of Marlborough, continued his policies. Anne put her full confidence in Marlborough, and his wife, Sarah, was also her best friend. Marlborough, together with Lord Treasurer Godolphin, conducted an administration which is considered to have been one of the most efficient and effective in English history.

Not only was Marlborough an able administrator; he was also perhaps England's greatest general ever. The victories he achieved were monuments to tactical genius and personal bravery. In this, however, Marlborough found his equal in Eugene, Prince of Savoy. The two together – they cooperated astoundingly well considering the potential for rivalry – became the scourge of Louis, and in their campaigns in France against the previously impregnable line of barrier fortresses brought France and Louis to their knees.

But the country squires of England cared little for victory over France and certainly not for the means by which it was achieved: standing armies and perpetual debts, with the threat of subjugation to a devouring war machine. Certainly all of England glowed with patriotic fervor upon hearing of the monumental victories; but that feeling quickly evaporated when the party aficionados and pamphleteers once again began working the base. Marlborough and Eugene were warmongers, it was said; they prolonged the war needlessly, just to fill their own pockets; they cared nothing about the poor soldiers being mowed down in droves. And the Allies were a worthless bunch, living off the English dime, neglecting their own responsibilities, never making good on their own promises, letting the redcoats bear the brunt of every battle. And Godolphin was running the most corrupt administration ever, running the country into ground, incurring a massive debt that could never be repaid. And the Whigs, why they were turning the country into a moral cesspool, with their occasional conformity making a mockery of the Established Church, tolerating all manner of perfidious sects.

This sentiment simmered under the surface, and a Marlborough, who was more Tory than Whig himself, at least in terms of background, would have to have known of it. What he did not realize – until it was too late – was that a conspiracy was brewing right in the very heart of government, a conspiracy which not only would bring the Tories back to power, but would bring down the Marlborough-Godolphin administration – an administration which did its best to rise above the party fray but was incrementally forced to give in to Whig demands; which would wreck the war effort just when it was bringing final success, and would destroy the bonds joining the Allies in terms of a common Christian order, finally replacing it with the new order of autonomous nation states pursuing naked national interests.

This conspiracy was the brainchild of Robert Harley, the future Earl of Oxford, a master politician who recognized that Tory sentiment could be ridden to establish political supremacy. Since the Whigs commanded a majority in both houses of Parliament, they demanded an increasing share of the government's offices, this despite Anne, who absolutely loathed them. Both Marlborough and Godolphin counseled Anne to give in to their demands so as to maintain Parliamentary support for the war effort. Harley saw the pain this gave Anne, and began to work on her through the offices of a cousin of Sarah Churchill's, the infamous Abigail Masham née Hill. It was Sarah's good offices that had brought Abigail into the Queen's service, and as lady-in-waiting Abigail was well-positioned to whisper into Anne's ear whatever Harley wanted Anne to hear. By this means Abigail was able to supplant Sarah in the Queen's affections – Sarah, herself a Whig sympathizer, only made things worse by railing against the inevitable. By subtle process Harley, working through the Queen, was able one by one to maneuver the Whigs out of office. And by working on the country's war weariness, Harley and his co-workers were able to return a Tory Parliament in 1710.

Back in France, Louis observed these events with scarcely believing eyes. Indeed, the dissolution of the Whig Parliament by Anne inspired scenes in Versailles as might have given her second thoughts, had she known of them. "It is impossible for me to describe the transport of joy the King was in upon reading that part, [viz.] the dissolving of Parliament; 'Well,' says the King, 'if Monsieur Harley does that, I shall say he is un habile homme, and that he knows how to go through what he has undertaken; Mesnager,' adds the King, turning to me, 'it is time you were in England;' I could not interpose for some time, the King was so full of this news, and talked so fast; sometimes to himself and sometimes to me...."[185]

English politics thus opened a door that Louis would surely not allow again to be shut. "Since the changes in London had first been perceived by the French Court... the whole policy of Louis XIV had been to gain time for the downfall of Marlborough and an English defection to break up the confederacy. Thus, and thus alone, could France be saved."[186]

And Louis found willing accomplices in Harley and his protégé cum Secretary of State, Henry St. John. St. John had been favored in his career by Marlborough, who even had gone to such lengths as personally to ensure that he received raises in his salary, as well as personally to repay his debts. For his genuine concern, and for his unparalleled service both to his country and the common cause of Christendom, Marlborough was repaid with the most horrendous form of vindictiveness and sustained lying, the likes of which it is difficult to find the equal of in all the annals of party politics. Both through his own acknowledged gift with the pen and that of his "partner in crime" Jonathan Swift (himself until recently a Whig – "Swift... was assailing all his old friends with merciless satire and invective, and proving that there was no malice like the rancour of the renegade"[187]), St. John blasted the Allies as horribly derelict, Marlborough as an ineffective pocket-liner, and the war effort itself as misguided and dangerous.

Behind the backs of the other Allies, Harley began negotiating with France about peace. But no sooner did Louis catch on to what was taking place than he immediately ratcheted up his peace demands. "Instead of dictating to a baffled and beaten despot, they were more like supplicants to this enemy, who had but a few months ago been ready to agree almost to any terms."[188] Marlborough had predicted that the peace party, far from ushering in peace, would find their goal increasingly difficult of attaining the more

---

[185] *Minutes of the Negotiations of Monsieur Mesnager at the Court of England towards the Close of the Last Reign* (1717), p. 61; quoted in Churchill, *Marlborough: His Life and Times,* p. 764.

[186] Churchill, *Marlborough,* Book II [Vol. IV], p. 837.

[187] Thomas Macknight, *The Life of Henry St. John, Viscount Bolingbroke,* p. 211.

[188] *Ibid.,* p. 179.

they pursued it: "Our extravagant behaviour has so encouraged the French, that they take measures as if the war was just beginning, so that our new ministers will be extremely deceived, for the greater desire they shall express for peace, the less they will have it in their power to obtain it."[189]

The accession of the Tories to power put one nail in the coffin of the final defeat of France; another came through the death of the young Emperor, Joseph, of smallpox in April 1711. Eugene had to rush from the Hague back to Germany to oversee the election of Joseph's brother, the Archduke Charles, as Holy Roman Emperor. "The death of the Emperor, so far from bringing peace nearer, drove it farther away. It completely ruptured... all plans for a decisive campaign in Flanders. It stimulated Louis XIV, and furnished him with a verbal argument against the logic of the Allies. It convinced him that he would be able to defend his northern fortress-line through the whole of 1711, and therefore that his remaining strength would outlast Marlborough's dying favour."[190]

This left Marlborough alone at the head of the Allied forces in Flanders, with his enemies in charge back in London. Though they, realizing their need of his good offices in order to keep the pressure on Louis, switched their rhetoric to that of sweetness and light, Marlborough knew the clock was ticking and that he did not have much time left for action. In the face of a revitalized French army and the incessant undermining of his command and his authority by his enemies in government, Marlborough nevertheless succeeded in pulling off what many consider to be his greatest military achievement, the penetration of the French "ne plus ultra" line and the capture of Bouchain.

It was a last hurrah. When he returned to England upon the conclusion of the campaign, he was forced to listen to a Queen's Speech opening Parliament including as its first sentence: "I am glad that I can now tell you that *notwithstanding the arts of those who delight in war*, both place and time are appointed for opening the Treaty of a general Peace."[191] The statement was directed, of course, at Marlborough, in lieu of the gratitude he truly deserved.

On December 30 Marlborough appeared at court for what proved to be the last time. "He was still Captain-General and a member of the Cabinet.

---

[189] Marlborough to Godolphin, Aug. 16, 1710, quoted in *ibid.*, pp. 179–180.

[190] Churchill, *Marlborough,* II, p. 803.

[191] *Ibid.*, pp. 904–905.

No Whigs attended, and he stood alone among his enemies. He was shunned by all. 'Nobody hardly took notice of him,' wrote Swift, who received an exulting account from his Ministerial friends. Such a spectacle, though entirely in accordance with the character of such tribes, is none the less unpleasant. There he stood, stared at and scorned, with no protection but his composure and his fame."[192] The next day the Queen dismissed him from all his duties and offices, using as an excuse trumped-up charges of corruption brought against him in the House of Commons. In fact, she had been prevailed upon by Harley and St. John to the effect that Marlborough wanted nothing less than to dispense with her in the manner of the Roundheads and Charles I, in order to assume the role of Lord Protector! So did his enemies have cause for rejoicing, for taunting, for laughter. "But the most pregnant comment was made by Louis XIV: 'The affair of displacing the Duke of Marlborough will do all for us we desire.'"[193]

It was now Eugene's turn to press the government on its newfound course of action. He arrived too late in London to have any influence on Anne's decision to relieve Marlborough, but still was determined to let the government know of Vienna's viewpoint regarding peace. He was sanguine about his prospects. "Already in writing his first memorandum he had in his report to the Emperor stated his conviction that 'no effect was to be hoped for,' that it was much rather certain 'that these fellows have already settled with France and perhaps may have gone farther than one might well believe.'"[194] And he would not leave his great friend and comrade-in-arms Marlborough in the lurch. As he put it to an emissary from the English court, "since it was known all over the world what a firm and intimate friendship I had fostered with the Duke of Marlborough, now finding him in misfortune, I could not do otherwise than uphold my friendship with him, lest the world should say, and I leave it as an evil echo after me, that I deserted and abandoned a friend in his hour of sorrow and stress when fortune had forsaken him."[195] This was the best he could do, for his official mission proved a failure. He returned to

---

[192] *Ibid.*, p. 912.

[193] *Ibid.*, p. 913.

[194] Braubach, vol. 3, pp. 91–92.

[195] Quoted in Churchill, *Marlborough*, II, p. 921.

Holland after two months, with only a magnificent diamond-encrusted sword – a present from the Queen – to show for it.

For their part, government ministers in conversation with their French counterparts by now had taken to referring to the Allies as "the common enemies." St. John took the lead in this. "St. John accepted this expression of 'the common enemies' as applied to all the allies of England who were unwilling to follow his lead. 'It is the desire of the ill-mentioned,' he wrote to Torcy [the French foreign minister – RCA], 'to arouse this mistrust both among us and everywhere else, but I am not worrying on that account, because it merely depends upon the All-Christian King to render all their efforts vain.'" How the tables had turned. "In fact, Oxford and St. John, dominated by their party struggle, now looked upon the French as friends, and upon their allies, by whose side they were standing in the field, as foes."[196]

Indeed, Eugene, who now assumed the Captain-Generalcy of the Dutch and the Imperial forces left vacant by Marlborough, would soon come to experience the reality of these declamations.

But the peace negotiations, which began in Utrecht while Eugene was in England, did not proceed as favourably as the conspirators had hoped. What did they expect, the Dutch Republic and the Empire simply to sign off on a peace tailor-made in the interests of England and France alone? "The anger of the Allies knew no bounds, and in England outside the Court circle widespread wrath was mingled with wider shame."[197] Beyond that, negotiations between England and France became hindered with the deaths in rapid succession of the heirs to the throne standing between Louis XIV and Philip V, thus paving the way to the union of crowns of Spain and France upon Louis' death. This was too much even for the peace party in England, and so the 1712 campaign proceeded.

The English contingent was still represented in the Allied armies even though Marlborough no longer led it; command over the English and the Allied forces in English pay was transferred to the Duke of Ormonde. Eugene thus led a force of divided allegiance into the field, for the English were waiting for a peace they felt was in the offing. In the meantime, the Allied forces moved deep into Belgium, placing themselves between the French

---

[196] *Ibid.*, p. 920.

[197] *Ibid.*, p. 939.

army under Marshal Villars and the road to Paris. With his superior forces, Eugene hoped either to provoke a pitched battle or to undertake a siege of one of the few barrier fortresses left between his armies and Paris.

But it was at this point that the perfidy of the Tory government manifested itself most clearly. For Ormonde had received orders from St. John, in the name of the Queen, to avoid all conflict with the French; and not only that, but to keep this order concealed from the Allied command. Even more: in a postscript that he "almost forgot" to mention, St. John informed Ormonde that the French were informed of this decision; and that it could not be changed without their knowing of it. This is the substance of the infamous "Restraining Orders" which one day would form a major article in St. John's impeachment.

Eugene, backed by the Dutch, proposed offensive actions; Ormonde refused to go along. Eugene then "in strong terms" reproached Ormonde, telling him "that this was no manner to allow us to march in enemy country in the midst of his fortresses, in order then to remain inert, which would encourage the enemy to action." If England had concluded a separate peace, it must make that knowledge public, "since, should it not be certain, it by such conduct puts both itself and all of Europe in danger of being lost."[198] But if Eugene knew to what lengths St. John had gone with the French, he would have put the matter in even stronger terms. When asked by the French go-between what Villars should do if Eugene went ahead with an attack, St. John responded that "there would be nothing to be done but to fall upon him *and cut him to pieces, him and his army.*"[199]

The significance of this cannot be expressed better than Churchill has already done:

> It would have been a grievous, though a permissible, measure to tell Eugene, the States-General, and other members of the Alliance that the British forces would not fight until the peace treaty was settled one way or the other. But for an English Minister, acting in the name of the Queen, to conceal from the Allies his intention, while disclosing it secretly to the enemy, was in fact

[198] Braubach, vol. 3, p. 107.
[199] *Edinburgh Review*, October 1835, p. 9; quoted in Churchill, *Marlborough,* II, p. 945.

to encompass the defeat of Eugene and the slaughter of the allies and comrades with whom the British troops had so long stood shoulder to shoulder. Nothing in the history of civilized peoples has surpassed this black treachery. The punishment meted out in after-years by their countrymen to the criminals concerned may lighten, but cannot efface, its indelible stain.[200]

So arose the image of "perfidious Albion" which has echoed through the ages. This event even served to gin up war fever against the English in the 20th century, as witness the book *Prince Eugene, His Life, His Work, and England's Betrayal,* published in Germany in 1942.[201]

But Eugene had received inside information from the English camp and had been apprised of these goings-on. The question now was, what to do with the English troops, which for all anyone knew might switch sides at any moment. The idea was even floated of disarming and arresting them: "the famous redcoats whose martial honour stood so high in those professional camps were to be seized as hostages against the faithlessness of their Government." St. John was indignant: "Some are even saucy enough to insinuate so far as to attempt seizing the British troops in Flanders." To which Churchill retorts, "to such a point had the Queen and her new friends brought the Common Cause."[202]

In the event, Eugene went ahead and captured Le Quesnoy, but soon thereafter Ormonde withdrew his troops from the Allied camp. The English ministry expected him to take the troops in English pay with him, but the Prussians, the Hanoverians, the Saxons, and the Danes all stood by Eugene, even though it would probably mean a cut in, if not a loss of, pay. "[Eugene's] long-time comrade-in-arms Leopold von Anhalt-Dessau, the commander of the Prussian corps in the pay of the Maritime Powers, came to him at Haspres and informed him that the English general had ordered him as well as Duke Karl Rudolph von Württemberg, the commander of the Danish contingent, the Hanoverian von Bülow und the Saxon General Wilckens to

---

[200] *Ibid.*

[201] Walter Elze, *Der Prinz Eugen, sein Weg, sein Werk und Englands Verrat* [Prince Eugene, His Way, His Work, and England's Betrayal].

[202] Churchill, *Marlborough*, II, pp. 947–948.

accompany him in the upcoming march in the direction of Dunkirk. As he had already informed the Imperial Field Marshal, the Prince of Anhalt declared that he would operate in terms of the instructions given him by his king and allow himself to be used for the best interest of the common cause;" the other generals answered in like manner.[203]

But it was here that the absence of Marlborough made itself felt. The Dutch had been unwilling to pay the added expense for forward supply centers; this led to extended lines of communications. Marlborough was too meticulous ever to have allowed his lines thus to be exposed; Eugene took the risk. "The explanation is no doubt the passion to achieve success, in spite of the manner in which he had been treated, which laid hold of Eugene and led him into risks which ought not to have been run. His was the strategy of exasperation."[204] A surprise attack by the French at the strategic location of Denain cut off the besiegers. The French victory was abetted by the removal by Ormonde of the pontoon bridges which would have enabled the Allied garrison to escape – yet another token, it was averred, of the English betrayal. It was the Dutch troops who suffered this defeat, which fed into the doom-and-gloom mentality of that country, which had come to bear the chief financial burden for the war after the departure of the English. Napoleon would blame Dedain, but Eugene blamed this defeatist mentality for the series of losses which followed, undoing three years' previous campaigning and freeing France from any threat of defeat.

What followed was the Peace of Utrecht, which when all is said and done is considered to have provided a net gain for both the Maritime Powers: the Netherlands, which gained its coveted line of barrier fortresses in Belgium; and England, which gained the *asiento*, or the right to conduct the slave trade in the Spanish Empire for 30 years, along with Gibraltar and Minorca, Nova Scotia, Newfoundland, the Hudson Bay territory, and France's commitment to destroy the fortifications at Dunkirk. In the subsequent Peace of Rastatt-Baden, Austria retained its gains in Italy while also gaining the Spanish Netherlands.

Historians have looked at these results and concluded that the War of the Spanish Succession established solid foundations for a European balance of

---

[203] Braubach, vol. 3, p. 108.
[204] Churchill, *Marlborough*, II, pp. 957–958.

power. France had been trimmed back, albeit by no means humbled. The Habsburgs were able to establish the Austro-Hungarian empire as a great power in its own right. England became the leading power in Europe, with its unrivaled navy, its colonial empire, and mastery over the Mediterranean. The Dutch Republic, having gained its barrier against France, ceased punching above its weight and succumbed to apathy.

But that is to view matters in accordance with the outmoded viewpoint of autonomous, absolute sovereignty, in which states are the more perfect the more they absorb power, both inward and outward, the more, in effect, they become laws unto themselves. This viewpoint triumphed in the 19$^{th}$ century and history has been written on its terms. Thus, the War of the Spanish Succession laid the foundations for a balanced order in which the "Big Five" of France, England, Russia, Prussia, and Austria called the tune. It is only in our day that German and hence European history is being rewritten, not in terms of these autonomous power entities, but in terms of the federal, post-feudal structure of integrated authority, of sovereignty under law, exemplified first and foremost in the Holy Roman Empire.[205]

In terms of this viewpoint, the Allied army composed of the various contemporary elements of the Holy Roman Empire, one-time members such as the Dutch Republic and Denmark, plus England and Portugal, Catalonia and Aragon, were fighting not merely to maintain a balance of power between autonomous power entities but to maintain the reality of a supranational order of nations united in terms of a common religion and law, to wit, Christendom. Marlborough and Eugene, like Leibniz, saw in France not merely a country out to establish primacy for itself in Europe, but to establish a different order altogether, the order of "reason of state" (*raison d'état*) in

---

[205] The German historian Georg Schmidt has lately coined the phrase "complementary imperial system" to describe the multifaceted reality of the Holy Roman Empire – see his *Geschichte des Alten Reiches: Staat und Nation in der Frühen Neuzeit 1495–1806* [History of the Old Reich: State and Nation in Early Modern Times 1495–1806]. Indeed, the various levels of collective responsibility from local to regional to national, along with the range of power centers from infinitesimally small to overweening large (Austria, Prussia, Bavaria, etc.) made of the Empire a system of complementary (and, of course, contradictory) loci of public power.

which narrowly construed interests triumph over considerations of the good of the whole, the "Common Cause" – a phrase which they used repeatedly and habitually. Marlborough in particular could never have held together the coalition of disparate forces over so long a period if he had not believed in more than just English national interests; it was this penchant for subordinating the interest of England to the interest of Christendom which proved his undoing back home. The Tories, ostensibly so zealous for the interests of Christianity – in the form of the established Church of England – by their policy so assiduously undermined the interests of universal Christendom.

The big loser of this war was the Holy Roman Empire itself, which if it had remained intact – and its collapse was by no means a foregone conclusion, despite the prejudices of subsequent historiography – and had been able to build on those institutions, such as the Imperial Circles,[206] which had contributed so greatly, in proportion, to the war effort, would have served as the central locus of Western Christendom, would have dampened the centrifugal energy of Prussia and Austria, and would have helped to avert the "German Catastrophe"[207] of the 20th century. As I argued in *A Common Law*, Germany was the key to Western Christendom; the fate of the former determined the fate of the latter. Leibniz shared this viewpoint, which is perhaps why he was held at arms' length by the interest-oriented princes of his day.[208] The War of the Spanish Succession settled the billiard-ball approach to international relations which culminated in the "Century of Warfare."

And today we have dinned into our ears the solution to this situation: we need to supersede the "nation-state." In fact, as I have seen it stated in a weblist exchange, it is sovereignty itself which is the problem, and sovereignty which must be eliminated. An entirely predictable,

---

[206] Roger Wines, "The Imperial Circles, Princely Diplomacy and Imperial Reform 1681–1714," *The Journal of Modern History*, vol. 39, no. 1 (March 1967), pp. 1–29. See also note 119, p. 117 above.

[207] Friedrich Meinecke, *The German Catastrophe*.

[208] P. Fransen, *Leibniz und die Friedensschlüsse von Utrecht und Rastatt-Baden* [Leibniz and the Peace Treaties of Utrecht and Rastatt-Baden].

and entirely disingenuous, response. The problem is not sovereignty per se, the problem is *which* sovereignty.

As Meyer makes clear in his seminal book *Leibnitz and the Seventeenth-Century Revolution*,[209] the struggle which took place in the late 17th century was a struggle over first principles with regard to religion, law, politics, and culture. The autonomous individual who was being established at the heart of philosophy and law had his correlate in the autonomous power-state, as exemplified first and foremost by France. The concept of absolute sovereignty, in which the sovereign makes the law, was superseding the concept of relative sovereignty, in which the sovereign is under law. The medieval *corpus Christianum* exemplified relative sovereignty; the most able exposition thereof was Johannes Althusius' *Politica Methodice Digesta,* "Politics Methodically Arranged."[210] The most able expression of the new order was perhaps Thomas Hobbes' *Leviathan.*

Ever since World War II it has been the studied conviction of "the international community" – the academic and diplomatic denizens inhabiting that shadowy world of international organizations and networks the center of which is the United Nations – that national sovereignty, and its seat the nation-state, must be superseded. Their goal is the establishment of a regime of *universal jurisdiction*, in which sovereignty has been swallowed up in a global government operating in terms of a universal administrative law. This would eliminate war, but also poverty, because wealth redistribution could then be carried out on a universal basis. But first things first – universal jurisdiction aims to eliminate warfare and in its place establish a universal penal law in which no criminals may hide behind walls of sovereign states.

Is this the kind of regime that Eugene and Marlborough were fighting for? Far from it. The question at stake was not sovereignty or no sovereignty, it was, and is, *which kind* of sovereignty. Western Christendom presupposed relative sovereignty, in which states recognized and upheld laws answerable to divine principles as summarized in the Decalogue. Absolute sovereignty came along which recognized no higher principle and would only submit to that to which it agreed; the law of nations or common law of Christendom,

---

[209] R.W. Meyer, *Leibnitz and the Seventeenth-Century Revolution.*

[210] Johannes Althusius, *Politica: An Abridged Translation of Politics Methodically Set Forth and Illustrated with Sacred and Profane Examples.*

which at one time served as the guiding light of legislation in all Western states, became transmuted into international law, a law composed of treaty obligations and nothing more. In the modern age, nation-states for the most part have adhered to the principle of reason of state in their dealings, especially with the triumph of Bismarck's *Realpolitik*.[211]

An exception to this rule, it must be said, has been – warts and all – the United States. Its Civil War was fought, at least in part, on the basis of idealism, of the desire to rid the country of slavery. Its entry into the two world wars of the 20th century stemmed – again, not entirely, but in part, if not mostly – from the desire to ensure that the world order remained one oriented to freedom rather than despotism. The Cold War was fought to maintain freedom over against Communist despotism. And the latest war, the so-called "War on Terror" – in fact, the war against resurgent militant Islam – is in no less degree a war for freedom, freedom from the rule of Sharia law. That such freedom is in the national interest, and thus serves the interests of the United States, is of course true; but it is no less true that Americans view this ideal as something good for all nations and which should be established for the good of all peoples, not just Americans. The hundreds of thousands, if not millions, of Americans who have shed their blood on foreign battlefields testifies to that.

America, therefore, has a rather healthy image of itself in its role of exercising sovereignty. It feels it has exercised sovereignty for the good not only of its own citizens but for the good of the world order. It therefore does not feel the qualms of guilt, the pangs of conscience, that a country like Germany feels upon looking back upon its own history as a nation-state.

But the "international community" is composed precisely of countless idealists of another sort, who view the wars the world has undergone, as well as the global problems, real or imagined, of poverty, environmental destruction, energy shortage, human rights violations, as problems which can and must be solved by eliminating national sovereignty, in its place establishing the regime of universal jurisdiction.

Most of the countries of the world for one reason or another – either out of guilt or out of greed (for the wealth of other countries), or both – have

---

[211] For details on this see my biography of Stahl: *Authority not Majority*.

lined up on the side of universal jurisdiction. But there is, of course, the 800-pound gorilla who has not yet wised up. And that is the United States.

This explains the opposition to the US which is so vociferously voiced at the international level. The US simply stands as a giant roadblock in the way of universal jurisdiction. The American citizenry certainly is in no mood to give in to such pressure from the international community, and the international community, supported by left-leaning academics and politicians, is in no mood to give up its quest.

Enter the "War on Terror." On the face of it, nothing could be more inimical to the ideals of the international community as currently construed than militant Islam, which despises the very rights and progressive social order the human rights advocates are pushing. Surely the Western intelligentsia would support the effort to rid the world of this virulent strain of repressive regime.

Certainly, opposition to the aims of the Islamicists was not lacking; but the method to combat it must needs be agreeable, must needs further the aim of universal jurisdiction. Hence, all authority and all hope was vested in the United Nations, especially with regard to the rogue regime of Iraq and Saddam Hussein. When the UN's efforts to bring Iraq to heel proved vain, America and its allies took matters into their own hands – to the chagrin, in fact the enragement, of the international community. For this approach, the approach of war, of "taking the law into one's own hands," was precisely what the international community had, and has, been trying to supersede.

Thus was resurrected the image of America as the global oppressor. Just as this image had been used by international leftism during the Cold War to defend Communism, it was brushed off and used again by the promoters of the New World Order of universal jurisdiction. Islamicism was not worse – Islamicism was simply a response to American "freedom," of globalism, multinational corporations, worker exploitation, energy gluttony, and the like. Islamicists simply wished to preserve traditional ways of life over against the dreaded almighty dollar. Not to mention the "just cause" of the Palestinians over against those global Shylocks, the Jews in Israel. In fact, the violence of the Jihadists could in fact be harnessed to a greater good, the humbling and supersession of national sovereignty, as represented first and foremost by America.

And so the circle has been completed. The proponents of universal jurisdiction today have stepped into the role of Louis XIV 300 years ago. Just as
he did, they now seek a new order, an order superseding one of obsolete restraint, an order answering to new demands and conditions, an order in
which the sovereign individual attains a new level of self-realization; most
importantly, an order in which they call the tune. The international community of today sees in militant Islam the same hammer to smash its enemy, the
US, as Louis did in the Ottomans, a hammer to smash his arch-enemy the
House of Habsburg.

But there is another parallel to be drawn: that of conservative opposition
to the war effort. Just as the Tories opposed the continental land war because
of the opportunities it afforded for the growth of the fiscal/taxation regime
and the threat to liberty of a standing army, just so today do conservatives
oppose the current War on Terror precisely because of the opportunities of
growth it affords the so-called military-industrial complex; the result, win or
lose, they say, is Big Government ever more firmly ensconced in power. And
the political benefits it provides the House of Bush are just as begrudged as
they then were by Protestants with regard to the Catholic, Counter-Refor-
mation-advancing House of Habsburg.

This, then, is what we are up against: as the Dutch say, a *monsterverbond*,
an "unnatural alliance" of internationalists, mainly left-wing, and Islamicists,
mainly prehistoric. Both seek a New World Order, one under a regime of
human-rights-inspired enlightenment, one under a Sharia-inspired Cali-
phate. They both have a common enemy: the order of sovereign nations, each
responsible inwardly for its own law, jointly responsible for maintaining a
shared order amongst themselves. And we have a conservative opposition
standing in the way of direct dealing with these threats. In the 18th century,
the Turks were put away once and for all by Eugene, but Louis was able to
stamp his image on Europe, an image which lives to this day. In our day we
face a different challenge. First, to see off the threat of Islamofascism; second,
to see off the threat of universal jurisdiction. And then, perhaps, in the Providence of God we may begin to restore Humpty-Dumpty Christendom,
which sat on a wall, and had a great fall.

# National versus Global Economy

The following articles were written in the leadup to and aftermath of the 2016 presidential election in the United States. This was a watershed event, because it signaled a changed in "business as usual," defined as the pursuit of global governance, neoliberal *cum* neocolonialist economic policy, and the ongoing delegitimizing of the nation-state as the fulcrum of erstwhile international, now transnational, soon to be supra- or even contranational law.

What they demonstrate is that a true understanding of the law of nations also emphasizes flexibility in the face of changed circumstances. The leading idea remains the same: as originally put forth by Vitoria (see pp. 67ff. above), it is communication. This communication, however, takes place for the mutual benefit of nations. This rules out relations of mere exploitation. Uppermost to this law is the well-being of the nations involved. That is why Vitoria mainlined the views of Las Casas; but that is also why he was so adamant about denying the existence of a world empire with pope and Holy Roman Emperor at its head. The nations are the sovereigns, not a universal order imposed over them, by which they become mere provinces, administrative regions. For this reason both the School of Salamanca and Althusius championed national sovereignty. This sovereignty redounded to the nation, for the benefit of the citizenry.

This balance was lost when the theocratic framework was jettisoned in the 17th and 18th centuries. A point which the book insufficiently brings out is that classical and neoclassical economics themselves are a product of this deracination. They took over only a part of the *jus gentium,* while jettisoning the other part. As a result, they turned free trade and open borders into a *means* for the attainment of a universal order of justice and peace, rather than what they really are, a *result* of the attainment of that order. In this sense, classical and neoclassical economics get things backwards. The abuse to which the world economy is put when this sequence is reversed is made manifest in the following articles. As such, they form a necessary supplement to the presentation.

# National Economy?

AT FIRST GLANCE the notion of a national economy would seem to be self-evident. After all, the lion's share of economic data comes in the form of "national accounts," which treat the nation as a self-contained economic entity, like a business. And the talk, when it comes to the economy, is always of how the nation is doing, or how other nations or countries are doing. Likewise, history revolves around the nations and their economic progress, as with the US and its "manifest destiny."

But the idea of a national economy does not extend to the level of theoretical category. Economic theory does not take it into consideration. It comes into play because of political, not economic, considerations. The fact of the matter is, because politics is concentrated at the national level, so also is fiscal and monetary policy. And this factual state of affairs determines the subject matter. It is at the national level that both fiscal and monetary policy takes place; it is the level at which results from these policies are expected.

Economic theory, however, is not discussed in terms of the nation but in terms of abstractions: the "market," "business," "consumers," etc. This is, or at least it used to be, referred to as "microeconomics." Then we have "macro-economics," which is essentially the economic role of the state with its aforementioned fiscal and monetary policies; in this way we smuggle the nation in through the back door, as it were.

But the nation never functions as a subject of economic theory in its own right. Economic practice, of course, cannot avoid it – the sovereign democratic state is the way things are, it delimits the subject matter at the "macro" level.

The unexamined presupposition in all of this is, what is the locus of the economy? It is actually a question of the utmost importance, because only in this way can we come to grips with crucially important notions – and realities that, like it or not, we have to deal with – like the "global" economy.

One person who, thankfully, did not leave this presupposition unexamined is Jane Jacobs. In her book *Cities and the Wealth of Nations*,[212] she puts the notion of a national economy, which she takes to be the reigning

---

[212] Jane Jacobs, *Cities and the Wealth of Nations: Principles of Economic Life*.

doctrine, squarely in the cross-hairs. In her view, such an economy is an artificial imposition: the real economy is city-oriented. Cities, not nations, form the watersheds of an economy. Which is to say, cities are the focus of integrated, mixed economies, involving all major sectors from agriculture to industry to finance. Within the city and its supply regions, a stable and integral economy is maintained.[213]

Therefore exporting and importing takes place between cities, not nations. By extension, cities perform the vital economic function of *import-replacing:* the replacement of imported goods with goods of their own making. In Jacobs' model, it is this import-replacing function that is the basic motor of economic growth.[214]

Jacobs adds to this import/export functionality the logical corollary: currencies. Currencies function as *feedback mechanisms:* they provide economies with information with respect to their productivity vis-à-vis other economies. A rise in an economy's currency indicates that it is more productive than other economies the currencies of which are falling in relative terms, while a fall indicates the reverse condition.

So then Jacobs draws the obvious conclusion. Since cities are the basic units of import and export, currencies, in order to best perform their function, should be geared to the city economy itself; their rise and fall would thus trigger the appropriate response in the city economy, because this currency fluctuation acts as both tariff barrier and export subsidy (a falling

---

[213] *Ibid.,* ch. 2.

[214] "Whenever a city replaces imports with its own production, other settlements, mostly other cities, lose sales accordingly. However, these other settlements – either the same ones which have lost export sales or different ones – gain an equivalent value of *new* export work. This is because an import-replacing city does not, upon replacing former imports, import less than it otherwise would, but shifts to other purchases in lieu of what it no longer needs from outside. Economic life as a whole has expanded to the extent that the import-replacing city has everything it formerly had, *plus* its complement of new and different imports. Indeed, as far as I can see, city import-replacing is in this way at the root of all economic expansion." *Ibid.,* p. 42.

currency acts as an export subsidy, a rising currency as a tariff barrier). Cities should maintain their own currencies.[215]

This also indicates a problem with this entity known as the national economy. A larger political unit such as a nation-state, when it imposes a common currency on a multiplicity of cities, short-circuits this feedback function of currencies. It favors the economies of some cities at the expense of others. Since cities not only import and export to foreign nations *but also to sister cities in the same nation,*[216] the automatic feedback information provided by the currency does nothing to allow cities within the range of the currency to adjust their economies to each other. They receive none of the feedback information that a city-based currency would provide them. Therefore, the cities whose economic position is favored by the national currency continue to grow, while the others stagnate.[217]

Clearly Jacobs is no friend of the nation-state. "Virtually all national governments, it seems fair to say, and most citizens would sooner decline and decay unified, true to the sacrifices by which their unity was won, than prosper and develop in division."[218] And she takes classical economics, especially as exemplified in Adam Smith's tellingly titled *Inquiry into the Nature and Causes of the Wealth of Nations,* to task for this. Smith "accepted without comment the mercantilist tautology that nations are the salient entities for understanding the structure of economic life. As far as one can tell from his writings, he gave that point no thought but took it so much for granted that he used it as his point of departure."[219] Smith's unthinking assumption of this assumption was subsequently passed from generation to generation without any further thought on the matter. "Ever since, that same notion has continued to be taken for granted. How strange; surely no other body of scholars or scientists in the modern world has remained as credulous as

---

[215] *Ibid.*, ch. 11.

[216] *Ibid.*, p. 43.

[217] *Ibid.*, ch. 11.

[218] ch. 13; the quotes are from pp. 212, 215–216.

[219] *Ibid.*, p. 30.

economists, for so long a time, about the merit of their subject matter's most formative and venerable assumption."[220]

So Jacobs agrees with us that the locus of the economy is an unexamined proposition. Nevertheless, her thesis that the nation was the focal point of classical economic theory is debatable. In fact, it is contradicted by an early proponent of "The National System of Political Economy," Friedrich List.[221] List certainly does not figure as an unthinking follower of Adam Smith. His description of Smith's school is telling: he calls it "the Cosmopolitical System." By which he means that, *pace* Jacobs, it is the *antithesis* of a "national system" of economics.

In line with the influential vision of "Perpetual Peace" put forward in the late 18th century by the celebrated Abbé St. Pierre, this "cosmopolitical system" of economics presupposes harmony and peace between the nations. In such a situation, nations *per se* have no interests; the human race is joined together as one; and for this reason, "for the most part the measures of governments for the promotion of public prosperity are useless; and that to raise a State from the lowest degree of barbarism to the highest state of opulence, three things only are necessary, moderate taxation, a good administration of justice, and peace."[222] Free trade is then the norm, and indeed, can only truly be implemented under the auspices of such a universal peace. But, argues List, this is to confuse a hypothetical goal toward which the nations should work, with a standing condition already attained.

> The [classical] School has admitted as realized[,] a state of things to come. It presupposes the existence of universal association and perpetual peace, and from it infers the great benefits of free trade. It confounds thus the effect and the cause. A perpetual peace exists among provinces and states already associated; it is from that association that their commercial union is derived : they owe to perpetual peace in the place they occupy, the benefits which it has procured them. History proves that political union always precedes

---

[220] *Ibid.*, p. 31.

[221] As elaborated in his book *The National System of Political Economy*, first published in German in 1841. The English translation was first published in 1856.

[222] *National System of Political Economy* (1856 ed.), p. 191.

commercial union. It does not furnish an instance where the latter has had the precedence. In the actual state of the world, free trade would bring forth, instead of a community of nations, the universal subjection of nations to the supremacy of the greater powers in manufactures, commerce, and navigation.[223]

While Smith and the other proponents of the classical school did recognize the existence of nations and national interests, List correctly assesses the basic orientation of the system. Much of this was inchoate; Lists's strictures served to stir up debate, generate criticism, and give rise to critical schools of economic theory, such as the so-called Historical School.

This is evident not only in the advocacy of free trade generally as panacea for all economic ills, but also, importantly, in the advocacy of free trade in the area of currency. As we explored in "Capitalism and the 'Modern World System'" (pp. 201ff. below), leaving currency to the free market is a key element in a cosmopolitan system that deemphasizes nations as economic actors and subjugates sovereignty, in order to establish a "center-periphery" system of exploitation. And Adam Smith's classical system established commodity money as a cornerstone of its economic order. As such, in its essentials List's construct holds true.

List is correct to point out that mercantilism, the target of the classical school's vituperation, took the nation to be the focus of economics. The system of commodity money, established to overcome mercantilism, is thus a product of the cosmopolitan system. Indeed, the latter found its justification in the fact that it overcame mercantilism, with its supposed framework of conflict of interests and the struggle between nations.

The system of commodity money came to be embodied in the gold standard. As I have argued elsewhere (*Follow the Money*, ch. 14: "The Great Transformation"), that system ended up in the shipwreck of two world wars and a great depression. As such, it is forever a thing of the past.[224]

Since then, we have had national currencies; and since 1971, ostensibly free-floating national currencies. Jacobs' polemic against the current system

---

[223] *Ibid.*, p. 200.

[224] "Weighing the Gold Standard," at commonlaweconomics.com. Link: https://wp.me/p7sx1H-sG

of national currencies has this to say for it, that it understands the role of currencies as feedback mechanisms. Furthermore, the understanding of economies as things that are city-oriented and city-generated. Where Jacobs goes astray is in her exclusive focus on currencies as the only way imbalances are rectified.

As I outline in the accompanying course (at http://www.commonlaw-investing.com), economic regions within national boundaries, which thus share the same currency, adapt to each other and resolve imbalances between each other by changes in wages and prices. These changes trigger flows between the economic regions, which are called factor flows: flows of mobile factors of production. Two such factors are labor and capital. They flow back and forth between economic regions, depending on such things as wage levels, price levels, and interest rates.

In the cosmopolitan system, these flows take place not only within countries but between countries. The world is then viewed as a unified, universal jurisdiction of provinces, with the free flow of mobile factors of production settling up regional imbalances.

The problem with this system is, of course, that it does not take nations into account as inescapable realities with inescapable, differentiated, often conflicting characteristics. Nations have different cultures, languages, religions, mores, values, levels of material development, and certainly different approaches to and attitudes towards getting and spending. This leads to evident differentials in things like rates of economic growth.

There is more. Nations have an unsettling penchant: inner drive to establish sovereignty. This was one of the great insights of the German Calvinist statesman and political philosopher Johannes Althusius (1563–1638). At the time, the doctrine of sovereignty was for the first time being fully developed in its modern form as the power that cannot be gainsaid, the power that stands above all other human institutions and authorities and "speaks the law" to them in a final manner. The Frenchman Jean Bodin (1530–1596), coincidentally one of the forerunners of the theory of commodity money, was also the developer of this new theory of sovereignty, which he located squarely in the ruler, whether king or national assembly of whatever sort.

Althusius accepted Bodin's doctrine of sovereignty but turned it on its head, as it were. It was not the ruler, but the nation as a whole which was the bearer and locus of sovereignty. The ruler was simply the administrator thereof, who exercised its power in the name of and in trust to the true sovereign, the people or nation.

> I have attributed the rights of sovereignty, as they are called, not to the supreme magistrate, but to the commonwealth or universal association. Many jurists and political scientists assign them as proper only to the prince and supreme magistrate to the extent that if these rights are granted and communicated to the people or commonwealth, they thereby perish and are no more. A few others and I hold to the contrary, namely, that they are proper to the symbiotic body of the universal association to such an extent that they give it spirit, soul, and heart. And *this body, as I have said, perishes if they are taken away from it.* I recognize the prince as the administrator, overseer, and governor of these rights of sovereignty. But the owner and usufructuary of sovereignty is none other than the total people associated in one symbiotic body from many smaller associations. These rights of sovereignty are so proper to this association, in my judgment, that even if it wishes to renounce them, to transfer them to another, and to alienate them, it would by no means be able to do so, any more than a man is able to give the life he enjoys to another. For these rights of sovereignty constitute and conserve the universal association.[225]

This key consideration is something that Jacobs and economists in general overlook. Sovereignty is a legal and political doctrine that fixes economic reality in a determinate and conclusive manner. It transcends economics while also acting as a basic datum that real-world economics must take into consideration. And it is nations that exercise sovereignty. As such, it is nations that establish and maintain a common law, the determiner of economic reality: hence, common-law economics. Currency, for one thing, is a function of this common law. No nations, no sovereignty; and no sovereignty, no common law. As this piece is already long enough, I will spare the reader any further elucidations. But this article[226] can serve to fill the gap.

---

[225] Frederick S. Carney (trans. and ed.), *The Politics of Johannes Althusius* (London: Eyre & Spottiswoode, 1965), p. 10. Emphasis added.

[226] "Rethinking the Foundations: How Economies Really Work," at commonlaweconomics.com. Link: https://wp.me/ P7sx1H-7s

# Capitalism and the "Modern World System"

WORLD SYSTEM ANALYSIS was first developed in the early 1970s as an alternative to the traditional nation-state-oriented analysis of the global economy. In its initial form (which has since been expanded – even, significantly, to ancient Mesopotamia[227]) the focus was put on the *modern* world system, as evidenced by the title of the pioneering work of the genre, by Immanuel Wallerstein: *The Modern World-System.* According to this version of events, the world system developed in the transition from medieval to modern times, with the key period being the 16th century.

What characterizes a world system is what is called a center-periphery relation. The center determines the flows and the rationale, while the periphery provides the means and materials. The center is the "why," the periphery is the "how." The whole thing exists for the benefit of the center; the periphery may derive some advantages from the relationship, but these are adventitious.

Wallerstein argues that such a system was set up by the Western colonial powers. Prior to this, the structure for economically connecting various regions was empire – a political method, not an economic one. In the imperial model, there is likewise a center-periphery relation, but it functions differently. Such empires "guaranteed economic flows from the periphery to the center by force (tribute and taxation) and by monopolistic advantages in trade."[228] That was the good news; the bad news was that these forced contributions required massive outlays in coercive apparatus in order to be sustained. "The bureaucracy made necessary by the political structure tended to absorb too much of the profit, especially as repression and exploitation bred

---

[227] For example: Barry Gills, Andre Gunder Frank (eds.), *The World System: Five Hundred Years Or Five Thousand?*

[228] Immanuel Wallerstein, *The Modern World-System I: Capitalist Agriculture and the Origins of the European World-Economy in the Sixteenth Century,* p. 15.

revolt which increased military expenditures;" the upshot is that empire was only "a primitive means of economic domination."[229]

As such, the new method of world system was a great improvement exploitation-wise. "It is the social achievement of the modern world, if you will, to have invented the technology that makes it possible to increase the flow of the surplus from the lower strata to the upper strata, from the periphery to the center, from the majority to the minority, by eliminating the 'waste' of too cumbersome a political superstructure."[230]

It was *capitalism* that enabled this great leap forward. Capitalism does not require political hegemony to realize these economic flows between the center and the periphery; rather, it makes use of political power to attain favorable terms of trade. "The state becomes less the central economic enterprise than the means of assuring certain terms of trade in other economic transactions." It stacks the deck in favor of the center, to ensure the center's superiority. Trade is the medium for accomplishing this. Not free trade, to be sure, but managed trade. "The operation of the market (not the *free* operation but nonetheless its operation) creates incentives to increased productivity and all the consequent accompaniment of modern economic development."[231]

"The world-economy is the arena within which these processes occur."[232] And so globalism came into being.

There have been many critiques of this framework. For one thing, was this really the first time such a world system has come about? There is good reason to believe that such a world system was already established in ancient Mesopotamia (at least, a far-reaching center-periphery arrangement based in capitalism and trade rather than conquest).

For another, does capitalism *necessarily* form such a world system? It can be argued that there are different forms of capitalism. Was it not a form of capitalism that participated in Wallerstein's empire? It would seem that capitalism of some form was alive and well in, e.g., the Roman Empire. And cannot capitalism function just as well within a domestic economy, under the thumb of sovereignty?

---

[229] *Ibid.*

[230] *Ibid.*, pp. 15–16.

[231] *Ibid.*, p. 16.

[232] *Ibid.*

Indeed, if there is a term subject to equivocal use, it is capitalism. Schumpeter referred to capitalism as "that word which good economists always try to avoid," precisely because of the range of meanings attributed to it. For his part, Schumpeter defined it as "that form of private property economy in which innovations are carried out by means of borrowed money, which in general, though not by logical necessity, implies credit creation." Those familiar with Schumpeter's theory of economic development will recognize the emphasis he puts on this function; those who aren't, might profit from the course in economics[233] which highlights this functionality. For his part, Schumpeter defends the importance he attaches to it. "It undoubtedly appears strange at a first reading, but a little reflection will satisfy the reader that most of the features which are commonly associated with the concept of capitalism would be absent from the economic and from the cultural process of a society without credit creation."[234]

Be that as it may, world system analysis is important, not as just another critique of capitalism, but as a critique of the form capitalism *can* take and the way in which trade, banking, etc., *can* be used to establish hegemonic exploitative regimes on a transnational basis.

One of the important aspects of world system analysis is the perspective it opens to the way sovereignty can be manipulated, even hijacked. For the center of the system is less a political power center than an amorphous, protean nerve center. Fernand Braudel, not quite a world-system analyst but a kindred spirit nevertheless, depicted this kind of capitalism quite starkly. From early on, he wrote, the great capitalists have seated themselves astride the currents of domestic and international trade; they have been able to make things happen for themselves in a major way. "This commanding position at the pinnacle of the trading community was probably the major feature of capitalism in view of the benefits it conferred: legal or actual monopoly and the possibility of price manipulation."[235]

---

[233] At commonlaweconomics.com.

[234] Joseph Schumpeter, *Business Cycles: A Theoretical, Historical, and Statistical Analysis of the Capitalist Process*, vol. 1, pp. 223–224.

[235] *Civilization & Capitalism, 15th–18th Century: Vol. II, The Wheels of Commerce*, p. 374.

Thus, "active social hierarchies" were constructed atop the market economy, and those at the pinnacles could call the tune in the great national and
international markets. The esoteric privileged area of large-scale and international trade represented a "shadowy zone" atop the market economy. "Certain groups of privileged actors were engaged in circuits and calculations that
ordinary people knew nothing of. Foreign exchange for example, which was
tied to distant trade movements and to the complicated arrangements for
credit, was a sophisticated art, open only to a few initiates at most." For
Braudel, this transnational perch is the linchpin of the arrangement. "To me,
this second shadowy zone, hovering above the sunlit world of the market
economy and constituting its upper limit so to speak, represents the favoured
domain of capitalism."[236]

This understanding opens the door to a critique of this world-system
analysis. The center-periphery framework with which it works, demands
strong states at the core and weak states at the periphery. "The world-economy develops a pattern where state structures are relatively strong in the core
areas and relatively weak in the periphery. Which areas play which roles is in
many ways accidental. What is necessary is that in some areas the state ma-
chinery be far stronger than in others."[237]

In the early-modern period, according to Wallerstein, it was absolute
monarchy which provided the strong state, benefiting the two main power
groups, the so-called capitalist bourgeoisie and the feudal aristocracy. "For
the former, the strong state in the form of the 'absolute monarchies' was a
prime customer, a guardian against local and international brigandage, a
mode of social legitimation, a preemptive protection against the creation of
strong state barriers elsewhere. For the latter, the strong state represented a
brake on these same capitalist strata, an upholder of status conventions, a
maintainer of order, a promoter of luxury."[238]

But as I have written elsewhere,[239] it was not any of the absolute monarchies but the Great Exception, the Dutch Republic, that functioned as the

---

[236] *Civilization & Capitalism, 15ᵗʰ–18ᵗʰ Century: Vol. I, The Structures of Everyday
Life*, p. 24.

[237] Wallerstein, *The Modern World-System*, p. 355.

[238] *Ibid.*

[239] See my *Follow the Money: The Money Trail Through History*, pp. 84ff.

core of the budding world system. This was not an absolute monarchy but a country in which the very concept of sovereignty and its location was unclear. It was a country the political power of which was divided between a *stadhouder* (a viceroy without a king) and a city-oriented gentry which might serve as the poster children of Wallerstein's capitalist bourgeoisie.

As I explained in "Isaac Newton and the Alchemy of Finance,"[240] the Dutch Republic was able to establish its trading network basically by poaching the silver circulation of its neighboring "absolute monarchies," which is one reason France invaded the country in 1672. In other words, it worked to undermine the sovereign attributes of its neighbors to establish this network. It also e.g. circumvented trade restrictions established by its more powerful neighbors. In other words, the world system functioned by weakening, not strengthening, national sovereignty.

This characteristic is overlooked by Wallerstein's analysis. It recurs on a regular basis. The entire commodity-money framework which the Dutch Republic and then England worked to establish on a world-wide basis, the monetary framework that fostered the world system such as it was, takes money entirely out of the hands of the state and puts in in the hands of a private capitalist elite.

Del Mar's scathing denunciation serves to highlight just how opposite to the notion of a "strong core state" this new monetary regime actually was:

> From the remotest time to the seventeenth century of our æra, the right to coin money and to regulate its value (by giving it denominations) and by limiting or increasing the quantity of it in circulation was the exclusive prerogative of the State. In 1604, in the celebrated case of the Mixed Moneys, this prerogative was affirmed under such extraordinary circumstances and with such an overwhelming array of judicial and forensic authority as to occasion alarm to the moneyed classes of England, who at once sought the means to overthrow it. These they found in the demands of the East India Company, the corruption of Parliament[,] the profligacy of Charles II., and the influence of Barbara Villiers. The result was the surreptitious mint legislation of 1666–7: and thus a prerogative, which, next to the right of peace or

---

[240] At Common Law Economics: http://www.commonlaweconomics.com

war, is the most powerful instrument by which a State can influence the happiness of its subjects, was surrendered or sold for a song to a class of usurers, in whose hands it has remained ever since.[241]

In a similar vein, the core of John Hobson's critique of British colonialism (taken over by Lenin in his *Imperialism: the Highest Stage of Capitalism*) is that colonialism serves the interests neither of the mother country nor of the colonies, but only the interests of certain specific parties who profit from the arrangement. It follows that such a world system is not necessarily benefiting the core countries at all – it might even be a serious drain on them. *Qui bono?* The answer is not so simple as the world system analysis might lead us to believe.

Fast forward to the contemporary situation. The arrangement in which we find ourselves, which has been gestating since the end of World War II and has settled into a familiar pattern since the 1980s, cannot be described in terms of this center-periphery arrangement. In fact, the argument can be made (and forcefully) that it has been the periphery which has taken advantage of the core. This has been accomplished mainly by pegging exchange rates at levels advantageous to exports from the periphery (production) paid for by the core (consumption). In this arrangement, the United States is referred to as the "consumer of last resort," the place where excess production can be most efficaciously offloaded.

This hollows out the production capacity of the consumption-oriented countries running the trade deficit. Obviously, this is not good for workers in those countries. Nor is it beneficial to the workers in the producing and exporting economies. As Michael Pettis makes clear in his extremely important book *The Great Rebalancing*, it is by a form of forced "savings" (i.e., expropriation) imposed on households and thus workers that this trade advantage is maintained. *Qui bono?* Not the workers, neither in the exporting nor in the consuming countries. Rather, it is our familiar friend, Braudel's "shadowy zone" (p. 204 above) of behind-the-scenes capitalist power brokers, which benefits from its "commanding position at the pinnacle of the trading community" to steer the profits in its direction and the losses to *both ends* of the trading network. In this arrangement, there is no core and no periphery

[241] Alexander Del Mar, *Barbara Villiers: or, a History of Monetary Crimes*, p. 7.

– there are only regions of exploitation. The difference is in the form the exploitation takes.

Having covered these arrangements more extensively in the accompanying course (at commonlaweconomics.com), I direct the reader there for further background. In the meantime, it is enough to confirm that the seismic rumblings now being felt among the various electorates in the West have a solid basis in reality. It is only to be hoped that the powers that be take heed of these rumblings and make the appropriate adjustments, before they turn into actual political earthquakes.

# Confessions of a Free Trade Advocate

EVER SINCE I can remember I have been a proponent of free trade. It seemed the logical thing: why should the government restrict economic activity which in itself is legal and aboveboard? And when I began exploring economic theory, lo and behold, free trade was at the forefront of most every exposition. It was the natural, the logical position to hold, and arguments against it seemed forced and, in fact, unfair, as if a basic principle of justice was being violated.

My instincts received even more validation from historical, moral theology. Francisco Vitoria, the Spanish theologian who was the first to flesh out a recognizably modern theory of the international community and law of nations, made freedom of trade one of the pillars of such a world order. As I wrote in 1991, "Freedom of trade Vitoria also includes among these rights of natural communication. This is quite noteworthy: remember, these rights belong to the 'primary' law of nations and as such may never be denied! National governments may infringe the right of neither their own nor of foreign private citizens and subjects to freely engage in trade, so long as trade and business may be carried on without prejudicing the health and safety of the community."[242] Free trade seemed to be a categorical imperative.

I continued along these lines in the first edition of *A Common Law*. There I articulated a twofold tradition in Western constitutional theory and practice, the common-law tradition and the civil-law tradition. Of these two, the common-law tradition espoused limited sovereignty and the primacy of private law over public law, while the civil-law tradition embraced absolute sovereignty and the subordination of private to public law. As an extension of this, I included freedom of trade versus restriction of trade as a dividing line between the two traditions. With regard to the unification of Germany's disparate states in the 19th century, I wrote that "The roots of German unification lay firmly in the civil-law tradition. Customs union lay the basis for further political union: free trade was established within the customs union, tariff barriers between it and the rest of the world.... In the civil-law tradition,

---

[242] "The Meaning of National Sovereignty: Part II: Vitoria and Althusius," at commonlawreview.com. Link: https://bit.ly/2vtn14C.

trade can only be securely established within an area controlled by the sovereign; the domestic economy is the only stable economy. In the common-law tradition, trade binds societies under law, a law which also binds sovereigns and commits them to enforce it. In the civil-law tradition, law is the servant of the sovereign; in the common-law tradition, the sovereign is the servant of law" (pp. 125–126). Here again, I made free trade a categorical imperative and one of the core elements of a "constitution of liberty."

As a final example, I wrote this in 1992:

> Today the world is faced with the choice between two kinds of democracy. One, liberal democracy, is the descendant of the theocratic *jus gentium*, upholding freedom of trade, open borders, restricted national sovereignty, and the primacy of the private sector, considering that human society at the level of private association basically furthers the harmony of interests of its members, and that coercive authority is necessary only to ensure that violations in this harmony are punished. The other, social democracy, is the descendant of divine right absolutism, championing economic nationalism, closed borders, absolute national sovereignty (unless that sovereignty can be transferred to a supranational body), and the primacy of the public sector to rectify the inherent conflict of interests which exists in human society.[243]

So my free trade bona fides are fairly impeccable. But what I didn't realize through all these expositions was something I only later began to uncover. It is a principle that already was elucidated by Friedrich List, one of the first post-classical economists to critique the doctrine of freedom of trade. The principle is this: trade between individuals and private entities is not the same as trade between nations, because it is nations that establish the framework within which trade can even take place. In the words of Karl Polanyi, markets are embedded. And this is of crucial importance. Nations establish currencies, laws, markets; they embody cultures and mores that impinge directly on economic performance; they embrace religions that, as Max Weber among others has shown, likewise are of crucial importance to economic activity. The public interest and the common-wealth are real factors that

---

[243] "Two Kinds of Democracy," at commonlawreview.com. Link: https://bit.ly/2J1ntyV.

transcend private economy. They condition all economic activity and they cannot be abstracted away as if irrelevant to economics. This is the besetting sin of the free-trade theories of classical and neo-classical economics.

"How!" questions List. "The wisdom of private economy is then the wisdom of public economy! Is it in the nature of an individual to be preoccupied with the business and the wants of the future, as it is in the nature of a nation and of a government?" Leaving everything to individual action could not possibly ensure that collective interests will be taken care of. "Consider only the building of an American city; each man left to himself would think only of his own wants, or, at the utmost, of those of his immediate descendants; the mass of individuals as united in society are not unmindful of the interests and advantages even of the remotest coming generations; the living generation, with that view, submits calmly to privations and sacrifices which no sensible man could expect from individuals in reference to the interests of the present, or from any other motives than those of patriotism or national considerations."[244]

The absence of an understanding of the role of nations, and the focus on individuals, led classical economics to consider the entire world as one great commonwealth, with no distinctions of nationality and sovereignty. This is what led it astray. Its basic principles are valid within the framework of the nation, in their own sphere; but they run aground when trade between nations is considered. "In representing free competition of producers as the surest means for developing the prosperity of mankind," List writes on p. 261, "the School is perfectly right, considering the point of view from which it regards the subject. In the hypothesis of universal association, every restriction upon honest trade between different countries would seem unreasonable and injurious. But as long as some nations will persist in regarding their special interests as of greater value to them than the collective interests of humanity, it must be folly to speak of unrestricted competition between individuals of different nations." List here speaks only of national interests, but elsewhere he discusses the whole range of relevant criteria by which nations are distinguished. And so, "The arguments of the School in favor of such competition are then applicable only to the relations between inhabitants of the same country. A great nation must consequently endeavor

---

[244] *National System of Political Economy*, pp. 245–246.

to form a complete whole, which may maintain relations with other similar unities within the limits which its particular interest as a society may prescribe." The social, public interests which obtain between nations are divergent; they differ from private interests and cannot be treated equally with them. "Now these social interests are known to differ immensely from the private interests of all the individuals of a nation, if each individual be taken separately and not as a member of the national association, if, as with Smith and Say, individuals are regarded merely as producers and consumers, and not as citizens of a nation" (p. 261).

So what does List propose as an alternative? Protectionism. This is his great failing. Because of this, his book has been neglected by those who realize the shortcomings of that doctrine, among whom I include myself. As I knew and still know, protectionism has its own set of problems.

Recall that "the School," as List refers to the classical school of Adam Smith and Jean-Baptiste Say, advocated a commodity-money regime, which in effect harnessed the nations to a single currency. Because of this, if a nation wished to effectuate some sort of insulation of the domestic economy, it could only resort to protectionism as a fall-back.

The United States pursued a protectionist policy throughout the 19th and into the 20th century. The problems to which this led were given powerful expression at the crackup of the commodity-money regime in 1931, by James Harvey Rogers. Rogers placed a good deal of the blame for the bleak situation on the regime of tariffs obstructing trade.

> The prominent part played by our high protective tariff in the present disastrous situation is beyond serious question. Aside from the political corruption which it has engendered in our national politics throughout more than a hundred years of our history, and aside, too, from the glaring domestic injustices which, since its inception, it has created and maintained; on it can now be laid the blame for a very important part in the extraordinary maldistribution of the money metal, in the recent drastic and rapid decline of prices, and therefore in the world-wide depression.[245]

---

[245] *America Weighs Her Gold,* p. 193.

Of course this would have to be the case. Tariff walls short-circuit the functioning of a commodity-money regime. The attempt to eliminate trade imbalances through what effectively is a single currency run up against the shoals of that irreducible datum, the national economy. Domestic interests, in particular labor interests, simply will not pay the inflation/deflation whipsaw price to be paid to keep that system running. And so came the inevitable resort to trade barriers, and the eventual collapse of the system.

It is unfortunate that List's exposition is known only for its advocacy of protectionism. Underneath that veneer lies a trenchant critique of the "cosmopolitan" system which is what unrestricted free trade embodies, which is valid now, as it was then. A common-law understanding of economics, which is what underlies List's work, recognizes that nationhood and national sovereignty entail a framework of laws and institutions that delimit all economic activity and set up "natural" trade barriers that schemes like free trade and commodity money cannot overcome. A truly "natural" economic framework understands that currency is a function of sovereignty, and that floating exchange rates will provide the balancing mechanism that nations need to conduct trade relations with each other.

So how do we save freedom of trade? Not by eliminating nations, national sovereignty, national boundaries, and the like, but by embracing them within a framework that recognizes rather than undermines national sovereignty. Free-floating currencies are one crucial aspect of such a regime; after all, this is nothing else than free trade in currencies. Another is the adoption of domestic fiscal and monetary policies that do not promote the advantage of one nation over another. This is what happens when, for example, countries like Germany and China inflict forced-savings regimes on their own citizenry, punishing consumption and promoting production. What then in fact happens is that other countries are forced to take on board their excess production, as Michael Pettis has demonstrated in his book *The Great Rebalancing*. It is here that international efforts need to be conducted, not in imposing transnational regimes that undermine and displace national sovereignty altogether, and make a farce of even the pretense of democratic rule.

# The Economics of the 2016 Election Cycle

THE CURRENT ELECTION CYCLE in the United States is like none other in recent memory. At least in terms of vitriol, it is no contest. But beyond the partisan slams back and forth lies a deeper fundamental reality which really lies at the heart of the contest.

In fact, despite surface appearances, this is not a typical Democrat versus Republican, left-wing versus right-wing, liberal versus conservative, election. It goes far deeper than that.

My own wish is that partisans on both sides would suspend judgement for a moment, follow me through a rather involved analysis of the economics underlying the current political situation, and think through the implications. In advance, the author thanks you for your attention.

Vantage points are everything. We have a good one provided us by the Keynesian economist, Thomas Palley. Palley's leftist credentials are impeccable, as might be expected from a former Assistant Director of Public Policy for the AFL-CIO. As such, the following exposition can make the claim, at any rate, to being something other than a mere partisan discussion. The hope is that we get beyond the left-right divide as it has manifested itself in the current political landscape, to the underlying realities that transcend that divide as currently manifested.

Back in 2009, Palley wrote a significant article[246] outlining the real underlying causes of the financial meltdown and credit crisis of 2008. In the course of explaining that catastrophic course of events, Palley ends up providing a succinct summation of the condition of the world economy generally, that retains its applicability to this day.

As Palley has it, the standard explanations of market failure do not go nearly far enough, which is a significant admission by a left-leaning economist. For the usual explanation of economic problems provided by economists of this persuasion puts the blame precisely on market failure. This time

---

[246] Thomas I. Palley, "America's Exhausted Paradigm: Macroeconomic Causes of the Financial Crisis and Great Recession," IPE Working Papers. Available at https://goo.gl/gRkfD7.

is different. "Most commentary has ... focused on market failure in the housing and credit markets. But what if the house price bubble developed because the economy needed a bubble to ensure continued growth? In that case the real cause of the crisis would be the economy's underlying macroeconomic structure" (p. 1).

In other words, the housing bubble was not an unfortunate unforeseen occurrence: it was fostered by deliberate, albeit blind, policy. How and why such a situation would actively be pursued, is the burden of Palley's article.

The roots of the said macroeconomic arrangement actually go back decades. Palley traces them to the onset of the Reagan administration of 1980. "Before 1980, economic policy was designed to achieve full employment, and the economy was characterized by a system in which wages grew with productivity. This configuration created a virtuous circle of growth .... After 1980, with the advent of the new growth model, the commitment to full employment was abandoned as inflationary, with the result that the link between productivity growth and wages was severed. In place of wage growth as the engine of demand growth, the new model substituted borrowing and asset price inflation" (p. 2).

We must register a quibble with the timing of events here. 1980 did not happen in a vacuum. The hyperinflation of the 1970s is what discredited these Keynesian policies and the Reagan policy responses were the fairly obvious policy response. Anyone who lived through that period knows just how helpless everyone felt at the inability to tame the inflation dragon. In that regard, the Reagan response was inevitable and welcomed.

What really precipitated the new macroeconomic arrangement was the abandonment of the previous such arrangement, the post-war Bretton Woods currency and trade setup. This occurred not in 1980, but in 1971, with President Nixon's abandonment of the dollar-gold link. What this meant was a switch from fixed to floating exchange rates, which together with the advent of OPEC and skyrocketing oil prices, deranged a hitherto relatively stable situation currency and trade situation.

A graph provided in another of Palley's articles[247] suggests the same correlation:

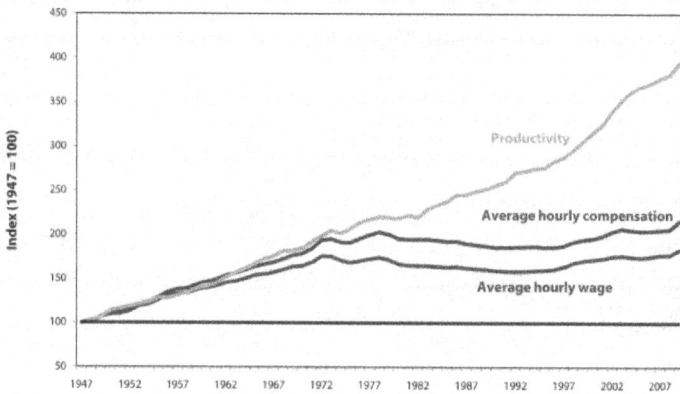

Source: EPI analysis of Bureau of Economic Analysis and Bureau of Labor Statistics data.

Figure 1: *Productivity and real average hourly wage and compensation of US non-supervisory workers, 1947–2009. Source: EPI analysis of Bureau of Economic Analysis and Bureau of Labor Statistics data.*

As can be seen in the accompanying figure, the divergence between productivity and compensation/wages begins in the early 1970s, corresponding with the breakup of Bretton Woods. So, it was the early 1970s and not 1980 that saw the change in fortunes of which we are speaking.

The new arrangement was characterized by a new priority: globalization. The preference for globalization expressed itself in a new attitude toward trade deficits. "Under the earlier economic model, policymakers viewed trade deficits as cause for concern because they represented a leakage of aggregate demand that undermined the virtuous circle of growth. However, under the post-1980 model, trade deficits came to be viewed as semi-virtuous because they helped to control inflation and because they reflected the choices of consumers and business in the marketplace" (p. 5).

---

[247] "Making Finance Serve the Real Economy," in Thomas I. Palley and Gustav A. Horn (eds.), *Restoring Shared Prosperity: A Policy Agenda From Leading Keynesian Economists*, p. 74. Available at http://goo.gl/1uJZv6.

This is a crucially important statement. It provides the kernel of what has been happening over the last 40 years. "The virtuous circle of growth" is Palley's way of formulating what we in our own model (as described in the accompanying course[248]) refer to as the circular flow of the economy. In essence, all economies are local, then regional, then national, and only then international. A "virtuous circle of growth" is what we understand as the domestic economy. But arrangements can be made that discombobulate this order. What we then have is the domestic economy subordinated to supranational interests. In essence, it is a form of colonialism. And that is what Palley is referring to when he speaks of a "leakage of aggregate demand." The circular flow is disrupted; supply and demand are disconnected from each other in the domestic economy, diverted toward an international economy characterized by trade deficits and surpluses, the ineluctable by-products of these "leakages."

This arrangement is papered over by appeals to free-market principles. Hence the epithet "neoliberalism." These trade deficits do indeed help to control inflation, but at a steep price. And they may reflect "the choices of consumers and business in the marketplace," but without consumers and business realizing that there is a flip side to these cheap imports, and that is the loss of employment and productive capacity.

For what do these trade deficits actually represent? For one thing, the systematic suppression of wages on both sides of the trade equation. "American workers are increasingly competing with lower-paid foreign workers." This is obvious and well-known. What is less well-known is what is going on with these foreign workers: "That pressure is further increased by the fact that foreign workers are themselves under pressure owing to the so-called Washington Consensus development policy, sponsored by the International Monetary Fund (IMF) and the World Bank, which forces them into the same neoliberal box as American workers." They are *both* being disadvantaged; they are being played against each other. For the loss of purchasing power on the part of American workers is not compensated for by increased demand from abroad, for foreign workers likewise are deprived of purchasing power, despite the fact that they are on the receiving end of the job-offshoring program.

---

[248] "The Two Markets," at commonlaweconomics.com: http://alvamail.synology. me/ commonlawinvesting/courses/the-two-markets/

*"Neoliberal policies not only undermine demand in advanced countries, they fail to compensate for this by creating adequate demand in developing countries"* (p. 7; emphasis added).

This is the double bind in which workers find themselves, both in developed and developing countries.

In developed countries this arrangement has hit the manufacturing sector particularly hard. The idea has been spread abroad that in the US the decline of the manufacturing sector is the result of inevitable trends, in particular, increased productivity. But this does not explain the loss of jobs: "A smooth long run declining employment share brought about investment and innovation that creates a more efficient manufacturing sector is a fundamentally different proposition from decline caused by adoption of a policy paradigm that dismantles the manufacturing sector by encouraging off-shoring and undermining competitiveness" (p. 4). It is the latter, not the former, that explains the loss of manufacturing jobs. That is to say, the new macroeconomic arrangement with its leakage of production to low-wage countries is the real reason.

Accompanying the loss of manufacturing jobs has been a steady divergence in income share. "Between 1979 and 2006, the income share of the bottom 40 percent of U.S. households decreased significantly, while the income share of the top 20 percent increased dramatically. Moreover, a disproportionate part of that increase went to the 5 percent of families at the very top of income distribution rankings" (p. 6). Palley also points to increased labor market flexibility and the abandonment of full employment as a policy objective as factors behind widening income inequality, but the obvious driver of the process is the pressure on the job market brought on by the off-shoring of jobs.

All of this has displaced what Palley terms the "stable virtuous circle growth model based on full employment and wages tied to productivity growth" (p. 9). What has taken its place? The new arrangement "based on rising indebtedness and asset price inflation." *These two, not productive activity, generate the income to fund consumption.*

In the new arrangement, production takes place in developing countries, while consumption takes place in developed countries. *Production has been divorced from consumption.* This is the reality behind the ever-present trade imbalances characterizing the modern global economy.

In the old model, in line with Say's Law, production funds consumption and consumption, production. This is the circular flow of the domestic economy, Palley's "virtuous circle growth model." The new model divorces production from consumption. Production no longer pays for consumption: the producers in developing countries have their wages suppressed, and so cannot provide increased demand, while the consumers in developed countries are not producing and selling enough to pay for their consumption. *The shortfall is paid for by taking on debt:* in terms of economic jargon, this is known as "financing the trade deficit."

This in turn leads to asset bubbles. "Since 1980, each U.S. business cycle has seen successively higher debt/income ratios at end of expansions, and the economy has become increasingly dependent on asset price inflation to spur the growth of aggregate demand" (p. 9). Various asset markets have done duty to generate this asset inflation and thus artificial prosperity, yielding the dot.com bubble, stock market bubbles, and housing market bubbles. These bubbles are self-feeding phenomena: increases in asset prices spur borrowing based on those asset prices, which in turn encourages further spending leading to further increases in asset prices. But they also provide income to sustain standards of living that essentially are beyond the means of the underlying wealth-producing capacity of the economy.

Palley speaks in particular of the "the systemic role of house price inflation in driving economic expansions." He points out that "Over the last 20 years, the economy has tended to expand when house price inflation has exceeded CPI (consumer price index) inflation." This is true for the Reagan expansion, the Clinton expansion, and the Bush-Cheney expansion, and so is "indicative of the significance of asset price inflation in driving demand under the neo-liberal model" (p. 10), which has truly been a bipartisan affair.

Of course, "The problem with the model is that it is unsustainable." It requires continued excessive borrowing and continued reductions in savings rates, which can only be sustained by ever-expanding asset inflation, which eventually must come to an end.

This dynamic lay behind the credit crisis of 2008, only this time things were different. Mainly, the degree of indebtedness, the breadth of participation in it – as might be expected from a bubble generated by the broader housing market – far exceeded previous instances and precipitated the enormous blow to the real economy, not to mention the carnage wrought to the financial economy.

Behind this macroeconomic structure lay the disruption of the production-consumption linkage of the domestic economy. It was this that made necessary the generation of artificial prosperity to maintain a standard of living, a level of consumption, without any connection to the level of production.

This macroeconomic structure was supported by trade policy. Palley points to the establishment of the North American Free Trade Agreement (NAFTA), the establishment of the "strong dollar" policy after the East Asian financial crisis of 1997, and permanent normal trade relations (PNTR) with China in 2000, as the "most critical elements" of the global economic arrangement. These were "implemented by the Clinton administration under the guidance of Treasury secretaries [*sic*] Robert Rubin and Lawrence Summers." The measures "cemented the model of globalization that had been lobbied for by corporations and their Washington think-tank allies" (pp. 12-13).

The upshot was a global economic arrangement featuring a "triple hemorrhage:" leakage of spending on imports, leakage of jobs overseas, and leakage of investment overseas.

We gained a new economic arrangement in which trade deficits became the rule and the world became the production zone for US corporations, which could turn around and sell this production to compatriot consumers. "At the bidding of corporate interests, the United States joined itself at the hip to the global economy, opening its borders to an inflow of goods and exposing its manufacturing base. This was done without safeguards to address the problems of exchange rate misalignment and systemic trade deficits, or the mercantilist policies of trading partners" (p. 14).

This created a "widening hole" in the economy "undermining domestic production, employment, and investment."

NAFTA in particular ushered in a new era of exchange-rate policy. "Before, exchange rates mattered for trade and the exchange of goods. Now, they mattered for the location of production" (p. 15). This worked to the advantage, of course, of multinational corporations, enabling them to pursue the policy of producing in low-wage markets and selling the production in developed markets. This in turn led to a strong dollar policy, likewise pushed by multinationals. "This reversed their commercial interest," as US corporations previously favored a weak dollar, for obvious reasons.

The collapse of the peso in 1994 was a direct result of this new policy. In the new arrangement, the cheap peso was a boon to US corporations producing in Mexico and exporting to the US. "The effects of NAFTA and the peso devaluation were immediately felt in the U.S. manufacturing sector in the form of job loss; diversion of investment; firms using the threat of relocation to repress wages; and an explosion in the goods trade deficit with Mexico .... Whereas prior to the implementation of the NAFTA agreement the United States was running a goods trade surplus with Mexico, immediately afterward the balance turned massively negative and kept growing more negative up to 2007."

The strong dollar policy was further implemented during the series of financial crises in the late 1990s, starting in East Asia. "In response to these crises, Treasury Secretaries Rubin and Summers adopted the same policy that was used to deal with the 1994 peso crisis, thereby creating a new global system that replicated the pattern of economic integration established with Mexico" (p. 16). The strong dollar increased the purchasing power of the US consumers: "critical because the U.S. consumer was now the lynchpin of the global economy, becoming the buyer of first and last resort."

One result of this policy was that "manufacturing job growth was negative over the entirety of the Clinton expansion, a first in U.S. business cycle history" (p. 18). Positive business cycle conditions obscured the underlying trends; to add insult to injury, "the Clinton administration dismissed concerns about the long-term dangers of manufacturing job loss. Instead, the official interpretation was that the U.S. economy was experiencing—in the words of senior Clinton economic policy advisers Alan Blinder and Janet Yellen—a 'fabulous decade' significantly driven by policy." Janet Yellen is, of course, the current Chair of the Federal Reserve Board.

The final step in this process was taken when China was granted the status of PNTR and then admitted to the World Trade Organization. "Once again the results were predictable and similar to the pattern established by NAFTA—though the scale was far larger."

Hence, all the pieces were put in place during the 1980s and 1990s, but they did not come to full fruition until the crisis of 2008. "From that standpoint, the Bush-Cheney administration is not responsible for the financial crisis. Its economic policies ... represented a continuation of the policy paradigm already in place. The financial crisis therefore represents the exhaustion of that paradigm rather than being the result of specific policy failures on the part of the Bush-Cheney administration" (p. 21).

G iven the above, it is obvious that the credit crisis of 2008 was not the result of the usual suspects, deregulation of financial institutions and banks pushing excessive lending for no other reason but greed. The excessive lending was built into the structure; the entire world economy depended on it, for only through this asset-inflation-induced debt could US consumption, the driving force of economic growth in developing countries, be paid for.

So what is needed is paradigm change. And in this context, Palley, writing in 2009, makes a prophetic statement.

> The case for paradigm change has yet to be taken up politically. Those who built the neoliberal system remain in charge of economic policy. Among mainstream economists who have justified the neoliberal system, there has been some change in thinking when it comes to regulation, but there has been no change in thinking regarding the prevailing economic paradigm. This is starkly illustrated in the debate in the United States over globalization, where the evidence of failure is compelling. Yet, any suggestion that the United States should reshape its model of global economic engagement is brushed aside as "protectionism. [sic]", which avoids the real issue and shuts down debate (p. 25).

"Shuts down debate," indeed. In the intervening period between 2009 and 2016, the topics of trade deficits, currency arrangements, and multilateral trade deals, have consistently been dismissed as matters of concern, denigrated as unworthy of debate; while proponents of such a re-evaluation have been routinely dismissed as cranks undeserving of serious attention.

As it happens, two candidates for the office of President have put this issue on the table, despite the bile they have received for it: Bernie Sanders and Donald Trump. The concerns of both have been dismissed out of hand by regnant opinion-makers. This should not come as a surprise. After all, "The neoliberal growth model has benefitted the wealthy, while the model of global economic engagement has benefitted large multinational corporations. That gives these powerful political interests, with their money and well-funded captive think tanks, an incentive to block change" (p. 26). Furthermore, "Judging by its top economics personnel, the Obama administration has decided to maintain the system rather than change it," and subsequent history confirms this. In fact, at the time of writing, President Obama is promoting the latest iteration of this neoliberal arrangement,[249] in the form of the Trans-Pacific Partnership (TPP).

It is not only the Obama administration that continues to push this arrangement. The entire Washington establishment, both Democrat and Republican, is fully behind the continuation of this unsustainable model. Given this intransigence, what is the logical next step? Palley points to it, and subsequent history has only confirmed it: "stagnation is the logical next stage of the existing paradigm" (p. 27). Ever-burgeoning debt that only gets rolled over and never repaid, leads, as the example of Japan teaches, only to economic stagnation, the so-called zombie economy.

Where does Hillary Clinton stand on this issue? Recent statements indicate softening in the direction of Sanders' position, including announced opposition to TPP. Besides the pronounced skepticism with which such proclamations have been greeted by the left wing of the Democratic Party,[250] there is the little matter of track record. After all, it was during her husband's administration that all the pieces of the neoliberal program were implemented, and on that, she was with him all the way. Nothing in her subsequent record either as Senator for New York, or as Secretary of State, would indicate otherwise. Quite obviously, her current registered opposition to TPP was driven by Sanders, Trump, and poll numbers.

But beyond this is her place within the framework of what has become the Clinton global network. This network is anchored by a range of institutions: the Clinton Foundation, the Clinton Family Foundation, and the Clinton Global Initiative, among others. The Clinton Foundation was

---

[249] "Obama to take trade battle to the heartland," https://politi.co/2vphn3q.

[250] "How progressives are putting Hillary Clinton in a tough spot on trade (again)," https://wapo.st/2ZHVdaD.

established in 1997 with the purpose to "strengthen the capacity of people throughout the world to meet the challenges of global interdependence."[251] The Clinton Global Initiative is part of this entity, although between 2009 and 2013 it was hived off, presumably in connection with Clinton's stint as Secretary of State, to avoid the appearance of conflict.

Articles such as this one from the *Washington Post*, providing "The Inside Story of How the Clintons Built a $2 Billion Global Empire,"[252] yield a glimpse into the global reach the Clintons enjoy within the current neoliberal framework. In fact, one might paraphrase Palley's characterization of the US by saying that indeed the Clintons are joined at the hip with the neoliberal framework. We might go so far as to say that Hillary Clinton is the poster child of this framework, which doubtless is part of reason she enjoys such favorable press despite the fact that she carries so much baggage, of the kind that would have eliminated just about any other candidate.

And so it can be argued that the globalist corporate elite, which props up, and benefits from, the neoliberal arrangement, is promoting the Democrats' progressive agenda, using it, exploiting it, the better to ensure that this pernicious arrangement remains cemented in place. Hillary Clinton is certainly progressive on social issues. The question is, is she progressive on economics? Let the record speak for itself.

---

[251] https://en.wikipedia.org/wiki/Clinton_Foundation
[252] https://wapo.st/2ZHWKgT.

# Immigration, Migration, and Imbalances

THE CURRENT FRACAS with regard to immigration through the southern border of the United States will die down in time, and another issue will replace it in the headlines, in breaking news announcements, in round-table discussions. There will not be a resolution any time soon. But what is important is to understand the underlying issues involved. The context is what we need to get a better idea of how to judge necessarily ephemeral events.

The first thing to understand is that at bottom, the motivation for these people movements is economic. For this reason, we can start our analysis by eliminating the category of refugees seeking asylum. The latter is not a function of economics but of justice and compassion. While this is important, it is dwarfed by the scale of economics-inspired movement.

We also need to distinguish immigration and migration. In the sense I intend, immigration concerns people going to the country of destination with the mindset of assimilating into that country. For example, hitherto when immigrants moved to the United States, they moved with the intention of becoming Americans, of leaving their home countries behind and entering into the civic compact that has defined the United States from its inception. Migration, on the other hand, is no so much concerned with assimilation, but rather with the maintenance of the original culture and religion in the midst of the new environment – the establishment of enclaves within a foreign culture, that while engaged, is not entirely received, and indeed is held at arm's length. In this sense, migration is a form of colonialism. And indeed, contemporary migrations are looked upon, approvingly or otherwise, as a form of retribution for the centuries of colonial relations the West imposed upon the rest of the world: these foreign peoples are now returning the favor, colonizing, and extracting wealth from, the host nations.

In the current climate, and in this analysis, it is migration with which we are concerned.

## Some economic principles to guide the discussion

Migration, then, is an aspect of a global confluence of factors mainly economic in character.

Certain basic economic concepts have to be grasped in order to get a proper view of this phenomenon.

First: the economy, whether viewed locally, nationally, or globally, is a *circular flow* of the production and consumption of goods and services.[253] This is a reflection of Say's Law: supply creates its own demand. Say's Law, which was most effectively employed in the work of Joseph Schumpeter, from whom the phrase "circular flow" comes, helps us understand how economies function.

The circular flow of goods and services concerns is the so-called *real economy*.

Second: not only is there a circular flow of goods and services, there is also a circular flow of payment, credit and debt, which is generated together with the other circular flow. It is both the result of that flow, and affects that flow. This is the so-called *financial economy*.

The two impinge on each other and determine each other. They cannot be viewed in isolation but as two parts of the same coin. The trouble with much of modern economics is that it does not do that, but treats them in abstract separation.

These circular flows are firstly local, comprising a local economy. A larger economy is a composite of smaller economies, and so comprises a confluence of circular flows. For this reason the economy, especially in other languages like French, is also called the *conjuncture*. The broader economy is a conjuncture of smaller economies operating more or less in sync with each other.

The component sub-economies do not move in lockstep. Rather, they develop at varying paces, some experiencing boom periods, others bust periods, others more or less stagnating.

What happens, then, is that factors of production flow towards areas of greater productivity: that is where the jobs are, that is, where capital receives a better return.

---

[253] See "The Problem of Saving" at commonlaweconomics.com. Link: https://wp.me/p7sx1H-v8

## Borders and exchange rates

Within a political unit, these flows can occur unhindered. Between political units, they are obstructed by borders. These borders are the product of law. Laws set up obstructions to the crossing of boundaries. Furthermore, currencies, which are the product of law, form hidden barriers. Because they fluctuate, they make it more difficult to judge relative values, such as wages, keeping investors and workers from making the move, especially if the move looks to be from a more valuable to a less valuable currency. But beyond all of this, language and culture form boundaries, so that even in the absence of legal or monetary hindrances, people are hindered from moving because of the difficulty in adapting to foreign conditions.

So how do adjustments occur between economies separated by boundaries? By adjustments in the exchange rate of the countries' currencies, so that areas with expanding economic activity see their currencies appreciate, while those with relatively contracting activity see their currencies depreciate. This is reflected in the current account, which is the sum of a country's economic activity as far as production of goods and services is concerned, as it relates to other countries. The current account is in surplus when exports exceed imports, and vice versa. And a current account surplus should result in an appreciating currency.

In a perfect world, this mechanism would proceed unhindered, and the balance between nations would be maintained, with current account surpluses and deficits continually issuing forth into currency shifts that automatically lead to their reversals. Outperforming countries would have more money to buy foreign goods and services, and underperforming countries would have relatively cheaper goods and services to offer. This would result in a reversal of flows, with the more expensive countries importing more (and producing less) and the less expensive countries exporting more (and consuming less). Wages would increase in step with the currency, allowing them to import more. This is not a static condition. Currency exchange rates would continue to shift, balancing flows through the fluctuations and reversals of economic conditions over time.

## Short-circuiting the feedback mechanism

But here is where problems arise. Particular interests are favored at any particular time, on both sides of the equation. On the side of the exporting country, there is the interest of the export industry, while on the side of the importing country there is the interest of consumers. Or at least, consumers can be led to believe that it is in their interest to have cheap goods available, although there is a hidden cost to this, which we will discuss shortly.

*This is the situation in our current regime of globalism.* Cheap-production countries are looking to lock themselves into exchange-rate and regulatory conditions favorable to their continued exports, even though such a regime is unfavorable to their own domestic economies. In those countries, domestic consumers face high prices on imports and production geared to foreign markets; workers see their wages artificially suppressed, rather than automatically rising vis-à-vis foreign competitors, as they would if currency exchange rates moved in step.

The gainers in such a situation are mainly multinational corporations which have relocated to low-wage countries and use their former home markets as dumping grounds for cheaper production. Other gainers are governments in the exporting countries, which book revenues from those corporations and their exports. Controlling elites on both sides of the equation benefit financially and politically.

The result in the importing countries is cheaper imports, but likewise a drain of production capacity, leading to an economy heavy on service-sector jobs.

Is such an economy – one lacking in production capacity – sustainable? It would seem that, given the demands and requirements of modern welfare states and the generation of revenues they require, that such an economy is not sustainable – for ultimately it is production capacity that generates wealth, while services only redistribute pre-existing wealth. Not to mention the utterly redistributionist nature of entitlement and benefit payments, which generate no wealth whatsoever, and in fact entail a form of friction which erodes wealth.

# The stubborn expansion of imbalances

In the event, such a regime generates what have come to be known as *imbalances*. And a lot of effort is expended to counter those imbalances without resolving them. For to resolve them would lead to favored parties – e.g., multinational corporations, exporting countries – losing their lucrative advantages.

One of the important consequences is reflected in money and banking. The regime of fixed or pegged exchange rates is realized by keeping currency exchange from taking place. Normally, cross-border trade is paralleled by currency exchange, which leads to shifts in exchange rates. But to keep those exchange rates stable, currency exchange has to be headed off at the pass, as it were. This is accomplished through what is known as "sterilization." Central banks act to keep foreign currency earnings from being released into the domestic economy. This holds down purchasing power and so eases pressure on the domestic currency to appreciate against the foreign currency. But this also leads to bloat in the currency of the importing country. Under our current regime, in which the US dollar serves as the reserve currency for international trade – and in which the US, not coincidentally, serves as the "consumer of last resort"—this has led to the buildup of massive amounts of liquidity which circulate aimlessly on financial markets without touching ground in real markets. This leads to bubbles in markets that traditionally serve as havens for excess liquidity, such as real estate markets and stock markets. Such asset "bubbles," when they burst, lead to massive failures in the banking system, as occurred in 2008–2009.

## Migration as a rectification of imbalances

This is one way in which imbalances are generated, and how they, by hook or by crook, get resolved. But capital flows comprise only one of the factors that resolve cross-border imbalances. The other mobile factor of production – labor – will likewise be drawn by the magnetic attraction of richer countries, especially where 1) those economies are lopsided toward service jobs, which cannot be exported and therefore draw low-wage labor to them rather than going to where low-wage labor is, like manufacturing capacity can; and

2) those economies maintain more or less lavish welfare and benefit regimes which *ipso facto* exert an attraction on citizens of less prosperous countries.

Therefore, in a world of fixed or pegged exchange rates – or especially, in the case of the European Union, a single currency – imbalances are rectified globally in the same way they are internally within a domestic economy. For the effect of the current globalist regime is to turn the entire world economy into a single domestic economy.

It would seem that this is a driving force behind current policy decisions being taken by Western nations, both in North America and in Europe. In the United States, border control lapsed and the government introduced a range of measures to accommodate inward migration, rather than making an attempt to stifle it. This is a tacit acknowledgement that a regime of floating exchange rates, the counterpart of nations able exert to effective sovereignty, has been set aside for all practical purposes, and that the great dream of cosmopolitan liberals everywhere is at hand: a global regime of universal jurisdiction, of a police rather than a military force, of a global welfare state in which ostensibly universal human rights move from the category of "ostensible" to "actual," and the entire globe is harnessed to a redistributionist regime in which equal rights for all becomes a reality, regardless of cost.

In the meantime, what this regime of more-or-less fixed exchange rates and open borders spells is mass migration. For able-bodied labor will move if it can move, and given the technical transportational possibilities that increasingly have become available to low-wage populations everywhere, this movement will only accelerate. This is even more the case where populations are stuck not only in low-wage situations but in crime-ridden or even war-ridden, dysfunctional countries. Muslim populations in particular seem to be caught inordinately in such situations. Not surprisingly, Muslim populations are on the move.

## The problem with this solution

But this points up the profound danger involved in these movements, and the misgivings they give rise to among "receiving" populations. For we are not dealing here with interchangeable parts; we are dealing with human beings, with cultures, mores, religions, in addition to whatever wealth or lack of it, health or lack of it, they may already have. Add to this the migration-orientation as opposed to immigration-orientation of these peoples, and the problem becomes all too apparent.

With migration, nationhood itself becomes problematic; instead of these groups being encouraged to assimilate, they become treated as victims of nationalistic jingoism, and encouraged to become integral parts of the grievance coalition.[254] Patriotism really does come to be seen as the last refuge of the scoundrel, at least for the idealist. Cosmopolitanism becomes *de rigueur*.

But that cosmopolitanism is only a façade covering over deep divisions. For example, to what degree is Islam compatible with liberal democracy? If Muslims ever were to become a majority, would they maintain Western liberal institutions, or would they impose the institutions peculiar to Islamic countries, such as Sharia law? These are questions that not only are interesting academic exercises, but which practice will answer unequivocally, sooner or later, and of which real people will feel the effects.

Another such question: to what degree can countries like the United States sustain influxes of low-wage labor for service jobs that already are under pressure from unemployed or underemployed citizens? How can revenues be generated to counter the massive amount of pressure being put on the health, education, and welfare systems these countries have built up over the years, especially given their aging populations? Is it not a form of collective suicide to allow these migrations to take place in the hope that the gravy train will continue to flow? For looked at purely in terms of economics, these flows look to be unsustainable.[255]

## The end game?

Perhaps that is what our contemporary global elites are after. The very destabilization of nations, the undermining of national sovereignty, only plays into the hands of those desiring to establish a global regime to replace, or at least gain dominance over, sovereign nations. Nationhood itself is at stake. Politicians seem to have placed the dream of universal jurisdiction and

[254] "Yes, Virginia, There Is Freedom of Speech" at commonlawreview.com. Link: https://bit.ly/2XUvJF4.

[255] "Prospects for the US Economy" at commonlaweconomics.com. Link: https://wp.me/p7sx1H-wx

the realization of every human being's inalienable rights to food, accommodation, livelihood, education, health care, and the rest of it, above the exigencies of national survival. Apparently, they will pick up the pieces left in the aftermath of conclusive national failure.

Indeed, this would seem to be end game of national leaders favoring and preferring foreign interests to those of their own nations (e.g., Barack Obama, Angela Merkel). They seem to be auditioning for leadership in the regime which is yet to come, a regime to supplement or even replace our current framework of internationalist institutions such as the United Nations. Will it ever come to that? Yet another of those questions that practice will answer. But it is looking increasingly likely.

But there is an alternative. The venerable tradition of national sovereignty, of laws and currencies which are the expression of that sovereignty, of national populations that determine their own destinies rather than having them determined by unaccountable elites at transnational levels – the infrastructure for this is still there. And the top priority to this end, quite simply, is floating exchange rates and maintenance of the institutions protective of national sovereignty. This is not rocket science. It is a simple choice. Nationhood, or globalism?

# The Economic Consequences of the Release (Brexit)

MUCH has been written on the decision by the UK to leave the European Union. Much of it is emotion-driven. But that is no way to assess such an important turn of events. The actual significance is, in significant degree, economic in nature. This calls for an economic analysis, to which we now turn.

The Organisation for Economic Co-operation and Development's (OECD) Report published in April 2016, entitled *The Economic Consequences of Brexit: A Taxing Decision*,[256] provides a competent summary of the disadvantages that might follow upon a British departure from the EU. We will use it as a reference for interaction.

## Initial objections

The initial objections the Report registers are based on circumstantial evidence.

This holds for "Since EU membership in 1973, UK living standards have risen more than in peers" and "A multipolar world implies that the UK is economically stronger as an EU member, and in turn contributes to the EU strength." (both on p. 9). Despite the graphs, such arguments, are, at best, suggestive rather than demonstrative. The same holds true for the objection that "Uncertainty has already begun to have a negative impact on the economy" (p. 10).

## Exchange rates and the balance of trade

The Report then claims that "Uncertainty about Brexit has led to capital outflows and a weaker exchange rate" (p. 12). For a country running a perennial trade deficit, this is anything but objectionable. The graph below

---

[256] Kierzenkowski, R., et al. (2016), "The Economic Consequences of Brexit: A Taxing Decision," link: http://dx.doi.org/10.1787/5jmolsvdkf6k-en

shows the development of the UK's balance of trade since joining the EU (then the European Economic Community) in 1973.

SOURCE: TRADINGECONOMICS.COM | OFFICE FOR NATIONAL STATISTICS

This shows a downward trend, and since the late 1990s, a persistent trade deficit. As such, a decline in the pound's exchange rate will only help matters, by encouraging exports and discouraging imports.

This will especially benefit trade with the EU. "The EU remains the main trade partner of the UK and the financial sector benefits from direct access to the Single Market, which has strengthened the comparative advantage of the City" (p. 14). Absolutely true. And by way of elucidation: "Exports to EU countries account for about 12% of UK GDP and about 45% of total UK exports, and for imports the EU is even a more important partner."

This is exactly the point. The persistent trade deficit shown in the above graph is primarily a result of trade *with the EU*. The graphics below shows the breakdown. The first shows the percentage per country of imports into the UK, the second the percentage per country of exports from the UK (source: Tradingeconomics.com).

The data is from 2017. As can be seen, the EU (Germany, France, the Netherlands, Belgium, Italy, Ireland) accounts for the lion's share of both imports and exports.

Taken together, these graphs show that 1) the EU accounts for the lion's share, not only of trade, but of the trade *deficit* the UK is running, and that 2) this makes the EU *more* dependent upon the UK as a source of income than the other way around, precisely for this reason. The EU has every reason to maintain existing trade relations with the UK. *It would be to the EU's disadvantage not to do so.* The EU needs the UK as a buyer of its goods more than the UK needs the EU.

## Renegotiating trade deals

The Report goes on to claim that "Negotiating a new trade agreement with the EU is likely to be complex" (p. 16). The various possibilities are laid out in a table, which we reproduce here:

The claim is that negotiations will be complex and that the UK will be on the outside looking in, with the very real possibility of being relegated to "Most Favored Nation" status, in which trade with the EU will be "subject to the EU's common external tariff."

For one thing, such a common external tariff will be reciprocated; and as we have just seen, the EU needs the UK market more than the other way around.

Secondly, negotiations need not be complex at all. The website Lawyers for Britain[257] has put together comprehensive, detailed research papers on this issue, of which we gratefully make use. On "Brexit and International Trade Treaties,"[258] it summarizes the issue both for the UK and for trading partners generally, with the following points (emphasis added to highlight key issues) :

- "Because of the EU customs union and 'common commercial policy', the UK is not able to negotiate its own trade agreements with non-member countries -- we can only do so as part of the EU. The UK will be able to participate in new trade agreements with non-member countries from the day after exit. The process of negotiating new trade deals can be started during the 2-year notice period leading up to Brexit, with a view to bringing them into force on or soon after the date of exit.

- "The EU has existing free trade agreements which currently apply to the UK as an EU member. Most of these EU agreements are with micro-States or developing countries and only a small number represent significant export markets for the UK. Both the EU and the member states (including the UK) are parties to these agreements. *The UK could simply continue to apply the substantive terms of these agreements on a reciprocal basis after exit unless the counterparty State were actively to object.* We can see no rational reason why the counterparty States would object to this course since that would subject their existing export trade into the UK market, which is currently tariff free, to new tariffs. *There will be no need for complicated renegotiation of these existing agreements* as was misleadingly claimed by pro-Remain propaganda.

- "The UK was a founder member of EFTA but withdrew when we joined the EEC in 1973. We could apply to re-join with effect from the day after Brexit. *There is no reason why the four current EFTA countries would not welcome us back, given that the UK is one of EFTA's largest export markets.* EFTA membership would allow us

---

[257] Link: http://www.lawyersforbritain.org/index.html

[258] Link: http://www.lawyersforbritain.org/brexit-trade-treaties.shtml

to continue uninterrupted free trade relations with the four EFTA countries, and also to participate in EFTA's promotion of free trade deals with non-member countries around the world.

- "The EU is seriously encumbered in trying to negotiate trade agreements by the large number of vociferous protectionist special interests within its borders. *After Brexit, the UK would be able to negotiate new trade deals unencumbered by these special interests much faster than the EU,* and with a higher priority for facilitating access to markets for our own export industries including services.

- "It is *completely untrue that you need to be a member of a large bloc like the EU in order to strike trade deals.* The actual record of the EU compared to that (for example) of the EFTA countries demonstrates the direct opposite.

- "The baseline of our trade relationship with the remaining EU states would be governed by WTO rules which provide for non-discrimination in tariffs, and outlaw discriminatory non-tariff measures. From this baseline, and as *the remaining EU's largest single export market,* we would be in a *strong position to negotiate a mutually beneficial deal providing for the continued free flow of goods and services in both directions.* We explain what such a deal would look like in a later post, Brexit - doing a deal with the EU."

All of this indicates that it will require no herculean effort for the UK to reestablish itself as an independent trading partner, neither vis-à-vis the EU, nor the world at large. After all, the other countries of the world are not members of the EU, and they are surviving. And it bears repeating that for the EU to impose a tariff on UK imports would make no sense at all, because the same kind of tariff would be imposed reciprocally on exports to the UK: all $420 billion of them (from all of Europe, 2014).

All in all, it would be in the EU's best interest to simply maintain existing trade relations, as they are eminently in its interest. It is otherwise with the UK, which for its part would benefit from a restructuring. For one thing, it could strengthen its manufacturing base thereby.

## Other near-term effects

Further near-term effects discussed in the Report, such as a putative "reduction in UK trade openness," "imposition of tighter controls on inward migration," leading to "a large negative shock to the UK economy, which would spillover to other European countries" (all p. 21), are either mere surmises or could serve to argue the exact opposite.

The argument that a decline in the exchange rate would have deleterious effects on the UK economy is an example of an argument that could just as well be used to argue the opposite. As discussed above, a decline in the exchange rate would bolster UK exports and inhibit imports, which would benefit the UK and disadvantage the EU. In other words, the neo-mercantilist export policy of the EU countries like German and the Netherlands would be brought more in line with equity.

## Long-term effect on trade

The Report goes on to discuss possible long-term effects.

The first one discussed is the trade situation. "The UK is the most attractive destination for FDI in the EU, partly owing to access to the EU internal market" (p. 24). Foreign direct investment would be restricted by withdrawal from this internal market. But again, as noted above, access to the single market is unlikely to be restricted, as the EU derives more advantage from it than the UK. Furthermore, the major inhibitor to direct investment is *currency risk*. But it's not like the UK is withdrawing from the euro; it is only rearranging its relation with the EU, with the relation between the pound and the euro (a free float) not changing at all.

## Effect of reduced immigration

Secondly, "Immigrants, particularly from EU countries, have boosted GDP growth significantly in the UK" (p. 26). Apparently, immigrants are more productive than native-born Britons. This is obviously a contentious statement; whether it proves anything is another question. Then there is this contention: "Immigrants from the EU make a positive contribution to the public finances, despite relying on the UK welfare system, which is also the case of UK migrants elsewhere in the EU" (p. 27). This is another statement difficult to rhyme with realities. Even if immigrants are all net contributors in terms of social welfare revenues and payouts, the jobs they take, leave other labor market participants without jobs and thus, at least in part, adds to the social welfare rolls (unemployment and other forms of social assistance). In addition, "immigrants from new EU countries have comparatively lower wages..." (p. 27), which means they depress wages, which may be beneficial to employers, but not to employees, and additionally reduce consumption.

The claim is made that reduced immigration would lead to reduced skills, and "A loss of skills would reduce technical progress." That may be true in the short term, but where there is demand for skills, there will be training and education to enable workers to acquire those skills, and there is no inherent reason why native-born Britons could not be trained up. It is in fact a curious prejudice and form of reverse discrimination to believe otherwise.

## The upshot

As a result of these putative disadvantages, the claim is made for a "central scenario" in which "UK GDP is more than 5% below the baseline by 2030." Just the opposite is at least as likely.

Objections in favor of withdrawal can also be made, of course, but the Report neglects to mention those. One is the fact that the UK is the second-largest net contributor to the EU's budget,[259] after Germany. Another is that the UK bears a major part of the costs of the EU's common defense. Yet another is the costs of an inherently cumbersome and inefficient, far-off, relatively unaccountable bureaucracy regulating so much of the economic life of the nation.

But the biggest problem with the EU is tangential to this particular debate. It has to do with the single currency, the euro, in which the UK, of course, is not a participant. The euro forms a massive net drag on the world economy, and the debt overhang to which it has contributed, by having

---

[259] Link: http://www.telegraph.co.uk/news/newstopics/eureferendum/12176663/ EU-Facts-how-much-does-Britain-pay-to-the-EU-budget.html

encouraged irresponsible, indeed unconscionable, North-South lending,[260] is a toxic inheritance that not only stifles current economic growth, but also forms a burden that future generations will be hard-pressed to alleviate.

That, however, is stuff for another discussion. For now, it is enough to re-emphasize that, in line with the position outlined in "Capitalism and the "Modern World System" (along with "National Economy?"), it is nations, not empires, that create wealth. And that should be kept uppermost in everyone's mind.

---

[260] See "Prospects for the European Economy" at commonlaweconomics.com: https://wp.me/p7sx1H-wQ

# Works Cited

Acton, John Emmerich Lord. *Essays in the History of Liberty: Selected Writings of Lord Acton*. Indianapolis: Liberty Classics, n. d. [1862].

Althusius, Johannes. *Politica. An Abridged Translation of Politics Methodically Set Forth and Illustrated with Sacred and Profane Examples*. Translated by Frederick S. Carney. Indianapolis: Liberty Fund, 1995.

Alvarado, Ruben. *Authority not Majority: The Life and Times of Friedrich Julius Stahl*. Aalten: WordBridge Publishing, 2007.

—. *Calvin and the Whigs: A Study in Historical Political Theology*. Aalten: Pantocrator Press, 2017.

—. *Common Law & Natural Rights: The Question of Conservative Foundations*. Aalten: WordBridge, 2009.

—. *Follow the Money: The Money Trail Through History*. Aalten: WordBridge, 2013.

—. *The Debate that Changed the West: Grotius versus Althusius*. Aalten: Pantocrator Press, 2018.

Andreae, S. J. Fockema. *De Nederlandse Staat onder de Republiek*. Amsterdam: Noord-Hollandsche Uitgevers Maatschappij, 1978.

Aristotle. *The Ethics of Aristotle: Nicomachean Ethics*. Translated by J. A. K. Thompson, & Hugh Tredennick. London: Penguin Books, 1976.

—. *The Politics*. Translated by T. A. Sinclair & Trevor J. Saunders. London: Penguin Books, 1981.

Augustine, Saint. *The City of God*. Translated by Marcus Dods, George Wilson, & J. J. Smith. New York: The Modern Library, 1950.

Barraclough, Geoffrey. *Factors in German History*. Westport, CT: Greenwood Press, Inc., 1979 [1946].

Becker, Carl. *The Heavenly City of the Eighteenth-Century Philosophers*. New Haven & London: Yale University Press, 1932.

Berman, Harold. *Law and Revolution*. Cambridge, MA: Harvard University Press, 1983.

—. *Law and Revolution: The Formation of the Western Legal Tradition.* Cambridge, MA, and London: Harvard University Press, 1983.

Bohatec, Josef. *Calvins Lehre von Staat und Kirche unter besonderer Berücksichtigung des Organismusgedankens.* Breslau: M. & H. Marcus, 1937.

Böhme, Helmut, ed. *The Foundation of the German Empire: Selected Documents.* Translated by Agatha Ramm. London: Oxford University Press, 1971.

Bonald, [Louis Gabriel Ambroise] Vicomte de. *Oeuvres complètes de M. de Bonald, Pair de France et Membre de l'Académie Française.* Petit-Montrouge: J.-P. Migne, 1859.

Braubach, Max. *Prinz Eugen von Savoyen: Eine Biographie.* 5 vols. Munich: R. Oldenbourgh Verlag, 1962–1965.

Braudel, Fernand. *Civilization & Capitalism, 15th-18th Century.* 3 vols. New York: Harper & Row, 1981–1984 [1979].

Brewer, John. *The Sinews of Power: War, Money, and the English State 1688–1783.* New York: Alfred A. Knopf, 1989.

Burke, Edmund. *Reflections on the Revolution in France.* Indianapolis & New York: Liberal Arts Press, Inc., 1955 [1790].

Burns, J. H., ed. *The Cambridge History of Medieval Political Thought c. 350–c. 1450.* Cambridge: Cambridge University Press, 1988.

Burns, J. H., and Mark Goldie. *The Cambridge History of Political Thought 1450–1700.* Cambridge: Cambridge University Press, 1991.

Butterfield, Herbert. *The Whig Interpretation of History.* New York and London: W. W. Norton & Co., 1965 [1931].

Chafuen, Alejandro A. *Christians for Freedom: Late-Scholastic Economics.* San Francisco: Ignatius Press, 1986.

Chesterton, G. K. *Orthodoxy.* New York: Dodd, Mead & Co., 1908.

Churchill, Winston S. *Marlborough: His Life and Times.* 4 vols. London: George G. Harrap & Co. Ltd., 1923–1938.

Czibulska, Alfons von. *Prinz Eugen: Retter des Abendlandes.* Rheda-Wiedenbrück: im Bertelsmann Lesering, n. d.

Daniel-Rops, H. *The Church in the Dark Ages.* Translated by Audrey Butler. London: J. M. Dent & Sons Ltd., 1959.

Del Mar, Alexander. *Barbara Villiers: or, a History of Monetary Crimes.* New York: Cambridge Encyclopedia Co., 1899.

Dillen, J. G. van. *Van Rijkdom en Regenten*. The Hague: Martinus NIjhoff, 1970.

Dumbrell, William J. *Covenant and Creation: A Theology of Old Testament Covenants*. Nashville, TN: Thomas Nelson Publishers, 1984.

Eksteins, Modris. *Rites of Spring: The Great War and the Birth of the Modern Age*. New York: Anchor Books, 1989.

Elias, Norbert. *Power and Civility: Volume 2 of The Civilizing Process*. New York: Pantheon Books, 1982 [1939].

Elze, Walter. *Der Prinz Eugen, sein Weg, sein Werk und Englands Verrat*. Stuttgart/Berlin: Deutsche Verlags-Anstalt, 1942.

Franklin, Julian H. *Constitutionalism and Resistance in the Sixteenth Century: Three Treatises by Hotman, Beza, & Mornay*. New York: Pegasus, 1969.

Fransen, P. *Leibniz und die Friedensschlüsse von Utrecht und Rastatt-Baden*. Purmerend: J. Muusses, 1933.

Frischauer, Paul. *Prince Eugène: A Man and a Hundred Years of History*. Translated by Amethe Smeaton. London: Victor Gollancz Ltd, 1934.

Fukuyama, Francis. *The End of History and the Last Man*. London: Penguin Books, 1992.

Gelder, H.A. Enno van. *The Two Reformations of the Sixteenth Century: A Study of the Religious Aspects and Consequences of Renaissance and Humanism*. Second printing. The Hague: Martinus Nijhoff, 1964.

Grice-Hutchinson, Marjorie. *Early Economic Thought in Spain, 1177 –1740* (. London: Allen & Unwin, 1975.

Groen van Prinsterer, Guillaume. *Groen van Prinsterer's Lectures on Unbelief and Revolution*. Translated by Harry van Dyke. Jordan Station, Ontario: Wedge Publishing Foundation, 1989.

Haines, Charles Grove. *The Revival of Natural Law Concepts: A Study of the Establishment and of the Intepretation of Limits on Legislatures with Special Reference to the Development of Certain Phases of Amserican Constitutional Law*. Cambridge, MA: Harvard University Press, 1930.

Hammerstein, Notker. *Jus und Historie*. Göttingen: Vandenhoeck & Ruprecht, 1972.

Hayek, Friedrich A. *The Fatal Conceit: The Errors of Socialism*. Chicago: University of Chicago Press, 1988.

Hayek, Friedrich. *Law, Legislation, and Liberty*. 3 vols. Chicago: University of Chicago Press, 1973–1979.

Hegel, G. W. F. *Hegel's Political Writings*. Translated by T. M. Knox. Oxford: At the Clarendon Press, 1964.

Herodotus. *The History of Heterodotus*. Translated by George Rawlinson. New York: D. Appleton & Company, 1862.

Hoedemaker, P. J. *Reformed Ecclesiology in an Age of Denominationalism*. Aalten: Pantocrator Press, 2019.

Huizinga, Johan. *Men and Ideas: History, the Middle Ages, the Renaissance*. Princeton, NJ: Princeton University Press, 1984 [1959].

Israel, Jonathan I. *Dutch Primacy in World Trade 1585–1740*. Oxford: Clarendon Press, 1989.

Jacobs, Jane. *Cities and the Wealth of Nations*. New York: Basic Books, 1983.

Jaeger, Werner. *Paideia: The Ideals of Greek Culture*. Translated by Gilbert Highet. New York: Oxford University Press, 1945 [1933].

Johnson, Paul. *A History of Christianity*. New York: Atheneum, 1976.

Justinian. *Justinian's Institutes*. Translated by Peter Birks, & Grant McLeod. Ithaca, NY: Cornell University Press, 1987.

Kagan, Robert. "Power and Weakness." *Policy Review*, no. 113 (June/July 2002): 3ff.

Kierzenkowski, R., et al. "The Economic Consequences of Brexit: A Taxing Decision." *OECD Economic Policy Papers, No. 16*. Paris: OECD Publishing, 2016.

Kunkel, Wolfgang. *Römische Rechtsgeschichte: eine Einführung*. Willsbach: Scherer, 1947.

Latourette, Kenneth Scott. *A History of the Christian Church*. New York: Harper & Row, Publishers, 1975.

Leibniz, Gottfried Wilhelm. *Leibniz: Political Writings*. Translated by Patrick Riley. Cambridge: Cambridge University Press, 1988.

List, Frederick (Friedrich). *National System of Political Economy*. Translated by G. A. Matile. Philadelphia: J. B. Lippincott & Co., 1856.

Macknight, Thomas. *The Life of Henry St. John, Viscount Bolingbroke*. London: Chapman & Hall, 1863.

Maine, Sir Henry Sumner. *Ancient Law*. London: John Murray, 1861.

McIlwain, Charles Howard. *Constitutionalism: Ancient and Modern*. Ithaca, NY: Cornell University Press, 1947.

McKay, Derek. *Prince Eugene of Savoy*. London: Thames & Hudson Ltd., 1977.

Meinecke, Friedrich. *The German Catastrophe*. Translated by Sidney Fay. Cambridge, MA: Harvard University Press, 1950.

Meyer, R. W. *Leibnitz and the Seventeenth-Century Revolution*. Translated by J. P. Stern. Cambridge: Bowes & Bowes, 1952.

Montaigne, Michel de. *Essays*. Translated by John Florio. London: Everyman's Library, 1980 [1910].

Moote, A. Lloyd. *The Seventeenth Century: Europe in Ferment*. Lexington, MA: D. C. Heath and Company, 1970.

Nef, John U. *Western Civilization Since the Renaissance: Peace, War, Industry and the Arts*. New York: Harper Torchbooks, 1963 [1950].

Neff, Stephen C. *Hugo Grotius on the Law of War and Peace, Student Edition*. Cambridge: Cambridge University Press, 2012.

Neuhaus, Richard John. *The Naked Public Square: Religion and Democracy in America*. Grand Rapids, MI: Wm. B. Eerdmans Publishing Co., 1984.

North, Gary. *Leviticus: The Book of Boundaries*. Tyler, TX: Institute for Christian Economics, 1994.

Oakeshott, Michael. *On Human Conduct*. Oxford: Oxford University Press, 1975.

Palley, Thomas I. "America's exhausted paradigm: Macroeconomic causes of the financial crisis and great recession." *IPE Working Papers*. Berlin: Institute for International Political Economy, 2009/2.

Palley, Thomas I. "Making Finance Serve the Real Economy." In *Restoring Shared Prosperity: A Policy Agenda From Leading Keynesian Economists*, edited by Thomas I. Palley, & Gustav A. Horn. n. p.: CreateSpace Independent Publishing Platform, 2013.

Pelikan, Jaroslav. *The Christian Tradition: A History of the Development of Doctrine*. Chicago: University of Chicago Press, 1983.

Perry, Richard L., ed. *Sources of Our Liberties: Documentary Origins of Individual Liberties in the United States Constitution and Bill of Rights*. Chicago: American Bar Foundation, 1978.

Plato. *The Laws.* Translated by Trevor J. Saunders. London: Penguin Books, 1970.

Pocock, J. G. A. *The Machiavellian Moment: Florentine Political Thought and the Atlantic Republican Tradition.* Princeton and London: Princeton University Press, 1975.

Ranke, Leopold von. *Geschichte und Politik.* Edited by Hans Hofmann. Leipzig: Alfred Kröner Verlag, n. d.

—. *History of the Reformation in Germany.* Translated by Sarah Austin. London: Longman, Brown, Green, and Longmans, 1845.

—. *Über die Epochen der Neueren Geschichte.* Darmstadt: Wissenschaftliche Buchgemeinschaft, 1954 [1854].

—. *Weltgeschichte.* Hamburg: Gutenberg Verlag Christensen & Co., 1928.

Reibstein, Ernst. *Die Anfänge des neueren Natur- und Völkerrechts: Studien zu den "Controversiae illustres" des Fernandus Vasquius (1559).* Bern: P. Haupt, 1949.

—. *Johannes Althusius als Fortsetzer der Schule von Salamanca.* Karlsruhe: Verlag C.F. Müller, 1955.

Rogers, James Harvey. *America Weighs Her Gold.* New Haven: Yale University Press, 1931.

Roover, Raymond de. *Business, Banking, and Economic Thought in Late Medieval and Early Modern Europe: Selected Studies of Raymond de Roover.* Translated by Julius Kirshner. Chicago and London: University of Chicago Press, 1974.

Rothbard, Murray. *Economic Thought before Adam Smith.* 2 vols. Cheltenham: Edward Elgar Press, 1995.

Rousseau, Jean-Jacques. *The Basic Political Writings.* Translated by Donald A. Cress. Indianapolis: Hackett Publishing Company, 1987.

Rushdoony, Rousas John. *This Independent Republic: Studies in the Nature and Meaning of American History.* Fairfax, VA: Thoburn Press, 1978 [1965].

Rüssel, Herbert Werner. *Antike Welt und Christentum.* Amsterdam-Antwerp: Akademische Verlagsanstalt Pantheon, 1944.

Schaeffer, Francis. *Escape from Reason.* Downers Grove, IL: Inter-Varsity Press, 1968.

—. *He is There and He is not Silent.* Wheaton, IL: Tyndale House Publishers, 1972.

—. *The God Who is There*. Downers Grove, IL: Inter-Varsity Press, 1968.

Schmidt, Georg. *Geschichte des Alten Reiches: Staat und Nation in der Frühen Neuzeit 1495–1806*. Munich: C. H. Beck, 1999.

Schumpeter, Joseph. *Business Cycles: A Theoretical, Historical, and Statistical Analysis of the Capitalist Process*. 2 vols. New York: McGraw-Hill Book Company, Inc., 1939.

—. *History of Economic Analysis*. London: Allen & Unwin, 1954.

Seelmann, Kurt. *Die Lehre des Fernando Vazquez de Menchaca vom Dominium*. Cologne: Carl Heymanns Verlag KG, 1979.

Stahl, Friedrich Julius. *Principles of Law*. Aalten: WordBridge Publishing, 2007.

Stanlis, Peter. *Edmund Burke and the Natural Law*. Ann Arbor, MI: University of Michigan Press, 1958.

Tellenbach, Gerd. *Church, State, and Christian Society at the Time of the Investiture Contest*. Oxford: Basil Blackwell, 1938.

*The Low Countries History Yearbook/ Acta Historiae Neerlandicae XI 1978*. The Hague: Martinus NIjhoff Publishers, 1979.

*The Old Reich: Essays on German Political Institutions 1495–1806*. Brussels: Les Editions de la Librairie Encyclopédique, 1974.

Tierney, Brian. *The Idea of Natural Rights: Studies in Natural Rights, Natural Law and Church Law 1150–1625*. Atlanta, GA: Scholars Press, 1997.

Tocqueville, Alexis de. *The Old Regime and the French Revolution*. Gloucester MA: Peter Smith, 1978 [1856].

Tuck, Richard. *Natural Rights Theories: Their Origin and Development*. Cambridge et al.: Cambridge University Press, 1979.

—. *Philosophy and Government 1572–1651*. Cambridge et al.: Cambridge University Press, 1993.

Ullmann, Walter. *A History of Political Thought: The Middle Ages*. Harmondsworth: Penguin Books, 1965.

—. *The Carolingian Renaissance and the Idea of Kingship*. London: Methuen & Co Ltd, 1969.

Vasquez de Menchaca, Fernando. *Controversiarum Illustrium aliarumque usu frequentium libri tres*. Translated by Don Fidel Rodriguez Alcalde. Valladolid: Cuesta, 1933 [1564].

Virgil. *The Aeneid.* Translated by John Dryden. New York: P. F. Collier & Son Company, 1909 [1697].

Vitoria, Francisco de. *Political Writings.* Translated by Anthony Pagden, & Jeremy Lawrance. Cambridge: Cambridge University Press, 1991.

Wallerstein, Immanuel. *The Modern World-System I: Capitalist Agriculture and the Origins of the European World-Economy in the Sixteenth Century, with a New Prologue.* Berkeley, CA: University of California Press, 2011 [1974].

Warfield, B. B. *Calvin and Augustine.* Phillipsburg, NJ: Presbyterian & Reformed Publishing Co., 1980 [1956].

Wines, Roger. "The Imperial Circles, Princely Diplomacy and Imperial Reform 1681–1714." *The Journal of Modern History* 39, no. 1 (March 1967): 1–29.

Wyduckel, Dieter. *Princeps Legibus Solutus: Eine Untersuchung zur frühmodernen Rechts- und Staatslehre.* Berlin: Duncker & Humblot, 1979.

# Original Index

# Supplementary Index

relations
  purpose in, 157
Rembrandt van Rijn, ix
rights
  as ethical power, 154
  as secondary principle, 157
  human, 145, 151, 158, 162,
    189, 190, 234
  natural, 147–54, 158, 159,
    160, 163
Rijswijk, Peace of, 173
Rogers, James Harvey, 216
Rousseau, Jean-Jacques, 158
Rubin, Robert, 224, 225
Sanders, Bernie, 226, 227
Say, Jean-Baptiste, 216
  Say's Law, 223, 230
Sharia law, 188, 190, 235
Smith, Adam, 161, 199, 200,
    201, 216
Sobieski, John, King of Poland,
  165
sovereignty
  absolute, 146, 147, 159, 185,
    187, 188, 213, 214
  Althusius, 202
  limited, 146, 162, 187, 188,
    213
  national, 143, 145, 151, 187,
    189, 190, 209, 214, 217,
    235, 236
  Althusius, 195
St. John, Henry, 178, 180, 181,
  182, 183
Stahl, Friedrich Julius, 154, 161
Stanlis, Peter, 146

sterilization of currency, 233
Summers, Lawrence, 224, 225
Swift, Jonathan, 178
Tacitus, ix
tariffs, 198, 199, 213, 216, 217,
    239, 240, 241
Trans-Pacific Partnership (TPP),
  227
Trump, Donald, 226
United States, 144, 158, 163, 188
universal jurisdiction, 141, 143,
    144, 146, 147, 151, 187, 189,
    190, 191, 202, 234, 235
Vasquez de Menchaca,
  Fernando, 154
  system of prescriptive rights,
    154–57
Victor Amadeus of Savoy, 173
Villiers, Barbara, 210
virtuous circle of growth, 219–
  23
Vitoria, Francisco de, 146, 147,
  213
Wallerstein, Immanuel, 205–9
War on Terror, 188, 189, 190
welfare state, 151, 232, 234
Western Civilization
  bifurcation of, x
Whig party, 175–80
William III of Orange, King of
  England, 166, 173, 174, 176
World Bank, 221
World Trade Organization, 225,
  241
world-system analysis, 205–10
Yellen, Janet, 225